UNDERSTANDING

RUSSIAN BANKING

Russian Banking System, Securities Markets,
and Money Settlements

Professor Mikhail K. Lapidus

and

Dr. Pyotr Joannevich van de Waal-Palms

Mir House International, Inc.

Kansas City, USA

UNDERSTANDING RUSSIAN BANKING
Russian Banking System, Securities Markets, and Money Settlements

Mir House International, Inc., Kansas City, USA

Design by:
Elizabeth Hayes
Terie Clement
Special Thanks to Arbat!

Printed by:
Gilliland Printing, USA

Library of Congress Catalog Card Number: 97-74538
ISBN: 0-9645464-2-6

Additional Contributors

Bukato, Victor I.
President of Mosbusinessbank

Burtsev, Sergei, V.
Department Head
Industry & Construction Bank

Corbin, Michael D.
Principal
Mir House International, Inc.

Drakhlis, Tatyana
Accountant

Dremin, Nikolay A.
Economist

Golovin, Yuri
President of
Petrovskiy Commercial Bank

Jezmir, Leonid
Researcher and Translator

Jickovich, Vladimir V.
President of Saint Petersburg
Association of Commercial Banks

Khokhlov, Alexander S.
Executive Secretary of the
Board of Directors of
Mosbusinessbank

Litov, Dennis O.
President of ZAO "Konto"
Investment Bankers

Lvov, Yuri I.
President of Bank "Saint Petersburg"

Mikhailova, Professor Elena
General Director of
Investment Company "Cartel"

Tabakh, Anton
Economist

Taraseivich, Prof. Leonid S.
Director of Saint Petersburg State
University of Economics and Finance

Traktovenko, David I.
Chairman of the Management Board of
Industry & Construction Bank

Trittin, Paul S.
President
Yang-Tri International, Inc.

Vasiliev, Vyacheslav N.
Economist

Table of Contents

Foreword

Introduction

FOREWORD

At the 1992 Yeltsin-Clinton Summit in Vancouver, during a discussion as to the amount that might be required to achieve reconstruction in Russia, I suggested the figure $3 trillion dollars. President Yeltsin's response was, "Just about right."

The global corporate business world knows from market economy experience what it needs to conduct business in Russia, and so do the Russian bankers. These bankers have taken upon themselves the responsibility to act as catalysts in accomplishing this economic reconstruction. To do this, Russian banks are undertaking the tasks of creating viable, reliable, dependable financial institutions to manage the currency of commerce which is the fertilizer of Russian economic life.

Both the Russian and U.S. governments depend upon their populations for the financial support to pay the costs of government. The Russian banking industry understands that it is the people who support the government and not the governments that support the people. Particularly in the United States, it is the people who have the wealth upon which government is dependent for its survival. It is the Russian banking industry's understanding that the essence of economic growth, to enable people to create and produce, is what offers Russia its place in the future global economy.

Russian banking is "inventing" a new Russian social process for individual and small group entrepreneurial pioneering, and it is providing people with new pathways for economic growth. Every decisive step in the history of economic development has been the result of deliberate decisions to open up space and enable people to pioneer. This deliberate incubation of the free enterprise of ordinary people has always worked to produce great results. This is not nostalgic, not romantic, not greed. It is the simple principle of applying "opportunity" to the great driving hunger of millions of people to transcend their inadequate past.

Many dwell on the negatives which did exist in the past. To proceed into the future, the Russian banking industry is finding and supporting the positive source of the strength of Russia. This source is the respect and enablement of the individual, the entrepreneurial every-person, who collectively constitutes "the unseen hand" of the wealth of Russia. It is their collective drive which transcends the past and is the irreplaceable motivational force of history.

Many in this generation have also written that the growth opportunity in Russia is gone forever. They would consign the Russian people to eternal political misery of grubbing over a perennially inadequate economic pie, which is constantly shrinking. Far too fashionable are the arguments that Russian resources are too limited, that the Russian environment cannot handle rapid growth, and that most Russians must look forward to a diminishing quality of life in increasingly servile jobs. To these, the Russian banking industry says,

"Humbug." These reasoned arguments are but the illusions of ignorance. Alignment with these arguments betrays the terrible struggle of the Russian forebears to bequeath to Russia a world made more dignified for each and every individual.

The Russian banking industry believes that Russian resources are essentially unlimited and that for every obstacle there is a solution. It believes Russia has the capacity to re-entrepreneurialize all goods and services which have ever been made. In short, it believes there are no arbitrary technical limits to the Russian capacity for economic growth. Russian bankers believe it is true that Russia cannot grow the same way as it did in the past, and that new ways must be found through which the limits of today can be transcended. Russian bankers believe that finding these ways is, in essence, the "job" of the Russian entrepreneur or, in its highest expression, his "profession."

The task of Russian banking is to design a coherent, integrated policy, a marketplace, if you will, for removing the barriers, all the barriers, to new venture formation, the principle one of which is trust.

Less than 30% of the population of Russia can presently make full use of its productive capabilities. The great entrepreneurial dilemma is reaching the point where sufficient tangible results have been created to interest formulae-oriented investment or loan capital. This in itself requires that the Russian banking industry acts as spokesman for the Russian people in obtaining greater freedom, flexibility and logic in regulatory policies.

As the Russian banking industry approaches the second decade of its participation in the development of a market economy, it offers this description of its own pioneering efforts of the past decade. It is a blueprint motivated by hope and expectations which it dedicates to its customers, the Russian entrepreneur. Together they face the challenges of rebuilding Russia's economy.

This book, Understanding Russian Banking, will benefit all parties interested in the Russian economy, including all international business students.

Dr. Pyotr Joannevich van de Waal-Palms
United States of America
August 7, 1997

INTRODUCTION

In the 1980's the Soviet Union found herself in a state of serious social and political crisis. Although the country contained enormous industrial and natural resource potential, it was suddenly on the verge of collapse. Due to failed management of a totalitarian centralized system, it was now necessary to begin the difficult transformation toward a proven privatized system, and a decentralized economic and political structure. By considering modern Western experiences and the national peculiarities of Russia herself, the gradual dismantling of the all encompassing Soviet bureaucracy began. At a level of reform unprecedented in human history, Russia methodically began her collaboration with the global market, encouraged by the incentive of economic survival. Additional reforms are yet to be realized in order to achieve a re-birth of Gross Domestic Product (GDP). Therefore, the real work of the Russian banking industry still lies ahead.

By the end of the 1980's, Gorbachev's perestroika, or restructuring, was beginning to be felt. The reality of a need for individual freedom in Russia had become very clear. Virtually all aspects of the economy were in need of revitalization. In particular, the banking system required extensive reorganization, because its function in the economy is similar to the importance of the circulatory system in the human body. For productivity to blossom in Russia, a fluid, stable network of banks and credit associations must be created.

At first, new commercial banks were founded and competition began with the previous government monopolies of production and distribution. Soon, privately owned businesses began to emerge. Defense plants had formerly been the manufacturers of consumer goods as a side-line. Efforts began to emerge which would eliminate military production from these facilities and convert them to making civilian products entirely. This transition is particularly challenging, because such industries require significant re-tooling to convert them to such dramatically different product lines.

It was not long until a new constitution was prepared and laws were passed providing for civil liberties. Changing a law does not immediately create the institutions and staff required to implement and enforce such laws. Nevertheless, such actions announced to the world Russia's intention to change the way her people would be governed in the future. Russian leaders had to take such steps on behalf of the Russian people. People who have always been governed from above require time to learn how to govern themselves. Voting of itself does not create a democracy. The concept of making elected officials responsive to their constituency, and thereby creating "public servants" to truly serve the electorate, can only be assimilated with time and practice.

In Russia, the politically powerful took control of the economy. With no precedent for dividing the largest and wealthiest country on earth among its former joint common owners, and with no memory of fiduciary responsibility, inequities have resulted, which have yet to be corrected. The capable are preserving, to the best of their ability, these early stages of "capital and income redistribution." Those disenfranchised in these early processes must look to the banking industry to make possible the full encouragement and development of their productive and creative talents, and the facilitation of their re-entry into Russian economic life. In the process of restoring GDP to its former levels, there will be significant opportunities to rectify injustices. Here the Russian banking industry can be the conscience for the social justice which was the original premise of the Russian revolution.

For the first time in eighty years, the opportunity for individual prosperity has become an achievable reality. A small middle class of self-sufficient citizens, which are long-term stability in any economy, has started to emerge.

Simultaneously, with these emerging changes throughout Russia's eleven time zones, signs of disruption appeared in the form of the sudden fall in production volume, increases in inflation, rising interest rates, and wide spread lawlessness. Those who have been governed need time to develop assertiveness to self-govern and to regulate anti-social, immoral, and exploitative freedom through community action. When people are accustomed to having decisions made for them, it takes time for a strong majority of law-abiding citizens to surmount these difficulties and exercise the power they now have. We must remember this power is still young, tender and untested. It is also a great disappointment to the Russian people that the West has not exercised moral, ethical and spiritual leadership to accompany its economic aid. Russians have been left to their own devices to discover that this is not a good time in their history to recreate the robber baron philosophy of the U. S. Wild West of the 1850's, nor, is it justified, necessary or productive. Russian bankers understand that pre-1933 U.S. banks were not reliable compared to today's standards and that the Russian economy needs reliable banks by today's standards to rebuild her economy. Accordingly, Russian bankers know that Russia needs, first and foremost, a rule of law, reliability, and the safety of person and property that will create the "trust" upon which all banking is based.

The time has come to put to rest the past failed economic experiments and learn that what works has now arrived in Russia. Understanding that the market is comprised of individual persons, each of which is an essential part of the whole, and that each of which must be safe if the whole is to be trusted, is a concept which must be adopted by all in this resurrection of Mother Russia.

The unique characteristics of a "market" is not that it is a communal or national group, but that it consists of individual autonomous units interdependent to some extent, which also make independent autonomous decisions that are synergistic and complementary. These decisions do not require consensus or consultation, for they are fiercely competitive, thereby achieving maximum efficiency. It is the intolerance of inefficiency and the resulting mortality of that inefficiency, which gives the market its productive power. This scenario requires that "one person" be "the market" and that the aggregate of these "markets" constitute THE MARKET.

The progress created by these changes implemented in the last ten years, give firm grounds to say that Russia is embarked on a new road which will lead to prosperity in direct proportion to its compatibility with the global economy and society. There is nothing threatening to Russian culture in this collaboration. Such collaboration enhances Russian stature and demonstrates Russian resilience. In this just cause, Russians have demonstrated that they are an heroic people. Russian bankers intend to face the facts, and our word must become our bond. Our Russian foundation must be altered to correspond to that pledge. That is the direction which the Russian banking industry chooses as the custodian of the finances of the Russian people.

The first stages toward the privatization of state property has been completed, in the sense that a transfer from communal ownership to private individual ownership has been made. The new owners are not all necessarily the rightful owners, but the inevitable direction of the economy has been set. When productivity has been restored, the inequities will have to be sorted out.

The commercial banking system has continued to develop in the past five years. A stock market has emerged in name, and is slowly beginning its development. Real estate and insurance markets are beginning to emerge. With all of these happenings, Russian commercial banking has played a growing role in each sphere of the developing economy. The government's former activities are slowly but assuredly being returned to the private sector, which has the real competence to deal with commerce.

Since 1992, more than 2500 new commercial banks have been created for the first time. Naturally, the quality of services provided by these infant Russian banks is in an embryonic stage compared to Western banks, but there is continual improvement of their operations as a result of training from experienced banking experts, and through acquisition of the latest electronic communication equipment and technologies. Gradually the Russian banking industry is becoming prepared to accept its real function in the economic revitalization of Russian economic life.

The job is not finished. Democracy is not solely defined as the opposite of Central Power. Democracy implies further the willingness to make government representative of the wishes of the peaceful law abiding majority of the population. Democracy also must provide and enforce laws consistent with economic reality, so that the productive and creative power of the people is allowed to fully function and flourish. That task remains, and it is a task to which the Russian banking industry pledges its full support.

The manner in which the individual Russian commercial banks are now active participants in commerce is encouraging. We realize that more needs to be done. Even a little unnecessary regulation is still a barrier to economic reconstruction. To whatever degree the "trust" of others is limited by regulatory policies, Russian bankers will create ways to make this "trust" unlimited. Banking in Russia will become focused upon fully supporting the business requirements of customers and to the furtherance of Russia's economic development. To this the Russian banking industry also pledges its support.

On the other hand, we welcome legitimate uniform requirements of the Government and the Central Bank in monitoring the solvency and financial conditions of Russian commercial banks as it is appropriate and in the interest of the general public. The ultimate focus should be on an absolute absence of any interference with the purely commercial decisions of the individual commercial banks. Government regulatory policies should be based on fiduciary obligations of the government to protect its constituents and not upon monetary policies which serve to finance the government through manipulation of emissions or currency devaluation.

The new Russian banks have learned to develop relations and contacts with international customers and suppliers in the international banking community. All major Russian banks have licenses and representative agreements to perform a broad range of banking services which we offer jointly with various international banks. Many have opened, on average, 30 to 40 correspondent accounts in the banks of Europe, America, and Asia. The leading banks among them have even established branch offices in many countries around the world.

A number of international banks have branches in Russia. As a result, Russian banks have come to understand the importance of exporting production to accumulate capital, as is evidenced in the Taiwan model. Russian bankers recognize that the Russian economy cannot continue to consume its own production until the per capita income of the Russian people increases. They also know that export is necessary to achieve that goal. It is further recognize that the justification for capital inflow is directly related to exports. There are no foreigners in a global economy.

The Russian economy is still very volatile, which is also true as it relates to commercial banking. Policies change, based upon an analysis of actual experience and the comparison of banks with more advanced practices. The pace of change in such an environment is slow, even though the realities of the need for action are clear. A pragmatic approach to a Russian bank's role in financing a Russian business lies in assimilating knowledge about the proper functions of banks.

The purpose of this book is to accurately present the recent situation in Russia's banking system and financial markets, and to provide an outline of the applicable legislation. Taking into account the fact that this book is intended primarily for an international audience, the authors considered it meaningful to provide a brief presentation of the development of the Russian banking industry during the past eighty years, and to describe the administrative system, as we now see it in Russia. For the sake of simplicity, $1 US dollar approximately converts to R5500 Russian rubles in this book.

UNIT 1

Russian Banking History and Development

Introduction

Unit One describes the internal banking system of Russia and its history and recent evolution, discovering that in a real sense, there can no longer be a purely internal banking system in a global economy. The global economy has been brought about through innovation, technology and de-regulation. To the extent the government prints more rubles than the equivalent of the hard currencies earned on exports, it will lower the real exchange rate value of the ruble. In effect, the government imposes a tax whenever it prints rubles for which there is no corresponding production of goods. By laws and policies, it transfers this money from the earner/owner to another party. Printing rubles is the same thing as collecting a tax. But it is a tax on the possession of money not the production of money, and is, therefore, parasitical.

Whenever any country runs a current account deficit, it needs to finance it with a capital account "surplus" (i.e. inflow). If it has a current account surplus, it must have a corresponding capital account "deficit" (i.e. outflow). Comparing 1979-81 with 1985-88, West Germany's capital balance moved from an inflow of $8 billion to an outflow of $40 billion. Japan's from an inflow of $5 billion to an outflow of $75 billion, and America's from an outflow of $2 billion to an inflow of $129 billion. But this yardstick is hardly of any use, for it is inaccurate and misleading. A balance of payments yardstick for capital flows gives a misleading impression, because it shows net rather then gross flows of capital.

For example, in 1980 total world bank cross border and international currency lending was $324 billion USD (United States dollars). By 1991 it was $7.5 trillion. The combined GDP (Gross Domestic Product) of the 24 industrial countries in 1980 was $7.6 trillion, and in 1991 it was $17.1 trillion. The 1996 GDP of Russia was half a trillion USD. During the past ten years, bank lending has risen from 4% of GDP of these 24 nations to 44%. From 1970 to 1988, the ownership of American bonds by international investors increased from 7% to 17%, and for Germany from 5% to 34%. Turnover in foreign exchange is now $900 billion each day. There are now 35,000 trans-national companies with 147,000 international affiliates. Finance has become totally global.

History shows that the countries whose governments do not involve themselves in business and have the fewest business regulations, attract the most investment. Russian budget "investments" are not investments at all, but subsidies. Neither are Western government budget allocations investment. Real investment of privately owned capital creates economic development, and there is no substitute for it. Elimination of the regulation of business (Freedom) is what develops economies. Currency risk is the greatest deterrent to investment. In an international economic system of global integration, differences between interest rates precisely match the expected changes in the relevant exchange rates. If a one year dollar asset yields 5%, and a one year ruble asset yields 600%, investors must expect the dollar to appreciate 595% against the ruble over the next 12 months. There is no longer any way for internal banking to avoid these global influences.

It is more difficult to steer economies using monetary policy and fiscal policy, now that capital flows freely in a global economy. Financial interdependence has neutered government economic policy makers. Monetarists believe that all you have to do to control inflation is to control the supply of money. The "quantity equation" of monetarists says that the supply of money in circulation multiplied by the number of times it turns over in the economy each year must equal the price level, multiplied by the amount of output produced. Under these conditions, slowing the growth of money will slow the growth of demand. The events of the 1980's have obliged us to disregard this theory. It has, however, been accepted that output is driven by supply-side factors and not by demand. For monetarism to succeed it must be possible for the government to control the supply of money and there must be a stable relationship between the amount of money and the amount of demand in the economy. Due to financial innovation and the expansion of global finance, neither of these conditions was met in the big industrial economies of the 1980's. Raising interest rates no longer controls the money supply. Domestic interest rate policy is undermined in a global economy. Higher interest rates increase exchange rates. If governments chose to limit exchange rate fluctuation, they cannot increase interest rates. The truth is, that there is no longer any such thing as money in the historic sense.

Charles Goodhart proclaimed the following law. "Any statistical regularity breaks down once pressure is placed upon it for control purposes." Governments change the way an economy works when they try to act upon it and control it. In a time of rapid innovation, expanding cross-border flows of capital, diminishing control through regulation, and the creation of new borders, give opportunities for statistical regularities to break down in unforeseen ways which are multiplied many times over. Loosening fiscal policy through budget deficits together with tightening monetary policies through currency exchange controls, higher taxes, and business regulation, creates high interest rates. Russian policy has driven $260 billion in capital flight out of Russia in the past five years, negating the effect of all international investment.

International capital has played a big role in supplying the needs of the American government. America's account balance worsened from a surplus of $1 billion in 1980, to a deficit of $160 billion in 1987, the mirror image of the country's inflows of capital. If capital controls had been in place, America would have had to finance its fiscal deficit domestically, which would have required interest rates to rise significantly. If the deficit had been financed by printing money, as Russia has done in 1991-1996, rising inflation would have resulted. Without open borders to capital and a free market economy absent of government's regulation of business, interests rates, or exchange rates, the choice facing Russia is the same. Since Russia has limited borrowing credit abroad, it cannot be irresponsible in spending or it will inflate the ruble. That is a useful reminder. The ability to borrow money can be harmful to an economy. Russia can follow the example of Baltic currencies or those of The Ukraine.

The greatest opportunity for Russian economic recovery is to eliminate all rules and regulations and allow business the opportunity to expand GDP and thereby pay more to the government at lower rates of taxation. This is the challenge facing the Russian banking industry in the 21st century. Such a monetary policy will permit the government to spend more of this revenue on social services and invest in the expansion of future production by providing credit to industry at affordable interest rates. To survive through the transition period, it will be necessary to substitute "compensatory finance" for the printing of currency and to concentrate on exports to earn international exchange with which to rebuild Russian industrial capacity and production. It is also necessary to repay debt by transferring ownership of industry in debt for equity swaps.

The market is self disciplining with punishment (bankruptcy) for failure. This is much preferred over government regulation by fiscal policy. Open capital markets let business men pass a vote of no confidence in the government by moving money abroad. Such exercise of discipline by the market over government, is the best self correcting economic policy. The threat of capital flight is a powerful sanction on the government and assures efficiency. It vetoes unaffordable programs and establishes priorities. It delays purchases until the purchase price can be earned by producing it.

Is the market vicious, frightening and unfair? So far those Governments who live by it, have survived, and reached the highest standard of social services for their citizens. The United States, which has increased its capital inflow to compensate for its trade imbalance, is surviving on the trust that it will not start the printing presses and inflate its currency, thereby settling its debts by inflating them away. The U.S. continues to attract capital because its creditors trust it not to inflate. Will Russia inflate? Currency appreciation continues to be a reward that investors expect to receive from investment at low interest rates. Does Russia have the courage to join the group of market economy nations. Do its leaders have the vision to take its people there by refusing to finance through printing money and rising inflation? That, only Russia can answer. Thus far Russia's answer has been wrong. The ruble has dropped to R5806 = $1.00 from R40 = $1.00 in 1990. But indications are that this course is being corrected.

The availability of overseas financing has altered the character of Russia's fiscal policy options. Budget-making is no longer simple. International flows of capital respond to changes in monetary policy and complicate the task of economic management by effecting the exchange rate. International flows of capital also respond to fiscal policy. The more open the Russian economy becomes, the more sensitive it will be to changes in interest and exchange rates. Unsurprisingly, the result depends upon the governments attitude toward exchange rates. Russian policy makers have to choose between monetary policy, which is strong under floating rates, ineffective under fixed, or fiscal policy which is weak under floating rates, strong under fixed. Preferred monetary policy, chosen with domestic inflation in mind, most likely will not conform to the preferred exchange rate, chosen with international competitiveness in mind. Often the two will conflict and one will have to go. Frequently the exchange rate must go to where the interest rate sends it. The notion that the exchange rate can be used to preserve competitiveness, even as monetary policy is fighting inflation, belongs to an earlier era, a time when current account imbalances, not interest-rate differentials, drove currencies. The expansion of global finance has tied money policy and exchange-rate policy inextricably together. So much so that shifts in competitiveness, as expressed in changes in current account balances, now have no detectable effect on exchange rates at all. It will be some time before economic policy and the new global market for capital learn to get along.

A drive toward more tightly regulated domestic markets, if attempted, would fail because financial markets have knitted themselves together and it will take more than the wit of governments to separate them. The country that tries to regulate more tightly, will find that it has delivered its financial industry into the hands of international competition. Governments themselves must not become a source of financial instability. Budget deficits must be kept small. Central banks must be allowed to go about their work unmolested.

So far Russia has never tried a real radical reform. It has not even tried a reform. What Russia's monetary policy has done, is try to support its existence by taxing assets rather than income, and by redistributing money. The results have been the removal of the tolls of production from the hands of the population. Such a policy suffocates Russian business before it can even get started. The result will be the death of the goose that could lay the golden egg. Existing production in Russia is simply inadequate to give the total population a decent living. Production must be increased. Nothing can be gained by redistributing existing GDP or by the cannibalism of assets. Industry must have sufficient capital to function. If it does not, Government will drag down industry and they will both have to deal with economic disintegration. For production to occur, investment is required. For investment to occur, economic freedom to produce and retain a fair portion of the results of labor is necessary. There is no other way. Government investments are not investments. They are subsidies, obtained from producers and given to non-producers. Such government transfers cannot last. Such rules will keep capital far away from Russia. Look at Taiwan and what it has accomplished in 40 years without any natural resources. The greatest resource of Russia is not what is in the ground, but what is in its people. The people will rescue the government if the government has the good sense to permit it.

Until such civilized norms are observed, export license auctions will result in the export of flight capital, decent housing will be provided only to the rich, and international investors will include in their expectation of return on investment and assessment of risks, the cost of arbitrary blocks on their bank accounts, fixed currency exchange rates, printing press inflation, withdrawal of work permits, suddenly legislated increases in their costs, retroactive cancellation of tax moratoriums and incentives and potential imposition of back taxes. Such risks will be added to the cost of their contracts during negotiations.

Why is Russian labor worth more money outside Russia's borders then inside Russia? Why are Russians successful, optimistic, positive, creative, competitive, and even joyous outside their borders, where they miss their home land. They are the same people in both places. Why can't their energies be freed at home, without a brain drain of the motherland? Why do Westerners, who are successful outside Russia fail inside Russia. The problems are the same. Could it be that something within the borders is the problem? If it is not the Russian people, then what and who is it that is causing so much difficulty? It is the exploration of these questions that has become the function of the Russian banking industry as it enters the 21st Century and attempts to become the "facilitator" for Russian industry and the GDP.

Chapter 1.1

Banking History from 1917 to Perestroika

Gosbank- State Bank of Russia

Before World War I and the 1917 October Revolution, Russia had a fully developed credit system and a stable monetary circulation. Russia's entire system of credit revolved around Gosbank, the State Bank of Russia. Though Gosbank was established in 1860, it was founded on the monetary and credit system of the previous State Bank, which was organized under Catherine the Great. In contrast to its contemporary central banks in Western-Europe, Gosbank not only issued government currency, but also financed the trade of several export goods such as cotton, sugar, and textiles. It was particularly active in trading wheat, rye, and cereals, which provided the government's main source of international currency. In 1913, for example, a full 50% of its commercial credit operations were connected to the export of grain. To facilitate these operations, Gosbank owned its own elevators and grain silos and, operating in areas without commercial banks, made futures payments for grain.

By 1914, the Gosbank network consisted of 10 regional offices with 125 divisions throughout the country. Gosbank served as a regional treasury for 791 localities and directed a system of more than 8,000 savings banks across Russia, with their deposits used for the financing of government operations. Gosbank was able to conduct and expand its operations without excessive monetary emissions. This type of growth was possible because the Russian state budget operated consistently without a deficit, and because the state treasury invested its surplus into Gosbank. The treasury monies became the fundamental resource base for Gosbank. Those deposits consistently rose and shortly before World War I, formed 73% of Gosbank's total holdings.

From 1895-1897, the Russian Minister of Finance initiated a series of monetary reforms which resulted in Gosbank being responsible for printing the nation's 5, 7, 10, and 15 ruble notes. Each ruble was backed by 0.7742 grams of gold, which was approximately equal to the gold content in a United States half-dollar or two German marks. From the beginning of these money reforms, the ruble began down the road to becoming one of the most stable currencies in the world. The ruble's stability was secured by the great reserve of gold in Russia and by an orderly emission of paper currency.

In addition to holding a substantial amount of gold abroad in international banks, the Russian government stored 1,528 million rubles worth of gold (which was approximately 1,200 tons) within its own treasury. This reserve of gold was used to back the printing of any paper rubles above Gosbank's own 300 million ruble limit for the emission of paper currency. Until 1913, the government did not draw on its gold reserves to print their currency. In that year, it printed only 163 million rubles, a full 137 million rubles below its established limit.

With the outbreak of World War I, the Czar's government was forced to regularly expand its monetary emissions. Then, in September of 1914, the government rescinded its system permitting the exchange of bank notes for gold. At that time, the printing of new money became such an important source in financing, for both the czarist and subsequent Kerensky regimes, that in the period from 1914-1917, the amount of bank notes in circulation rose 12 times. Additionally, the gold content of ruble coins was lowered to 5.5% of their total content.

Private Banking System

By 1917, there were also 47 commercial banks with 744 branches in larger cities spread across Russia. Since the early 1900's, these banks had also been establishing branches in London, Paris, and Zurich (some of which are once again operating in the 1990's).

Inside Russia, the banking system was well-developed. Provincial cities without branches of a commercial bank were served by city banks. In all, there were over 300 separate city banks which were founded by local authorities through the deposits of their residents. These banks provided loans to cover short-term financing and administered local mortgages.

Community of Mutual Credit (OVK)

Also prominent in the provincial areas was an investment network known as the Community of Mutual Credit, or "OVK" by its Russian acronym. The OVK served small industrial and commercial enterprises whose owners were members of the organization. By the beginning of 1914, there were over 1,108 separate OVK branches, with a total of about 600,000 members. Every member of an OVK branch had the right to participate in decisions and to apply for credit from the organization. Credit limits were usually in the amount of ten times a member's investment balance in the OVK.

Mortgage Banks

During the early 1900's, the large volume of construction in housing and other non-industrial infrastructures' helped support growth in mortgage banking. Government mortgage banks, divided into two spheres, for peasants and nobles, operated by granting loans from reserves accumulated through mortgage note revenues and annual profits on their securities. The Peasant Land Bank, for example, took an average annual profit of 5.5% on its securities alone.

In addition to government mortgage banks, there were 10 land banks and 36 regional mortgage banks. Many of the securities issued by these banks were also guaranteed by the government. Those that were, became highly quoted in domestic and international markets. The entire mortgage banking sector was so strong that it came to control over one-third of Russia's cultivated land.

Rural Cooperatives

Financing in the agricultural sphere was also facilitated by credit, as well as savings and loan cooperatives. From the period of 1905-1914, the number of these two types of cooperatives rose from 1,600 to 14,600. Both types of cooperatives provided loans primarily for the purchase of land, livestock, agricultural equipment, and fertilizer. They also financed rural retail trade. In addition to credit operations, the cooperatives sometimes sold members' products on commission and backed members on mortgage purchases of necessary agricultural equipment.

Bolshevik's and Gosbank

With the October Revolution of 1917, it was the Bolshevik's goal to take control of all aspects of the nation. As a part of this goal, they attached great importance to seizing and ultimately controlling Russia's well functioning banking system. A takeover of the banking system would logically begin with a takeover of Gosbank. Serving as "the bank of banks," Gosbank held accounts for commercial banks across the nation. It provided these banks with their own bank notes, and it conducted operations with their deposits. The finely tuned plan of the Bolshevik's consisted of first capturing Gosbank and all of its assets, then placing under its complete control the activities of all commercial banks and other credit organizations. The final step was to nationalize all banks and its entire support system.

On November 7, 1917, about 40 soldiers took control of Gosbank without any spilt blood. After the takeover, they simply left a few guards to join and supervise the bank's existing security guards.

The bank's officers, however, refused to recognize Soviet power and announced a strike, which was supported by the employees of the commercial banks. They began their strike by issuing themselves paychecks and then withdrawing their pay in cash, which caused a shortage of rubles among the general population. As the employees and officials of the banks continued to ignore all Soviet decrees, the Soviets responded by arresting the bank's top officials. In further response, on November 29, 1917, by armed assault, the Soviets took the key to the central monetary deposit safe. Soon afterward, without the use of any accounting methods or the registering of documents, the Soviets transferred 20 million rubles from Gosbank to their headquarters in Smol'nyi. Having taken over Gosbank, the communists moved to the second stage of their plan... nationalizing all commercial banks.

When officials went to open their commercial banks on the morning of December 28, 1917, they found them to be occupied by armed Soviet regiments. Each bank was also assigned a commissar who was required to personally approve all banking operations. Shortly after this, a decree was issued that nationalized all banks and changed the name of Gosbank to the National Bank. All commercial banks in Petrograd (Saint Petersburg) were reorganized into four divisions of the National Bank, which began operation in February 1918. By September of that year, the nationalization of all other commercial banks across Russia and their subsequent absorption into the National Bank system was completed.

When it first began operation in December of 1917, the National Bank limited its credit operations to financing war needs and to providing the largest cities with heat and various production requirements. At that time, the bank also ceased trading in securities as the Soviet government had annulled all internal and foreign government debts, and declared all government bonds and securities to be invalid. Soviet decrees from January 21-26, 1918, annulled 87 internal debts, 13 debts to international banks, and 137 railroad debts which had been guaranteed by the previous imperial and provisional governments.

War Communism

In 1918, with the beginning of the Russian Civil War, the Soviet government enacted a new set of economic and social policies known as War Communism. In 1919, the government ended the credit system for industry and stipulated that all industrial profits, which were being held in banks, were to be transferred to the treasury. If an industry were to require monetary funds, they would be provided by the National Bank. Though a national budget was maintained, it existed only fictionally on paper.

Eventually, ideologue's in the Communist Party and in Russia's leadership pushed for more extreme monetary changes. These communist believed that the newly created socialist society should live, develop, and perfect itself without the use of money. This fictitious idea took hold in government thinking when the communist succeeded in forcibly issuing the "Decree of the Soviet National Commissars" on January 19, 1920. This decree abolished the National Bank and transferred its operations to the National Committee of Finance. This committee retained exclusive rights to print money and abolished all other credit agencies in Russia.

At the same time, other measures were taken to effectively destroy the monetary system. Soviet authorities believed that the Russian currency system would become worthless if they accelerated the production of money without any effective limits. These central Soviet authorities gave to local organs of Soviet power the right to print money in accordance with their own needs. By today's standards, the subsequent events resulted in reaching absurd inflationary proportions. In a few regions of eastern Siberia, where they did not have printing presses, drinking alcohol labels were used in the place of money. For example, the labels of "Three-Star Cognac" were signed "three rubles--guaranteed," stamped by the local powers and the local bank, and issued as money. In all, over a trillion rubles (traditional and improvised) circulated in the economy by 1920. This became evidence to the reality that without cash, other items would take its place for trade or barter. Naturally, people will trade for the goods and services they need, with or without governmental backing.

From July 1921 to January 1922, the National Finance Committee issued an additional 14 trillion pieces of paper money. The rubles inflationary depreciation reached such a level that it was difficult to review accounts, or to carry out any trading because of the unfamiliarity of the large sums involved. As a result, barter became more common among the people in the street.

During this period of War Communism, industry fell into decline. Surviving industries were expected to hand over their production to the government and to rely on the government for providing them with raw materials, heat, and food provisions. Placed in a system that chose not to reward them with material or monetary bonuses for higher production rates, many workers left the industrial sphere and began producing handicrafts. These handicrafts could be traded with peasants for food products, which were becoming scarce in the larger cities.

The food shortages stemmed from the fact that the peasants had been cutting down on the amount of land that they cultivated as a result of the Soviet confiscation of their harvests. These confiscations were needed to meet the required allotments under War Communism. Officially, the authorities took from the peasants all of their harvest except for what would be required for the peasants' personal needs and for planting the coming year's crops. Often, however, even these future necessary provisions were eventually confiscated.

New Economic Policy (NEP)

The collapse of industry, frequent peasant uprisings, and the blockade of the channels to the Gulf of Finland by the navy in the Kronshtadt Rebellion against Lenin, were all evidence that War Communism had failed. The country's young leadership needed to resurrect a credit system and a trading system based upon a realistic relationship between goods and money, and do it quickly. In October of 1921, Soviet authorities created Gosbank RSFSR (Government Bank of the Russian Socialist Federation of Soviet Republics - whose name was changed to Government Bank of the Union of Soviet Socialist Republics-- Gosbank USSR--in July of 1923). The new Gosbank RSFSR was enjoined with the task of providing credit and other banking operations for the development of industry, agriculture, and the turnover of commodities. It was also empowered to reverse inflation and establish an acceptable level of monetary circulation.

To reverse inflation, Gosbank was instructed to issue a new series of currency. It was hoped that within a few issues, this new currency would become accepted and the current, increasingly worthless old currency could be withdrawn.

In October of 1922, Gosbank introduced into circulation, the "chervonets" coin. The name chervonets was taken from a type of gold coin minted in Russia in the eighteenth century. In terms of content, one chervonet contained the same amount of gold as a 10-piece imperial ruble coin, or 7.7423 grams of pure gold.

By producing the chervonets, Gosbank had at its disposal a large part, 900 tons, of Russia's gold reserves. When issued, it was understood that each chervonet was backed by the government with its vast gold reserves. Specifically, 25% of these reserves were in gold, international currency, and gems, while 75% was in what was considered to be highly liquid assets. The government issued the chervonets by taking loans on liquid assets and repaying them in chervonets. At the same time, the government declared the free exchange of chervonets for gold and manufactured corresponding gold coins. Exchange for the chervonet, however, hardly occurred and the government was forced to conduct international currency interventions on the black market, while supporting a higher exchange for the chervonet.

Gosbank then turned to three deflationary monetary reforms from 1922-1924. In 1922, the government issued a new ruble which was exchanged for the old one at the rate of 1:10,000. In 1923, another new ruble was issued. This time one ruble was exchanged for 100 rubles of the 1922 variety. In January 1924, treasury notes valued at 1, 3, and 5 rubles were issued and the chervonet was designated as the equivalent of ten rubles. After three months, these rubles were exchanged for the 1923 variety at a rate of 1:50,000. Thus, in the course of two years, Gosbank reduced the monetary circulation by 50 trillion units. The new monetary base helped establish a stable relationship between goods and currency, and it also increased the importance of Gosbank in the national economy.

By the beginning of 1922, Gosbank had 21 branches. By 1929, it had grown to over 589 branches. During that time, it had also moved beyond its original 1921 mandate, to fulfill the nations credit-accounting needs. As the years passed, Gosbank USSR emerged as the foundation component for an expanding credit system in Russia.

From 1922-1925, numerous banking structures were organized, including the All-Russian Cooperative Bank, the All-Ukrainian Cooperative Bank, the Russian Commodities-Industrial Bank (Prombank), the Far-Eastern Commercial Bank, the Northern Caucus Commercial Bank, the Central Asian Commercial Bank, the South-West Commercial Bank, the Electrification Bank (Elektrobank), and an additional 45 communal banks under the auspices of the

Central Committee Bank. Also, a system of agricultural credit was organized under the auspices of the Central Agricultural Bank, six republic banks for agricultural credit, 71 associations for agricultural credit, more than 9 thousand agricultural credit partnerships, and the renewed Communities of Mutual Credit.

A majority of these reestablished banks were registered as commercial enterprises. For example, Prombank, the newly-created commodities-industrial bank, was created toward the end of 1922, with beginning capital of 5 million gold rubles. It soon emerged as the largest credit-issuing bank after Gosbank USSR, and it eventually issued over 50,000 bonds at 100 rubles apiece. Though it was listed as a commercial bank, all of its bonds were held in the hands of governmental organizations, such as the National Committee of Goods and the High Soviet for the National Economy. In effect, Prombank was under government control and a government organ.

In September 1922, a reorganized OVK, Community of Mutual Credit, was established under a new charter. During the period of 1922-1926, over 300 separate OVK branches arose and expanded their composition of clients to include private merchants and independent craft specialists.

On December 12, 1922, Ruskombank (Russian Commercial Bank) was formed with the aid of Swiss capital reserves amounting to 10 million rubles (at that time equivalent to $5.2 million U.S. dollars). This was the first bank created in Russia with the help of international capital. The principle task of Ruskombank was to help commodities-industrial production enterprises to develop the internal domestic economy. In 1924, Ruskombank's bonds were redeemed by the National Committee of Internal Enterprise and by Gosbank, and the bank was reorganized and renamed Vneshtorgbank (Internal Enterprise Bank).

By the end of 1926, OVK's activities decreased as they were overshadowed by a rise in consumer cooperatives in both towns and rural areas. These consumer cooperatives became, in turn, displaced by private retail merchants. The OVK organizations were also squeezed out by handicraft-producer cooperatives, which were more attractive for people within the craft industry and which could supply them with more favorable raw materials, terms and services. Thus, people that may have otherwise joined an OVK went into these handicraft cooperatives, creating a new form of competition.

Retreat from the New Economic Policy (NEP)

By the late 1920's, the liberalized economic and monetary policies of the NEP were again curtailed as the government once again expanded its control. With the transition from War Communism, a large group of powerful communists had remained disapproving of the NEP. This block disapproved of the fact that the NEP tolerated private trade, the strengthening of monetary relations, and that the accumulation of private capital had been a reversal of the fundamental principles of socialism. They were vocal in their fears that this liberal course would lead to the restoration of capitalism in Russia.

Political disagreements about the NEP's effect were also fueled by infighting and the subsequent bids for power after Lenin's death in 1924. Policy debate centered around the best approach for securing an estimated 16-17 billion rubles in gold (more than $150 billion dollars by current rates), which was needed to fund the nations industrialization and to increase agricultural productivity.

There were many communists that believed it would be most effective to increase market relations, and to continue expanding the New Economic Policy. Advocates of this approach explained that a considerably high level of life and a gradual accumulation for investment in hard industry could be brought about by an expansion of light industry and the development of related commercial areas. They also favored the path of reliance on the private sector for agricultural production. Empower the people to produce on their own terms, and their prosperity would fuel growth throughout the country. Tax and control them to death and you will kill them and the economy.

Another group, which was headed by Joseph Stalin, believed that maximum collectivization of agricultural production, complete government control of light and heavy industry, and the liquidation and confiscation of private commerce would be the best means for directing resources into fulfilling the nation's goals under his leadership. In the second half of the 1920's, opponents of the NEP gained control and began to reverse once again the direction of economic and monetary progress.

The credit system, most notably the OVK organizations, were the first to be scrutinized and targeted. In 1927-1928, authorities in Russia and other Soviet republics began to discuss whether or not workers and functionaries should withdraw their memberships in the OVK organizations. They believed that OVK organizations would drive a wedge in society by creating a class of private capitalists apart from regular workers and functionaries. This alleged destruction of "class principle" was considered criminal behavior at that time. By the end of the 1920's, the majority of the OVK's once again ceased business activities.

Meanwhile, the banking system was also reverting to collective centralization as a result of market events and by policy design. In June 1927, the national leadership issued a decree, "On the Principles of Creating a Credit System." Previously, small branch banks had concentrated on short-term loans and the Gosbank had serviced most long-term loans. This decree allowed banks to pursue parallel activities with each other and to go beyond their fixed framework within specified branches of the economy. When a great amount of banks competed against one another to gain clients for short-term loans, it resulted in the bankruptcy of several banks. In the beginning of 1928, Prombank (named changed to Russian acronym BDK) was reorganized to provide accounting services as a specialized bank of long-term credit for industry and energy divisions of the economy. Its short-term operations were transferred to Gosbank. At the same time, Electrobank was liquidated and its active and passive long-term credit activities were transferred to BDK.

The government continued to speak out against private enterprise and as the bank's pushed for more autonomy, the state sought to mold them back into instruments of a centrally-directed economy. Toward the end of 1930, the NEP was abolished and the banking system once again endured tremendous changes.

Large scale industrialization started early in the 1930's, and in order to reinvest in capital construction, the government required that all money resources be centralized. The NEP credit system, which included most banks and credit organizations as well as commercial lending institutions, was not able to adapt to the new situation. A majority of the banks which made short-term and long-term commercial loans, paid no attention to government policy.

Credit reform in 1930-32, changed the overall structure of the banking system. First, by ending reform, commercial lending which prevented the government from having closer control over certain businesses was abolished. The only form of lending now became a Central Bank loan. The purpose and order of issuing loans was highly controlled, and an entire system of credit transfers was implemented.

The banking system of the country was divided into two strictly limited tiers. The core of it became the State Bank, which performed lending to all industries (except for construction). The second tier was a number of state specialized banks, which were centers for financing and for long-term capital investment. At this time, the banking system became the conductor of the state's centralized economic policy. It was the tool of direct planning, rather than an instrument of free economic relations. This total control over the economy and any banking systems remained stagnant and completely unchallenged for the next forty years. All efforts to make any changes and free up the system of tight controls were silenced.

By the 1970's, there was a deep growing gap between declared statements and real actions. The use of the infamous false statistical data was common practice throughout the economy. All reforms were required to fit the criteria of reinforcing the basis of socialism - state ownership. All international policy pursued the goal of global superiority over the Western capitalist countries, and massive economic help to the USSR-Indoctrinated countries of the third world. At this time, it was becoming clear that the government was over spending on its military superiority efforts and neglecting civilian needs.

In all industries, except for the military, there was an ever widening gap between the USSR and Western countries. Corruption and theft became common features of the state institutions. Additionally, the export of non-recoverable natural resources, such as oil and gas, were sold at dumping prices.

This made it possible to sustain a satisfactory level of consumption in the leading industrial centers. To make matters worse, in several regions there was a sharp deficit of foodstuff and consumer goods. Then finally, in 1985, the government officially announced that the country's economy was in a crisis. Perestroika (restructuring and rebuilding) and the search for a way out of this terrible experiment began. It was finally time for glasnos (openness) and the acknowledgement of the need for change.

An important part in accomplishing this transformation was through the use of the financial economic system. At that time, the entire banking system consisted of the State Bank and subordinate savings offices, which were the formally independent Stroybank and Vnesheconombank. Additionally, there were some Soviet commercial banks overseas, which were fully controlled by the State Bank Management Board and the Ministry of Finance. False accounting figures of credit investments were set up simply to balance the budgets of industrial growth, and to indicate that there were available monetary resources. The budget deficits were fully covered by banknote issues. However, no real account was ever taken of the available credit resources, because the deficit in the State Bank and Stroybank budgets were refunded by artificial inflation of the country's credit capacity. Thus, the State Bank system was able to make unlimited loans with no impact on its own liquidity.

There was no anti-inflationary procedure in the State Bank or in Stroybank, because all loans increased the customers account balance. In this condition of a single State Bank, unlimited deposit emission of rubles was possible, which were basically open credit lines. Therefore, heavy attention was focused on preventing bank "credit" money from being converted into cash.

In 1987, new state specialized banks were established which were focused on the main industries, thus setting up stronger relations between credit institutions and production. This is how the present banking system began its development. There was need in the economy for commercial banking services and that gap was filled. The rate of development in the economy has paralleled the growth in those banking services fulfilled by the commercial banks.

However, looking back, we see that these banking reforms were accomplished too fast, without the time needed to set specific strategic and operational goals. This also led to a duplication of some of the state banks' responsibilities. The number of administrative staff members increased, settlement operations were deferred, and document turnover became an overwhelming burden. When non-business competition appeared between banks, at times their relations became antagonistic. While during this fast moving time, local specialization failed to develop. Some banks were not able to open local branches because there was an insufficient number of companies to service. Thus, one branch might run business on behalf of one, two, or even three different specialized banks.

An attempt to make local branches self-running businesses also failed, because it was hard to quantify the resources available for their operations. The organizational structure of many of these banks was also unclear. The system of specialized banks could no longer support the emerging demand for free economic relations and services.

In 1988, the government lost its firm control over money turnover. With the first signs of galloping inflation coming to light, the Soviet republics started demanding more economic freedom. The response of the government was to announce overall economic and democratic reforms. This they felt compelled to do without having a well defined strategy, to say nothing about the need for fine tuned tactics. Part of this reform was to establish needed changes in the banking system. However, the ever expanding complexities of the internal Soviet economy continued to overwhelm the central control imposed by the communist leaders in Moscow.

This chaos called for a totally different banking system, which soon began to sporadically emerge. In 1988, new commercial banks were founded following established Western methods. This was the beginning of the liberalization of the banking system in Russia and the start of true economic reform.

Chapter 1.2

Banking Infrastructure Development

A nation's banking industry is an aggregate of its banks, the banking infrastructure, banking law, and the banking market. All are in close relationship with one another, the economy, society, political philosophy, and the environment. Being a part of the economy, the banking industry reflects economic relationships and growth at all levels of the society.

The new improved informational technology and systems have proven crucial to the successful development of Russian banks in these changing conditions. With the market economy encouraging strong competition, the existence of an economic crisis, and the instability of state and corporate financing are a real threat without the use of this technology. It is impossible to finance any project without using technology as a research tool and as a vehicle for organization and communication. The availability and accuracy of information and its analysis have become an indispensable attribute of all banking services. The information necessary to the bankers is normally provided by special agencies called credit bureaus. In some countries, the data required by the banks can be received from many reference books (trade and industrial registers), journals, special publications, or be solicited from the head bank where the customer's file is kept. In Russia, this new sphere of the market economy is quickly developing and improving. Open access to this economic activity information has become necessary for the successful development of healthy bank loans and stable securities markets.

The effects of any articulate market research touches the functioning of the banking industry as a whole, as well as the individual banks. Before 1995, few economic research centers had been established in Russia, and the research work of these few economic centers were not even coordinated. As a rule, the organizational structure of many commercial banks did not include those analytical units which could investigate the effective marketing of banking products and the efficiency of banking operations. Currently, almost all large banks in Russia now have a research division.

During the transitional period in Russia's economy, when the instructions of the former State Bank of the USSR became out of date, a new set of regulations and planned directives were implemented. A startling peculiarity in the development of Russian commercial banks is that there was not a unified legal system for banking until 1995. Thus, in the beginning, the bank's dictated their methods of operation based upon their own understandings and organizational activities. Now this situation has been corrected, as the Duma (Russia's legislature) and the Central Bank work together to adopt new laws and give concise operational instructions to all commercial banks. The playing field is now being plowed for an environment of trustworthy normal commercial banking activities in Russia.

Human resources are a very important element of any banking infrastructure. In Russia, there is now a network of vocational institutions of higher educational and technical colleges, which provide training for specialists in finance and banking. There is also a growing network of primary institutions, financial schools and academic colleges. The new generation is studying general sciences and special disciplines such as financing, banking, and accounting. The retraining of existing personnel and the subsequent improvement of their skills is now concentrated in special commercial schools, with both courses and training centers set up and financed within the large banks.

Hundreds of Russian banking clerks have gone abroad to study banking business and practice in the United States and Europe. By 1996, Russia had many banks which could compete effectively with Western banks in the area of customer services.

The sudden increase in the number of participants in the market economy, and the subsequent volume of transactions performed by the banks, has given them an incentive to install new communication lines and instill a higher level of technical maintenance for their banking operations. The Russian banking industry is gradually being equipped with these advanced means of communication, which will result in an acceleration of payments and settlements.

The banking industry cannot exist without the banking market, which organizes banking resources and provides banking products. Under the conditions of economic crises and the high inflation present in Russia today, it seems impossible to accumulate major resources for needed material investments. In banks throughout Russia, the share of public savings in disposable cash income accounted for only 6.4% in 1995, compared to 6.8% in 1994. Today, the situation is slowly improving. Inflation is now under better control, and savings in disposable cash income has increased to account for 7.5% at the beginning of 1996.

Early in 1995, one quarter of all Russian business entities were unprofitable, and with only small balances in their bank accounts. This naturally, impeded the proper development of the banking industry. Credit trading and short-term lending have not yet become a significant part of this growing market of banking activities. However, the balances on deposit are increasing and in the last ten months of 1996, balances rose an average of 24%.

The development and introduction of new types of services based on credit cards and electronic payments has slowed down since 1995, due to the reality that the technical base of Russian banks was not powerful enough to handle them properly. The situation is rapidly changing however, and several Russian banks can now comply with the technical requirements of an average Western bank.

For example, recently Mosbusinessbank increased its plastic credit card operations. Specifically, it introduced ETN (European Travel Network) and IAPA discount credit cards, which entitle their holders to discounts on hotels and car rentals. In addition, the holders of the VISA-Mosbusinessbank Credit Card are entitled to policies of the Gesa Assistance French insurance company. The Bank has aggressively issued plastic cards, including VISA-Mosbusinessbank and Mosbusinessbank-Union Credit Cards, bringing the total in early 1997 to 5,700 cards, which was 2.7 times higher than the previous year's figure.

For its more reliable clients, Mosbusinessbank has developed and implemented a VISA-Mosbusinessbank Business Credit Card program, which can be used as a true credit card as well as a credit line. The program provides short-term credit for clients, and renders the cardholder a supplementary set of services including discounts on hotel bills and travel discounts, in addition to accident, medical, and loss of luggage insurance. In Russia, VISA credit cards turned over an amazing $110.6 million USD in 1996. In 1995, among those Russian banks who were members of the VISA payment system, Mosbusinessbank accounted for 21.8% of the total volume of payment. Currently, Mosbusinessbank continues to service Visa, Diners Club and Eurocard/MasterCard holders.

Mosbusinessbank will cash for its clients, traveller's cheques drawn on ETC-Thomas-Cook-MasterCard, VISA, American Express, Bank of America, City Corp., Bank of Tokyo, Fuji Bank, Mitsui Bank, Sumitomo Bank, in addition to selling ETC-Thomas-Cook-MasterCard, VISA, and American Express traveller's cheques. The cash equivalent of the accepted cheques are deposited into either the client's or the bank's account on the same day they are handed over to the cash department of the bank's Head Office. In Mosbusinessbank's exchange offices, private individuals can even have their traveller's cheques cashed either in rubles or in an international currency.

This new and exciting Russian banking system includes the Central Bank of Russia, commercial banks, credit organizations, and the representative offices of many foreign banks. It is a system which is developing quickly and is now entering into a stage of improved stability.

Chapter 1.3

Saint Petersburg Association of Commercial Banks

The Saint Petersburg Association of Commercial Banks is a non-commercial public organization that was established by 28 banks in that city more than four years ago, during the process of reconstruction of the Russian banking system. It's purpose was to consolidate their efforts for efficient banking development in the city of Saint Petersburg and the Leningrad Region. Today it consists of 34 member banks.

The President, Vladimir V. Jickovich, is the head of the Association. The Council of the Association, which consists of 8 bankers, works under his leadership. The Association also has an Executive Committee which assists the President in fulfilling his duties and realizing decisions of the Council. Members of this committee include experts and consultants in finance, jurisprudence, electronics, public relations and international links.

The primary purpose of the Association is to promote the interests of the Saint Petersburg banking community in contacts with the Legislative Assembly, the Mayor's Office, and various public organizations. As it functions, the Association takes into account the real situation in the financial and political environments of the city, enabling it to evaluate existing problems and foresee the future development of events. The Association issues its own quarterly, "Bulletin of the Association of Commercial Banks," with balance-sheets of its members and other information of interest. One of the aims of the Association is to make the banking sector more open, thereby facilitating an environment of trustworthiness and stability between all the participants in the market.

The Association of Commercial Banks has continually developed contacts with various analogous associations and institutions internationally, and therefore welcomes additional connections.

Saint Petersburg faces a very complicated situation in the banking sector today. After a period of extensive development, banks have tended to encounter difficulties. Some of these difficulties have even brought on bankruptcy. These instances of instability have naturally shaken the depositor and creditor faith in our banking system.

The main problems which are now faced by the Association of Commercial Banks are as follows:

- Develop an optimum organizational structure, including modern methods of management.
- Establish proper directional priorities for the activities of the Association.
- Organize the work of Association members in the various Committees, on a volunteer basis.
- Organize the information distribution and publication activity.
- Determine the Association's role in the process of banking standardization.
- Determine practical implementation of staff improvement programs.
- Increase participation in internship programs in the banking sphere.

UNIT 2

Central Bank of Russia

Introduction

The challenges facing the Central Bank of Russia are unique. That it has the power to meet these challenges is made clear by this chapter. Seemingly big problems often have very simple solutions when you eliminate limiting beliefs. The Central Bank has the means to settle Russia's $80 billion national debt and create full employment and industrial recovery.

While Russian Foreign Debt totaled slightly more than $80,000,000,000 at the start of 1994. It is not an extraordinarily large amount considering the potential productivity of the population. Nor is it a large sum considering the wealth of Russian resources. By comparison, American government debt is presently $4,136,500,000,000 or 5100% the amount of Russian government debt. What presently makes the Russian government debt seem large and impossible to pay, is the present low productivity of the population.

On a per-capita basis, the Russian debt is much smaller than the per-capita debt of the U.S. population. Per capita debt of Americans is $16,221 as of the beginning of 1994. So, Americans owes 29 times as much per capita as do the Russians. But, as a percentage of per capita Gross Domestic Production, Russians owe more than Americans. The Russian government owes 20% of per capita gross domestic production in debt, while the American government owes 15% of per capita gross domestic production.

There in lies the problem, and the solution, facing the Central Bank of Russia today. It is clear that Russian assets, resources and potential labor productivity are not producing adequate GDP by global norms. But Russian citizens are not responsible for this because they have not been allowed control over the actualization of their potential for production.

About $32 billion of interest and principal payments were due in 1994. The Budget Committee of the Lower House of Parliament of Russia said in 1994, that the repayment figure for that year, which includes some obligations carried over from 1993, is far too high for the economy to bear. The Russian government budgeted $4.7 billion for all debt repayment in 1994. The decision of the Russian Parliament about the limited ability of Russia to pay its debts was probably an accurate appraisal of the facts, but it does not answer the citizens questions of how this has happened and is continuing to happen. It does not answer citizens questions about what could be done about it and why it isn't being done.

What normally happens when assets which have a potential value of producing 100%, produce only 50%? In private industry for example, such a business either becomes bankrupt or new managers are selected to do a better job. But governments cannot become bankrupt, so the absence of responsible management can continue, while the employers, sponsors, and citizens of such a government must pay the price by losing their jobs.

If you own an automobile and it sits in your garage and you do not use it and you owe money to the bank for this automobile, then it is logical to return the automobile to the bank and let them lease it to a taxi chauffeur to use. He will earn the money to pay the bank for the auto. You will not owe the money anymore. The taxi driver will have a job and pay taxes. The Russian Government will receive the taxes of the income of the taxi driver.

This brings up the point that idle assets have no value. Only the proper use of assets in producing turnover and cash flow gives the asset its value. The best Russian hotel, if it sits empty in the dessert, is worth nothing, even though it costs a lot to build it there.

Industrial production of Russian industry fell 25% in the first quarter of 1994, and compared to 1989, it may be as low as 50% today. More than 5000 Russian industries are closed and idle. More than 12 million Russian are unemployed and this figure may increase to 24 million if these assets are not properly managed.

Why not then give the automobile to the bank? Why not transfer the ownership of some Russian industry and resources to the creditors around the world? They will not let these assets sit idle. Such industry will have value only if they create turnover by production. If such an automobile needs a new motor before it can be used, the new owner will see to it that it receives a new motor. If a factory needs new technology or machinery or management, the new owner will provide it so that turnover can be created. Then the factory which has been received in payment of debts will become worth something. It can now produce cash from turnover and repay the debt, instead of sitting idle and worthless. And, it will employ Russian citizens no matter who owns it.

If the Russian government transfers industry in payment of debt, it will solve the problem of unemployment. Is it better management to have an automobile in the garage, or give it to a bank in settlement of debts and have the government receive income tax payments from an employed taxi chauffeur? Which gives the most national pride?

For many years Europeans and Asians have been buying industry in America. Is America any less American? Does it matter who owns the factories in which American earn the highest salaries in the world? Do not American workers use their savings and pensions to buy shares of these companies on

American stock exchanges? Rich workers are the ultimate owners of everything. Governments who have a rich population find their budgets well supported by the profits of such workers. The wise government follows a policy that creates rich citizens who can take good care of the government, for such citizens can pay in taxes for all the services that a caring government wishes to provide its citizens. A government cannot give away what its citizens have not yet produced. That creates debts. If, at the same time the government prevents its citizens from being economically creative and productive, it is committing financial suicide. It is the highest priority of government to create rich citizens. It is impossible to properly govern poor people. Poor people cannot pay for a government. And whatever a government gives must be paid for by its citizens. The only way for a government of poor people to survive is to compete with its citizens for survival by taking from its citizens instead of performing the will of its citizens, with the surplus production and savings of the people. Which choice gives more national pride and satisfaction? Who can be proud of serving in a government if it does not fulfill its highest priority function, the welfare of its people?

If Russians truly want to own Russian industry, they first need a high salary with which to buy shares of their industries. For this, they require global partners to provide machinery and increase the workers productivity. What better way to get such investment, then to pay Russian debts with its industry. If the bank has the automobile, it will make certain the credits are repaid that are owed to it for the automobile's financing. The solution is obvious and simple.

Of course, if Russian citizens prefer that their government own industry instead of its citizens, then this is also easy to accomplish. By being employed and paying income taxes, citizens can provide the government with the money to buy back the automobile later. But, if the government exists only as the elected representative of the people and the people own the government and it is their government, isn't it simpler to let the people buy the shares instead of the government? The Russian government already sees this as the correct policy by the support it has given to the policy of privatization. The Government already recognizes that industry in the hands of people will produce the most. Why not follow this to its logical conclusion by paying government debts with industry. It is called "Debt for Ownership Exchanges" or "Debt for Equity Swaps" to use the normal expression. The nationality of people, makes no difference in economics. Those who think otherwise suffer economic consequences such as Russia now experiences.

The only logical form of support of the government by citizens, is the payment of income taxes on profits. VAT (Value Added Tax), tariffs, import and export duties, license fees, export permit auction fees and all other forms of taxes are a withdrawal of capital from the production process before the profit of the activity can be measured. The only place to tax production activity is after the process is complete, and it can be measured to see if there is a profit. If there is a tax before that, it constitutes a confiscation of citizens working capital and demands a penalty for trying to support the government. This is counterproductive to the long term interests of the people and, therefore, of their government. It makes it more difficult for people to try to support the government. It encourages people to stop trying to produce for themselves and instead leads them to depend upon the government to support the citizens. That is of course an impossibility. Governments do not produce anything with which they can support citizens. Governments are spenders not earners. Citizens are the only ones who can support themselves, and their government can only be given some of the profits to provide services more economically to some citizens. A central source of road construction is more logical compared to each one personally building his own highway. But a central source of production is a contradiction with reality. Each citizen himself is the only one in control of his life energy and he or she alone can produce something with it. A government can only help to encourage productivity and divide some of the profits, willingly entrusted to it by its citizens, fairly among the citizens, for the mutual benefit of all its citizens and to take care of those who physically cannot help themselves.

Can every citizen eat if the government eats first and eats more than is produced? To eat more than is produced means eating capital. Eating capital results in closing factories and that produces 12 million unemployed. It's a simple question to solve. Everyone in the world uses experts to solve questions. Let Russia's creditors solve the unemployment problem by making Russia's creditors responsible for creating employment. Give the creditors the industry as repayment. It can be bought back later with the profits of the workers, made from collaboration with the creditors as partners.

Is this really the solution or another experiment? For this we have only to check the accounting experience of other governments. It is interesting to look at the government budget of The United States and see that American citizens, when left largely free of economic laws and rules and regulations to be creative in production in any way they please, produce $102,376 in goods per capita compared to the per capita production of Russians of R5,029,166.

Since Russians are equally educated as Americans, we can only assume something is interfering with the normal creative capability of Russian citizens. America has no VAT, no export duties of any kind, and generally no export license requirements. Mostly anyone can make anything and export it with only the responsibility to pay an income tax. Americans have new machinery and the latest technology. Could this maybe be the difference? It certainly isn't any inherent superiority. Maybe it is the superiority of freedom of access to economic tools?

The Russian government budget for 1994 estimated that 16.6% of GDP will be paid by the Russian people in taxes for a total amount of

R120,700,000,000,000.

Americans paid their government about 12% of GDP (Gross Domestic Product) in taxes, but it amounted to $2,533,248,000,000.00. So the country with less economic laws and lower taxes received more money from its citizens. Forget for the moment the exchange rate which distorts things and complicates things. Even if the ruble/dollar exchange rate were still today R120 =$1.00 instead of R5806 = $1.00, both citizens would still have paid the same even though Americans pay 25% less than Russians pay in income taxes. Considering all the other forms of Russian taxes, Russians of course pay far more than Americans. Of course, when in 1994 R120 trillion could be exchanged on the Moscow Exchange for about $60 billion dollars, it is easier to operate a government when you receive $2,533,248,000,000 than R120,700,000,000,000.

Transferring Russian industry to creditors and creating full employment would probably bring the value of the ruble back to its 1991 value, if the government also stopped printing money. This would become possible with the higher production, lower taxes and greater payments in absolute quantity of money.

It is also interesting that Americans received a much greater share of GDP in wages. The Russian government gave their workers only 18% of production value (GDP) in income. Americans received 80%.

So, from a comparison of other government budgets, it is clearly proven that government finances are solved by first taking care of the finances of the people. The competence of creation belongs to the citizens. Only people can create the monetary means to support their government.

Of course it can be argued that a great deal of the real value of Russian GDP is hidden in below world market domestic prices. What then is the real world market or human consumption value of Russia's 754,375,000,000,000 GDP? If the total value of exported Russian GDP in world market prices is $50 billion, what is left over for domestic consumption? It is very hard to say. But we do know that the per capita income of Americans is $82,785, and the average wage of Russians was reported by the Russian government in 1994 as R1.92 million rubles. The cost of basic foods was reported as R444,000 per year in 1994, or 23% of annual wages. Maybe it also costs Americans 23% of their salary. Maybe not. That is not the important question. The question is, *"If Russian wages are kept at the present level, what must the exchange rate become before Russians have the same buying power to live as Americans Have?"*

My guess is R120 = $1.00. What do you think? At that point, "At world market prices," the per capita GDP of Russian would be 40% of the American per capita GDP. If, when this is accomplished, life is not good enough, it can be increased further. It is clearly not a mistake to start, even if we do not know the exact figure. The direction that must be taken is all that is necessary to know in order to begin. There is only one way to accomplish this, permit the Russian worker to make Russian industry more productive. Transfer some Russian industry to Western creditors and together with Russian workers let them accomplish this together. In the process they will solve the financial problems of their government as well. God let this sanity happen.

These then are some of the questions facing the Central Bank of Russia as it prepares for the 21st Century. There is plenty of information available that indicates which practices work in a market economy. It remains for the Central Bank to bring about consistency in monetary policy, with the known phenomena of universal economic life. There is no need to reinvent the wheel.

Chapter 2.1

General Provisions of the Central Bank

The Central Bank of the Russian Federation (CBRF) is the principal bank in the country today. It is the issue center of Russia responsible for all cash and credit regulation, the administration of commercial banks, and the international exchange policy. The status, objectives, functions, discretion and guidelines for organization and work of the Central Bank are determined in the Constitution of the Russian Federation, under the section, "About the Central Bank of the Russian Federation."

On April 12, 1995, the State Duma confirmed the federal laws on the activities of the Central Bank, but with several amendments added. As stated, the main objectives of the Central Bank are the protection and provision of stability for the ruble, including its purchase power and rate of exchange in relation to international currencies. Additionally, the Central Bank influences the development and enforcement of the banking industry regulations within Russia, and the insurance of an efficient and continuous performance of the clearing system (the settlement of debts between the banks).

The Central Bank maintains exclusive legal status, in comparison with other legal entities under Russian law. This unique status is based upon its double nature, both political and economic in the domestic economy. On one hand in the economy, the Central Bank plays the role of the authoritative body which implements the economic policy on behalf of the government. On the other hand, it performs the role of an ordinary participant in national trading activities. Thus, it combines the features of both public and private institutions. Having a particular legal status which is not related to either the organizational or legal forms known to the civil law, the Central Bank is not a state bank, but at the same time it takes a special place in the system of the government of Russia. Ideally, there is a separation between the Central Bank and any "political" decisions.

Within the rights given to it by the Russian Constitution and subsequent federal laws, the Central Bank is relatively independent in its work, as can normally be expected in times of transition. Federal and local authorities have no right to interfere in the operation of the Central Bank, or in the implementation of its legal functions and its efforts of stability for the banking community. The relative independence of the Central Bank is ensured by the impossibility to divide or to alienate it from its Charter capital and other property owned by the federal state and entrusted to it. The Bank is also self-financing, as all costs are covered by its own income. The Bank maintains its independence from accountability for state obligations, except in cases when it is stipulated under a prior agreement or law. It has been granted the availability of special mechanisms to regulate the national cash and credit system, and is free to choose, at its discretion, the specific forms and methods of that regulation.

It is also made clear that the actions of the Central Bank cannot be contrary to federal law. The effective activation date of any Bank actions is stated when they are published in the official paper of the Central Bank of Russia. The following excerpts from *Vestnik Banka Rossii* (the Bulletin of the Central Bank of Russia), are accepted rules maintained by the Board of Directors of the Central Bank. The acts of the Central Bank do not have a retroactive force, as dictated by the provisions of the constitution.

Any of the Central Bank's decisions, which directly affect the rights, freedoms, or duties of the Russian citizen, must be registered at the Ministry of Justice. This claim must be made in the procedure established for the registration of the acts of all federal ministries and departments.

The decisions of the Central Bank are sent, when necessary, to all registered commercial banks by the postal service, or by an advanced technological communication medium. The normal acts of the Central Bank may be appealed in the proper established procedure.

The Central Bank has no right to give loans to the Russian government for use in covering the budgetary deficit or to buy government securities at initial issue, except for those cases when this is permitted by federal law and as it relates to the federal budget. Within its own legal ability, the Central Bank has the right to do any lawful banking transaction with local Russian banks and international credit organizations.

The Central Bank has no right to perform a banking transaction with legal entities and individuals that do not have a valid license for banking operations within Russia. The Bank is open, within the law, for the constructive cooperation with all authorities. In conjunction with the government of Russia, it develops and maintains a consistent state monetary and lending policy.

The Chairman of the Central Bank, or by his order one of his deputies, takes part in the meetings of the federal government. The Minister of Finance and the Minister of the Economy participate on the Board of the Central Bank as a consultative vote. The Bank and the Government are to inform each other of all presupposed policies that are of some significance to the state as a whole, and are to assist in the coordination of these policies. This is to be done with regular consultations and study.

Under the Central Bank's authority is the National Banking Council. This council includes representatives from the Ministry of Finance and Ministry of Economics, the President of Russia, the Duma, the Central Bank, various commercial bank representatives, and other independent experts. This pluralism of representation from the many spheres of influence in Russia come together for major economic and financial banking decisions.

The Central Bank is accountable to the State Duma of the Federal Assembly, which in part means:

- The appointment to, and the ouster from the post of Chairman, upon presentation of a candidate by the President of Russia.
- The appointment to, and the ouster from the post of the Members of the Board of Directors.
- The presentation of the annual report for their consideration and auditing opinion.
- The appointment of an independent accounting firm for auditing.
- Parliamentary hearings on the activities of the Bank, including the participation of all its representatives.
- A minimum of two times a year, the Chairman of the Bank reports to the State Duma on its activities, the annual report, and the basic lines of the single State monetary-credit policy.

Basic objectives of the Central Bank's activities are:

- The protection and insurance of the ruble's stability, including its purchasing power and rate of foreign exchange.
- The development and strengthening of the Russian banking system.
- The insurance of an efficient and uninterrupted functioning system of payment settlements.

Chapter 2.2

Functions and Governing Departments

The Central Bank of Russia, in interaction with the Government, maintains a single state monetary-credit policy. Its aim is to protect and ensure the stability of the Russian ruble. Additionally, one of the most important functions of the Bank is the printing of cash. By law, the Central Bank has the exclusive right to issue rubles, to organize their circulation and removal.

The separation of political and fiscal policy decisions is still the goal. Therefore, it is prohibited to introduce other monetary units, or to issue their substitutes within Russian territory. Also, the law does not foresee the introduction of a formal standard rate between the ruble and gold, or any other precious metal.

By arranging the cash circulation around the Russian territory, the Central Bank exercises the following functions:

- the forecasting and organization of production, transportation and safe-keeping of bank notes and coins
- the creation of reserve funds
- the introduction of rules for safe-keeping, transportation, and collection of the cash money for commercial banks
- the identification of signs of payment capacity for banknotes and coins, and the introduction of rules to replace and destroy defectives
- the creation of regulations for commercial banks to perform their cash operations

The Central Bank establishes rules for carrying out settlements in Russia. To regulate the aggregate needs and demands for cash in Russia, and to support the ruble's foreign exchange rate, the Bank purchases and sells foreign currency on an organized foreign exchange market (the Moscow Interbank Foreign Exchange). The Bank states and publishes formal rates of exchange of foreign currencies to the ruble, and takes other actions of intervention and regulation aimed to ensure stability of the ruble.

The Central Bank is responsible for determining the procedure for making financial settlements with other countries. The Bank organizes and exercises currency control, both indirectly and through authorized banks, in accordance with government legislation.

The Central Bank establishes rules for the following:
- banking operations, bookkeeping, and accounting for the national banking system
- the state registration of commercial banks
- the issue and recall of the licenses of credit organizations and auditing organizations

The Bank is also a creditor of last resort for commercial banks, and must follow the established system of refinancing.

Since February 1994, the Central Bank has been organizing and holding credit auctions, through which former state resources are distributed on a competitive basis. The auctions are held through banks with good financial standing, and are aimed to ensure the maintenance of a liquid state of the market. From July until September 1996, the Bank sold over 685 billion rubles in resources at these auctions.

An important component of the Central Bank's monetary and credit regulation, is its function and participation in the organization and operation of the treasury bills market. This serves as a non-inflationary source to finance the federal budget, and to cover the state debt. Together with the Finance Ministry, official dealers, and the Moscow Interbank Foreign Exchange, the Central Bank forms the infrastructure of the market for treasury bills. This is done by implementing the functions of a representative agent (commercial bank) for the Finance Ministry, by servicing the debt, acting as a dealer, and also as a body for regulation and control of the market. In addition, the Bank backs up the technical and organizational side of the operations for short-term coupon-free treasury bills (GKO). It also carries out auctions, repayment, preparation of necessary documentation, and remittance of cash to the account of the Finance Ministry.

The Central Bank takes part in the preparation of the forecast of the Russian balance of payments, and organizes the transactions of these balance of payments within Russia. In order to perform these functions, the Bank analyzes and forecasts the conditions of the national economy on the whole, and locally by region. This involves a review of the monetary-credit relations, and the currency-and-financial price relations. The Bank must openly publish the relevant materials and the statistical data for public review.

As a body for the state cash and credit regulation, the Central Bank is empowered by law to use a broad range of instruments to ensure the strengthening and stability of the ruble. For example, the Central Bank can change interest rates on its transactions and regulate proposals for resources by commercial banks. These mandatory provisions are done by means of reserve requirements, setting performance standards for transactions on the open market, refinancing of the banks, foreign exchange regulation, setting up of breakpoints for the cash mass, and through direct quantitative restrictions.

Because of the transitional stage of the Russian economy, and the existence of criminal elements, there is underdevelopment surrounding market relationships in production and lending financing. The Central Bank cannot fully use the market tools of regulation, such as re-endorsement of the bills and performance of Lombard operations and transactions on the open market. That is why, in its practical work, the Central Bank applies both administrative and market methods. This is especially evident at the current stage of anti-inflationary regulations.

With an aim to limiting credit issues by banks, on January 1, 1991, the Central Bank introduced the discount rate on loans given to commercial banks which took into account the ruble's devaluation. The ruble's value has continued to change many times since 1991. The following chart demonstrates a sample of how the discount rate has changed in the last six years:

Figure 1. Central Bank

	Discount Rate
January 1991	20%
March 1992	50%
June 1992	120%
October 1993	210%
August 1994	130%
January 1995	200%
February 1996	120%
October 1996	60%
January 1997	48%
February 1997	42%
April 1997	36%
June 1997	24%

This information is evidence that the Central Bank is very flexible in responding to the economic situations of the Russian market. From January 1991 to December 12, 1996, the Bank changed the discount rate 29 times. All varied functions of the Bank are reflected in its current statement of assets and liabilities. The following chart demonstrates the changes in that statement from March 1995 to November 1996:

Figure 2a.
Central Bank of Russia
(millions of rubles)

ASSETS		
ITEM	MARCH 1995	NOVEMBER 1996
GOLD	4,361,189	29,811,534
FOREIGN CURRENCY	23,591,294	80,709,545
CASH	410,868	905,338
LOANS TO FINANCIAL MINISTRIES	62,004,039	58,740,587
LOANS	21,652,846	9,242,172
SECURITIES	7,266,591	60,392,142
INTERSTATE SETTLEMENTS	5,945,756	4,641,676
OTHER ASSETS	15,225,856	54,497,300
TOTAL ASSETS	**140,458,439**	**298,940,294**

In Figure 2a and 2b, we can see that the totals more than doubled from March 1995 to November 1996. The amount of gold and hard currency has increased more than 14 times, which are signs of growing favorable conditions for Russia's Central Bank. In January 1997, the hard currency reserves of the Central Bank were $15 billion, and in July 1997, that amount was $23.8 billion.

Figure 2b.
Central Bank of Russia
(millions of rubles)

Liabilities		
	March 1995	November 1996
Registered Capital	3,000	3,000
Reserve Capital	2,989,266	25,662,224
Hard Currency Account	4,123,700	14,038,192
Cash in Circulation	34,048,694	99,644,868
Means Commercial Banks	22,593,696	39,632,044
Means of Budget and Client	16,975,738	20,274,732
Means in the Settlements	5,017,661	7,964,874
Other Liabilities	54,706,784	91,720,360
Total Liabilities	**140,458,439**	**298,940,294**

The Central Bank is a centralized system with a vertical structure of management. The organizational structure includes the head office, 60 head departments, and 19 national banks. It is composed of 29 regional centers of information, 1356 cash centers, 3 computer centers, 13 banking schools and 21 other institutions. The territorial administrative departments of the Central Bank do not have the status of a legal entity nor do they have the right to make decisions of a normative nature. They operate on the basis of following those Regulations established for them by its Board of Directors. The field departments of the Bank provide banking services for military units, institutions and organizations of the Ministry of Defense, as well as other state bodies and legal entities which protect the safety of Russia and of Russian citizens living abroad. The total staff of the Central Bank and its subsidiaries accounted for 62,805 people in January of 1995.

The Board of Directors comprises of the Chairman of the Central Bank, and 12 others who work on a permanent basis in the Bank. The Chairman of the Bank is appointed to his post by the State Duma, for a term of four years. This appointment requires a majority vote from the total number of the deputies. All candidates for appointment to the post of Chairman are submitted by the

President of Russia, not later than three months before the expiration of the powers of the current Chairman. In the case a Chairman is relieved of his post before the end of the term, the President of Russia submits a new candidate within two weeks from the moment of such relief.

The primary duties of the Chairman of the Central Bank include the following:

- Act on behalf of the Central Bank and represent without a proxy its interests in relations with bodies of state power, commercial banks, organizations of international states or organizations, and all other financial institutions and organizations in Russia.
- Preside at the meetings of the Board of Directors. In the case of equally divided votes, the voice of the Chairman is the casting one.
- Sign the decisions of the Central Bank, the decisions of the Board of Directors, the minutes of the meetings of the Board of Directors, and any agreements concluded by the Bank.
- Appointment and relief of the deputies of the Central Bank, and allocation duties and responsibilities amongst them.
- Sign orders and give obligatory directions for all employees of the Bank, its enterprises, institutions and organizations.
- Bear full responsibility for the activities of the Central Bank.
- Ensure the realization of the activities of the Central Bank are in conformity with current Russian Federal Law.

The 12 additional members of the Board of Directors are also appointed to their posts for a period of four years by the State Duma. The Chairman presents all candidates to the Duma after consultation and agreement with the Russian President. The functions of the Board of Directors include the following:

- in cooperation with the Russian government, they elaborate and ensure the performance of the basic directions of the single state monetary-credit policy
- approve the annual report of the Central Bank and submit it to the State Duma
- consider and approve estimates of the expenses of the Bank for the forthcoming year, not later than December 31 of the preceding year, and also those incurred expenses not stipulated in the budget
- determine the continually evolving structure of the Central Bank
- establish the qualifying requirements and hiring procedures for the Chairman, the members of the Board of Directors, the Deputy Chairman, along with other employees
- submit to the State Duma all proposals dealing with the change of the authorized capital of the Central Bank and commercial banks
- approve the procedure for the meetings of the Board of Directors

- appoint the Chief Auditor of the Central Bank
- approve the internal structure of the Central Bank, the regulations on the subdivisions of the Bank, the statutes of the organizations of the Bank, and the procedure for the appointment of the heads of the subdivisions, institutions, and organizations of the Bank
- determine the conditions and amounts of foreign capital within the Russian banking system, in conformity with Federal Laws

The Board of Directors also makes the following decisions:
- the creation and liquidation of all institutions and organizations of the Central Bank
- the establishment of norms for the commercial banks in accordance with current Federal Law
- regulations concerning the reserve requirements of commercial banks
- changing the prime interest rate of the Central Bank
- determining the influence of the its operations on the open market
- the participation with international financial organizations
- the participation of branches of the Central Bank and their role in the activities of the Bank, its institutions, organizations, and employees
- the application in the Russian banking market of direct quantitative restrictions
- the issuance and withdraw of banknotes and coins from circulation, and on the total amount of cash in circulation
- the procedure for forming the reserves of the commercial banks

The National Banking Council was created to improve the monetary-credit system of Russia. The Chairman of the National Banking Council is the Chairman of the Central Bank. The National Banking Council comprises of two representatives from each house of the Federal Assembly, one representative from both the offices of the President and the Government of Russia, and the Ministers of Finance and Economics. The other members of the National Banking Council are appointed by the State Duma on their presentation by the Chairman . The number of members on the National Banking Council is preferred to be no more than fifteen persons. The meetings of the National Banking Council are to be held at least once every three months.

The National Banking Council performs the following functions:
- consider concepts for improving the banking system
- consider draft theories on the basic directions of the single state monetary-credit policy
- consider the policy of currency regulation and control
- give opinions on and analyze the results of their decisions and the degrees of their fulfillment

- conduct an analysis and examination of all draft legislation and any other normative acts in the field of banking
- consider the most important matters of regulation and activities of the commercial banks
- participate in the elaboration of the basic principles of organizing the system of settlements within Russia

The Central Bank is a complex organization which is continually working to improve the banking system in Russia. With limited experience in both free market relations and early developmental levels in the economy, the increasing importance of responsible decisions by the central authority is crucial to the nation's future prosperity.

Chapter 2.3

Relations with Commercial Banks

The Central Bank of Russia register's commercial banks in the *Book of the State Registration of Credit Organizations*. The Central Bank can issue and revoke licenses of commercial banks, cooperate with the commercial banks, their associations and unions, and carrying out consultations with them, before adopting important decisions of a normative nature.

With the aim of cooperating with the commercial banks, the Central Bank creates committees and working groups composed of representatives from the commercial banks. These committees operate on a voluntary basis for the research of certain problems within the banking system.

The Central Bank does not bear any responsibility for the obligations of the commercial banks, with the exception of rare cases in which it chooses to assume such obligations. Likewise, the commercial banks do not bear responsibility for the obligations of the Central Bank. This relationship is ideally a mutually beneficial one where all voices are heard and respected.

The Central Bank as a body of banking regulations, supervises the activity of the commercial banks, banking legislation, and its own normative actions. This applies particularly to those obligatory norms established by the Central Bank. The main objective of its banking regulation and supervision is the maintenance of stability within the banking system and the protection of depositor and creditor interests. These functions may be exercised by it directly, or through a body of banking supervision created under it.

The Central Bank has the right to place qualifying requirements upon the heads of the executive bodies, and on the chief accountant of any credit organization in Russia. The rules, which are obligatory for commercial banks, are those about conducting banking operations, accounting procedures, and the presentation of statistical data to Central Bank state auditors.

The Board of Directors of the Central Bank must follow the established procedures when requesting information from commercial banks. This information must be presented to the Central Bank, with explanations about the commercial bank's activities and their opinion of the banking environment throughout the country. Additionally, the Central Bank has the right to request and receive information from federal bodies of executive power, in order to prepare banking and financial statistics and to analyze the economic situation. The data coming from the commercial banks on recent operations are not openly available without the consent of the relevant credit organization, but with exceptions of cases stipulated by Federal Law.

Regular reports must be published by the Central Bank summarizing the statistical and analytical information of the current banking situation in Russia. This provision applies to the information collected and transferred by the Bank, by order of the Russian Government to relevant international financial lending organizations (i.e. World Bank and International Monetary Fund).

The Central Bank does not have the right to demand that commercial banks fulfill functions alien to them. This primarily includes control over the manner of investing and lending to the commercial bank's clients. Each bank is able to perform the functions and banking activities it feels are most beneficial for its own prosperity and to meet the demands of its customers. In order to ensure the stability of the commercial banks, the Central Bank has established obligatory requirements for them. The following are examples:

- The minimum amount of registered capital for newly created commercial banks.
- The minimum amount of stock capital for commercial banks to operate. This is established as the sum of the registered capital, the funds of a credit organization, and the undistributed profit. The Bank officially announces the change of the minimum amount of the stock capital not later than three years before the time of its introduction. Beginning in 1996, the minimum amount of capital necessary to establish a commercial bank was six billion rubles. In 1999, the amount of capital is targeted to be a minimum of five million E C U (European Currency Unit).
- the limit of liquid assets in relation to the amount of registered capital
- the maximum amount of risk per borrower, or per group of related borrowers
- the maximum amount of risk per depositor
- the amount of liquidity of each credit organization
- the minimum amount of capital
- the maximum amount of attracted monetary deposits from the population
- the amounts of currency, interest and other risks
- the minimum amount of reserves created for high-risk assets
- the procedures for using the banks' internal funds for acquiring the shares of other businesses
- the maximum amount of credits, guarantees, and warranties given by a bank to its shareholders

The Central Bank also establishes the norms of liquidity for a commercial bank, which are partially determined as follows:

- the ratio between its assets and liabilities, taking into account the periods, sums and types of assets and liabilities and other factors
- the ratio of liquid assets (cash resources, on-call orders, short-term securities, and any other easily cashable assets) and gross assets.

For example, the Figure 3 lists several standards set by the Central Bank in the past.

Figure 3.

Standard Name	Standard Value
S1: ratio of Bank's capital to total risk-weighted assets	Over or equal to 0.04%
S6: ratio of Bank's liquid assets to total assets	Over or equal to 0.20%
S7: ratio of liquid assets to Bank's total liabilities on demand accounts	Over or equal to 0.20%
S8: ratio of Bank's assets of over one-year maturity to Bank's liabilities on deposit accounts, loans and liabilities with a repayment period of over one year.	Less than or equal to 1.50%
S9: ratio of maximum risk exposure per borrower to Bank's capital	Less than or equal to 1.0%

Beginning in the middle of 1996, the Central Bank changed its standards to bring them more in line with international practice. Different norms for different types and sizes of commercial banks have also been established. The Central Bank carries out audits of the commercial banks and their branches, and sends them orders which are obligatory for execution. One aspect of those orders is the elimination of any violations previously revealed in their activity. The audits may be conducted by representatives of the Central Bank, authorized by the Board of Directors and on its instructions, by auditing firms. The Central Bank reserves the right to review and check the accounts and other documents of the commercial banks, and where necessary, make copies of relevant documents.

In cases where there is a violation by a commercial bank of federal laws, the normative acts and directions of the Central Bank, or the nonsubmission of information or submission of incomplete or untrue information, the Central Bank has the right to intervene. The Central Bank may demand from the commercial bank the elimination of the revealed violations, to exact a fine at the rate of up to one tenth of one percent of the amount of the minimum authorized capital, or to restrict the conduct of certain operations for a period of up to six months.

In cases of nonfulfillment and failure to correct the violations within the period established, and also if such violations or operations conducted by the commercial bank have created a real threat to the interests of the depositors, the Central Bank has the right to exact from that commercial bank a fine of up to one percent of the amount of the paid authorized capital, but not more than one percent of the minimum amount of the authorized capital.

Concerning a change in the minimum amount of the registered capital of a commercial bank, the Central Bank can demand that it:

- carry out the arrangements dictated for its own financial improvement, including a change in the structure of assets
- replace the directors
- reorganize
- change its obligatory requirements for a period of up to six months
- prohibit the conduct of certain banking operations stipulated by the issued license for a period of up to one year
- appoint a provisional administration for the management of the credit organization for a period of up to 18 months

If these actions have not improved the situation of the failing commercial bank, the Central Bank has the right to revoke its operating license.

UNIT 3

Commercial Banks

Introduction

What is described throughout this book, and particularly in this unit, is the history of Russian banking and its rejuvenation in the past decade. It as been a dauntless task requiring courage and vision, and much has yet to be accomplished. Understanding what preceded today is important to those who would participate in Russian commerce tomorrow.

Trade finance has become easier to obtain in Russia as international lenders continue to gain confidence in Russian bank guarantees. The gradual improvement in the climate for forfeiting, factoring, declining inflation, and stabilized currency exchange rates have bolstered confidence levels. The result has been a dramatic increase in financing available to Russian importers. International financing of Russian imports totaled $2.4 billion, up 153% in the first quarter of 1997 compared to the first quarter of 1996. Exporters still need to work closely with their Russian customer's banks and European forfeiting providers to finance such transactions.

Russia's successful placement of three eurobond issues and the fall in Russian treasury bill (GKO) yields to below 20 percent, have caused a shift in interest from passive investment in Russian equities to trade finance of receivables. Much new lending and financing of Russian privately owned industry is coming from syndicated loans and other debt instruments issued by international financial institutions, often tied to export/import trade. In April, for example, Mazhkombank secured a one-year $30 million credit facility for pre-export finance syndicated by a group of 17 European banks. The credit line carried a rate of 5.25 percentage points over the "London Interbank Offered Rate" (Libor). While such rates are high by international standards, they compare very favorably to domestic interest rates in Russia. American banks also have a growing business in discounting trade receivables, such as promissory notes secured with a guarantee from a major Russian bank.

Public-sector financial institutions are also making financing available on more liberal terms than previously available. The European Bank for Reconstruction and Development and the World Bank are together extending a $300 million credit line to finance industrial reconstruction of Russian enterprises. The Export Import Bank of the United States has recently begun accepting private-sector risk in Russia on a case-by-case basis. On June 16th

1997, the Central Bank of Russia cut its re-financing rate from 36% to 24%, making returns on commercial financing more competitive with other alternatives.

All these changes indicate that progress is occurring from the embryonic stages of 1992-1996, and that inevitably Russia will create the financial industry that will support and release the full productive potential of its well-educated and highly-trained labor force, and the wealth of its natural resources, so that its Gross Domestic Product may reach levels similar to per-capita income of the industrialized nations.

Chapter 3.1

Commercial Bank Establishment

A commercial bank is a legal entity entitled to carry out banking operations. With permission from the Central Bank of Russia, their main objective is aimed at earning a profit. Banks are commercial organizations that can select from several forms of ownership. They operate in a competitive market with a limited, but growing pool of potential clients.

In 1990, radical changes took place in the Russian banking system. Over 1300 banks were established in one year. In the three following years, this process continued smoothly at an average rate of 240 new banks per year. By the beginning of 1994, the total number of banks exceeded 2000.

In 1988, the total number of branches of all state banks was 2500 (not including SBERBANK). By March 1995, 5680 commercial bank branches had been established. From January to April 1995, 194 branches were set up. In total, including the SBERBANK system , by that time in 1995, there were over 50,000 bank branches in Russia. In quantitative statistical terms, the Russian banking system has about the same number of banks as does the United States. On average, there are now 300 banking institutions for every 100,000 Russians.

Yet, in some isolated regions with territories equal in area to certain European countries, there are still far to few banking facilities. The density of banking institutions is very high in the large industrial centers, particularly around Moscow and Saint Petersburg. For instance, 500 banks currently operate in Saint Petersburg (including SBERBANK), which is approximately one bank per 10,000 people.

Further expansion of branch networks is proceeding, with the development of new branches and the takeover of small unprofitable banks. Banking licenses are no longer issued by the Central Bank to new banks if their charter capital is less than 4 billion rubles. The objective of the Central bank is to increase the amount of required charter capital to 5 million ECU by 1999. International banks are offering higher levels of services to the Russian financial market, making it more difficult for small and medium sized Russian banks to compete. The Central Bank has adopted the policy that the number of international banks in the Russian market shall not exceed 12% of the total number of banks. This figure includes banks with 50% international ownership. As of July 1995, the Central Bank estimated that the number of international banks had reached 6%.

In the Russian commercial banking system, there have been two periods of development. The first was from 1990 to 1995, which is known as the time of extensive development, a time of building the physical banking structure and network. And the second from July 1995 to today, a time of intensive development, technological and educational upgrading of services and internal processes. The following table shows evidence of these definitions:

Figure 4.
Grouping of the Russian Commercial Banks
by their declared Charter Funds

Charter Funds (rubles)	1/1/94	1/1/95	1/1/96	7/1/96	11/1/96
Up to 100 million	272 13.5%	93 3.7%	42 1.8%	33 1.5%	32 11.5%
100 million to 500 million	1320 65.4%	1160 46.1%	698 27.4%	480 22.3%	396 19.1%
500 million to 1 billion	201 12.9%	403 16.0%	282 12.3%	218 10.1%	192 9.3%
1 billion to 5 billion	138 6.8%	698 27.7%	841 36.6%	769 35.7%	709 34.2%
5 billion to 20 billion	28 1.4%	133 5.3%	410 17.9%	521 24.2%	577 27.8%
20 billion to 30 billion	- -	22 0.3%	28 1.2%	42 1.9%	56 2.7%
Over 30 billion rubles	- -	8 0.3%	64 2.8%	91 4.2%	111 5.4%
Total Number of Banks	2019	2517	2295	2154	2073
Percentage	100%	100%	100%	100%	100%

Unions and associations, in order to protect and represent their members interests, may form non-profit financial organizations. Throughout the country, both interregional and international financial links and relationships continue to be developed. The exchange of scientific information, technological standards, and common professional interests continue to improve. Substantial efforts have been made to utilize recommendations about conducting financial activities and solving common problems of financial organizations. The financial organizations owned by unions and associations are prohibited from carrying out commercial banking operations.

To establish a commercial bank in Russia, it is necessary to prepare several documents and apply to the Central Bank. The following are important components in the process of commercial bank establishment:

- an application requesting state registration and acceptance of a license for operations
- the commercial bank's Charter
- minutes of the meeting of the founders which adopted the Charter and endorsed the candidates for the executive officers' positions and the Chief Accountant
- the certificate confirming payment of the government licensing fee
- copies of the certificates of government registration for a regional legal entity
- audited statements confirming the validity of the submitted financial reports, which differ significantly from western Generally Accepted Accounting Procedures (GAAP)
- a certificate from the agencies of the State Tax Services of the Russian government, confirming fulfillment by the legal entity of its registration for purposes of filing and satisfying future tax obligations to the Federal Government
- the balance sheet of the entity for the past three years
- income declarations certified by bodies of the Russian State Tax Service confirming the sources of income contributed to the registered capital of the commercial bank. (Sources of income do not have to be confirmed for illegal flight capital being repatriated to Russia.)
- completed questionnaires by candidates for the executive officers positions and the Chief Accountant of the commercial bank containing the following information:
- Level of higher legal or economic education, supported by copies of a diploma or substantiating documents.
- Description of related working experiences, which must include work as a manager of a department or other division of a credit organization engaged in banking operations for at least one year.

- When appropriate education is absent, proof of managing experience in such related division of no less than two years.
- Disclosure of any past and present illegal criminal problems.

One of the most important documents is the bank's Charter. It must contain the following information:
- company's full and official name
- indication of organizational and legal type of institution
- information about the postal address of location of all management departments and separate divisions
- list of banking operations and transactions to be carried out
- information on the formation, proposed system, and authority of executive officers and directors

The registered capital of a commercial bank is the combination of all contributions from its participants, and shall constitute the amount of property guaranteeing the interests of its depositors. During the evolution of the development of the Russian banking system, the minimum registered capital required for the commercial banks has increased step by step:
- In 1991 the amount was 25 million rubles.
- In 1993 the amount was 100 million rubles.
- In 1994 the amount was 2 billion rubles.
- In 1995 the amount was 6 billion rubles.

In the period from 1991 to 1997, the value of the ruble decreased from RR40=$1.00 USD to RR5806=$1.00 USD (RR=Russian rubles USD=United States dollars). The requirement increased from approximately $600,000 in 1991 to approximately $1 million in 1995.

Borrowed money cannot be used to form the registered capitalization of a commercial bank. Additionally, resources of the Federal Budget and state non-budget funds, free monetary resources, and other property objects controlled by federal instrumentalities of government may not be used to form the registered capital of a commercial bank, except as envisaged by Federal Law.

The purchase of more than 5% of stock shares of a commercial bank by a legal entity, a group of legal entities, a Russian citizen or group of citizens under an agreement, or a group of legal entities acting as subsidiaries or dependents on each other, requires the submittal of a notification to the Central Bank. A purchase of more than 20% by any combination of the above listed, requires preliminary consent from the Central Bank. The Central Bank reviews applications for banking licenses and upon acceptance, issues the license.

Chapter 3.2

Domestic Operations

As stated, commercial banks are subject to federal registration with the Central Bank. All registrations are recorded and maintained in the *Book of Government Registration of Commercial Banks*. Only registered licensed commercial banks have the right to carry out banking operations in Russia.

According to Federal Law, a commercial bank's license to perform banking operations can be revoked under the following circumstances:

- proof of false statements of information used to obtain a license
- suspension for any reason within one year of receiving its license to begin operations
- proof of falsification of reporting data or balance sheets
- conducting banking operation outside the area stipulated in the license from the Central Bank
- failure to observe the requirements of the federal laws regulating banking activities, as well as regulations of the Central Bank
- unsatisfactory financial standing of the commercial bank
- failure to fulfill its obligations to depositors or creditors, which eventually could serve as grounds for an insolvency or bankruptcy suit against the commercial bank in a court of arbitration

A commercial bank is entitled to address the Central Bank with inquiries and applications pertaining to decisions and actions taken by the Central Bank, which is obligated to reply to such inquires on the essence of the raised issues within one month.

A commercial bank has the right to carry out in the aggregate the following banking operations:

- attract monetary resources from citizens and businesses in the form of deposits, whether demand or fixed-term
- invest deposits in its own name and for its own account
- open and maintain banking accounts for citizens and businesses

The Central Bank has issued regulations that state accounts of non-citizens must be restricted as to disposition in the following ways:

- Accounts opened in rubles, purchased with imported dollars, may be converted back to and repatriate such dollars only to the amount of dollars invested in Russian equity.

- Dollars imported for non-investment purposes may be used only to pay bills in Russia, and may not be converted back into dollars or repatriated.
- Ruble revenues received in Russia may only be deposited in accounts with repatriation restrictions, unless it can be demonstrated that such revenues are a return on invested capital in the form of profit distributions.
- Revenues earned from expenses incurred from business activities are not construed convertible profits.

The Central Bank may and has issued mandatory instructions to commercial banks to close any account at any time without explanation or rule of law, and to transmit the account balance to the Central Bank. The commercial bank can also do the following:

- clear payments ordered by citizens and legal entities, including those of correspondent banks, within their bank accounts
- collect cash, bills, payment documents and cash services to citizens and legal entities
- buy and sell foreign currencies in cash and non-cash forms (Such transactions are restricted and dollars obtained must be used to purchase and import tangible goods. Failure to do so results in fines which may exceed 100% of the value of the currency exchanged.)
- attract precious metals in the form of deposits and for security and investment
- provide bank guarantees
- issue guarantees for third party's, realizing the fulfillment of monetary obligations
- purchase the right to demand fulfillment of monetary obligations from third persons
- trustee operations for monetary and other property under agreements with citizens and legal entities
- carry out operations with precious metals and precious stones in compliance with legislation of the Russian Federation
- lease dedicated safety deposit space to citizens and legal entities
- leasing operations
- render consulting and information services

Under the license for banking operations issued by the Central Bank, a commercial bank is entitled to issue, buy, sell, register, keep, and carry out transactions with securities. Securities can be used as collateral for loans. There are other securities not requiring a special license in compliance with federal laws, as well as entitlements to act as trustee for the securities under an agreement with citizens and legal entities. A commercial bank may fulfill individual orders of the Russian Government, the executive authorities of Russian citizens, and various bodies of local government.

Under agreements concluded on a tender basis, commercial bank's may carry out activities with government funds, the funds of citizens, and local budgets and clear payments within them. The key role of the commercial bank is to ensure that federal funds are allocated to and used for the implementation of federal and regional programs. The resources available from the Federal Budget for commercial banks is now limited and being reduced.

If a commercial bank admits to violation of Federal Law or instructions of the Central Bank, measures are taken to solve the problems. One option for regulatory enforcement that the Central Bank can take is the revocation of the banking license.

To ensure financial reliability, a commercial bank must create reserve funds, including those for anticipated losses incurred on investments in securities. The procedure for forming and using reserves is determined by the Central Bank. The amount taken from pre-tax profits for the creation of reserves is determined in the Federal Laws on taxation. Commercial banks are obligated to classify their assets by isolating the high-risk and bad debts, and to create reserves to cover possible losses in compliance with the procedure established by the Central Bank.

A commercial bank is obligated to observe the standard rate of mandatory reserves to be deposited with the Central Bank, including the requirements pertaining to deadlines, volumes, and types of deposits. The procedure for depositing mandatory reserves is determined by the Central Bank in compliance with Federal Laws regarding the Central Banking system.

Maintenance of reserves by commercial banks on interest free accounts with the Central Bank is also a method of cash and credit regulation. The maintenance of commercial bank reserves at the Central Bank gives it the purpose to regulate the money and credit supply. By maintaining reserves, commercial banks assist the Central Bank in managing inflation. The amount of required reserves is set at a percentage rate proportionate to the volume of credit extended by the commercial bank, and the norm of provisioning is determined by the Board of Directors of the commercial bank.

Currently, the Central Bank requires reserves from domestic liabilities of 13%, and for international liabilities of 5%. These are average reserve requirements. Since inflation is affected by the monetary policy (emission of new printed currency - money supply), the bank reserves in effect can be utilized by the Central Bank to offset its inflationary policy.

Chapter 3.3

International Investment Operations

State registration of international financial organizations has facilitated an international banking presence. The introduction of international bank branches has created competition for better services. The steps which an international bank must take to obtain a license for banking operation requires, in addition to those documents listed in the previous chapter, the submission of the following:

- its decision to participate in the creation of a credit organization or in the opening of the bank branch within Russia
- the document which confirms registration of the entity and balance sheet statements for the past three years certified by a statement of professional audit
- written consent of the respective controlling body of the country of origin for its participation in the creation of a commercial bank within Russia, or for the opening of a branch of the bank. This is only required in cases where such permission is required to comply with the legislation of the country of origin.
- the entity shall present a confirmation of solvency of itself by a first class international bank.

The aggregate amount of participation of international capital in the Russian banking system is limited and established by Federal Law, subject to the suggestion of the government coordinated with the Central Bank. This quota is expressed as a ratio of the total Bank capital belonging to non- Russian owners and the capital of Russian owners. Upon reaching this fixed quota, the Central Bank periodically suspends the issuance of additional new banking licenses to banks with international investment capital and for the operation to branches of international banks.

A commercial bank must obtain preliminary permission from the Central Bank for an increase in the percentage of ownership by non-Russian investors. Sale of stock to non-Russians made without approval of the Central Bank, shall be invalid except for in special cases.

The Central Bank has the right to prohibit an increase of the registered capital of a commercial bank with money from non-Russian investors, if the sale would result in exceeding the quota of participation of international capital in the Russian banking system.

A commercial bank's application for an increase in the registered capital by investment from non-Russians must be acted upon by the Central Bank within two months of the date of the submission of the application. The result of this action is assumed to be either the granting of permission by the Central Bank to carry out the transaction indicated in the application, or a justified refusal in writing. In case the Central Bank fails to report its adopted decision within the two month deadline, the proposed transaction is considered permitted.

The Central Bank, in coordination with the government, is entitled to impose restrictions on banking operations for commercial banks with foreign investments and the branches of international banks, if the government of origin of such banks apply restrictions to banks with Russian ownership and branches of Russian banks within their country. The Central Bank may also designate the segregation of, and the designation of international funds brought into Russia as "expense accounts" and "investment accounts." Dollars converted to rubles and deposited in expense accounts are not permitted by law to be converted back into dollars, and may only be spent in Russia. Investments may only be made from bank accounts characterized as investment accounts.

The Central Bank is also entitled to establish additional requirements for commercial banks with international investment, and branches of international banks as they pertain to mandatory standard procedures for providing reports, approval of management, and their list of approved banking activities, as well as the minimum amount of the registered capital of the newly registered commercial bank or newly registered branches of an international bank.

International Credit Programs in Russia

Internal shortages of money within Russia is aggravated by government competition for credit, which offers domestic banks higher returns and lower risk compared to investment in business and industry. Under some circumstances, Western financing as well a capital investment have now become available in Russia, although all demand has not yet been fully met.

Interest rates in Russia are high. Long term lending for industrial development does not compare favorably with purchase of government securities. Credit demand has continued to increased due to the termination of Russian government subsidies and an inefficient regulation of Russia's credit market by the government.

As a result, the demand of large enterprises as well as small and medium businesses for long-term investment credits has not been satisfied. Even if several Russian banks were inclined to participate jointly, there is not sufficient bank credit available for industry to finance re-tooling that will cost billions of US dollars. And it is projects of this scale that large industrial businesses need for their development. Medium and small businesses also cannot count on obtaining long or medium-term loans, because of their inability to provide banks with the appropriate collateral for their loans, and because high interest rates exceed projected profit margins and ability to service such debt.

The construction industry, in particular housing, does not have a deed recording mechanism, title insurance, nor a market of consumers able to repay mortgages from their income. Most existing housing is still government subsidized. Farms do not produce the cash-flow to service the debt on the large values attributed to their fixed assets. There is no existing legislation regarding mortgages and collateral.

Therefore, no solution has yet been conceived for meeting housing needs in a manner consistent with a market economy. The main constraint is still the low per-capita income resulting from the decline in GDP, government competition for available resources, the privatization of existing GDP from which potential homeowners have been excluded, extensive export of *flight* capital, the wiping out of the savings of the population as a result of past inflation and devaluation, all of which have reduced the ability of the general population to pay mortgage financing. Under certain conditions it would be possible to create a housing program by hypothecating future projected higher per capita income, if such hypothecation were backed by government guarantees. Such programs would reflect a different prioritization of the distribution of national resources. Such a program has not as yet been promulgated or endorsed. In many cases, back wages of existing per capita incomes have not as yet been paid.

While Russian banks will not as yet guarantee housing finance, they will guarantee some commercial finance, and therefore some opportunities exist for eliminating commercial credit risk by lending with a guarantee from selected Russian banks. It is in this way that most foreign import finance has taken place. Currently there are approximately 15 Russian commercial banks which have sufficient assets to be acceptable to international financing organizations for non-recourse factoring. A characteristic feature of the international credit programs is their clear target orientation towards specific segments of the credit market or specific final borrowers.

Among the leading international lenders or guarantors of such lenders active in Russia today, are the International Bank for Reconstruction and Development (IBRD), the European Bank for Reconstruction and Development (EBRD), The Overseas Private Investment Corporation, The Export Import Bank, and various Western investment banks and factoring companies such as Palms & Company, Inc..

In addition to trade finance, equity capital syndication is provided by a number of investment funds to which capital has been provided for this specific purpose by Western governments. International commercial banks have also recently become more active, especially those from Germany, Holland, and England.

The longest existing credit programs, are two programs of lending to small businesses conducted by the European Bank for Reconstruction and Development, whose shares were purchased and are owned by various governments of the world and which was provided with capital by them specifically for the purpose of reconstructing the economy of Russia. One of them, which is called the Russian Small Business Fund, provides small businesses the opportunity to borrow money in the amount of up to $125 thousand US dollars for a term up to 3 years. Another, the Micro Loans Program, is also oriented toward small businesses and will consider making loans of up to $30 thousand US dollars for a period up to one year. There are more than 200 privately managed investment funds which have received more than $2 billion dollars of capital from governments and private investors specifically earmarked for investment in Russian industry, which are additional sources of equity capital, generally in larger amounts than $125 thousand dollars.

For several reasons, Russian small business credit requirements receive support from these programs. Russian small businesses have continued to develop and grow during the difficult years of economic transformation. This has been possible because the small businesses make possible the productivity of private individual initiative toward the production of goods. It is small private businesses that have proven to be the most economically viable due to the ability of the individual to make quick rational decisions about producing and delivering a product for which a need exists. Based upon the experience of small businesses in countries with well-developed market economies, it is possible to predict a long and substantial development of the small business sector in the Russian economy for years to come. In developed markets, small businesses play a most important role by producing more than half of the volume of the gross domestic product and by providing employment to a majority of the able-bodied population. It is small and medium-size business undertakings that ensure the stability of the economic system that supports the political system, by generating a large number of proprietors, a considerable part of the developing middle class, all of whom are interested in the preservation of political stability.

Western governments support young Russian businesses, sometimes without requiring that they meet the norms of privately owned financial institutions, because such Russian businesses form the foundation for democracy and stability in Russia. Privately owned international financing institutions, while sympathetic to these ideals and objectives, correctly maintain their commercial objectives of financing only those businesses which have an acceptable level of risk consistent with their mandate to protect their investor's capital and earn interest on such capital. Their requirements are therefore more pragmatic.

According to a decision by the Board of Directors of the European Bank for Reconstruction and Development, $300 million USD have been allotted for lending to small Russian businesses. The initial total capitalization of EBRD, for all investment in Russia for both large and small business and infrastructure, has been $20 billion dollars and has been augmented by further participation of many international banks worldwide. The money for this small business program was provided from the capitalization of the EBRD, jointly with 50% of the financing committed by the governments of the Big Seven countries. The program was started simultaneously in seven Russian cities in the summer of 1994.

In conformity with the terms of the Program, the EBRD concluded Loan Agreements with a number of Russian banks. These banks received funds for granting small loans. The terms of these agreements vary slightly for each bank, and therefore the lending conditions for small
loans and micro loans also vary accordingly.

Potential Russian borrowers, such as small businesses or individual businesspersons, deal only with the Russian commercial bank when applying for such loans. Only businesses that do not have a significant share of international or government ownership in their capital are eligible for a loan under this program. The number of employees in the company should not exceed 100 people for a small loan, and 30 people for a micro loan. Small loans are not granted to trading companies with the purpose of increasing their working capital, but a micro loan may be used for this purpose. According to the terms of the Program, the money cannot be used for funding the production of weapons and other military equipment, operations with foreign currencies and securities, speculative deals with real estate, production of alcoholic beverages and tobacco products, gambling business or any activity that cause damage to the environment. The interest rate on the loans are set by the Russian banks themselves, but for small loans, the EBRD stipulates the maximum amount of the margin Russian banks may receive as not more than 10% annually in USD. Thus, the interest rate on the loans granted to the final borrowers range from 16% to 24% per year. For the Russian market, this figure is considered relatively low.

Direct loans of trade finance from privately owned financial institutions, when guaranteed by a Russian bank, may be available directly at a rate of 12%. In this case however, the cost of the guarantee from the Russian bank must be added to the loan.

When receiving a loan from the EBRD and using the proceeds for crediting a small business, the Russian commercial bank has full responsibility for the repayment of the loan. However, as far as small loans are concerned, the EBRD may partly assume the risk of non-repayment of the loan by the final borrower during the first year or two of the Program's implementation. But, the commercial bank that granted the loan has to prove that all reasonable measures have been taken in order to recover the debt.

The objective of the Program is not only to develop small businesses, but also to help the Russian commercial banks organize their lending activities in accordance with international standards. For this purpose, the EBRD appoints its representatives who work directly with the staff of each Russian bank, and stipulates the procedure of decision-making in the lending sphere. The EBRD representatives are employees of international banks or financial institutions who are experienced in lending to small businesses in their country or origin. Each of those banks enter into an appropriate contract with the EBRD. The primary EBRD representatives currently in Russia are South Shore Bank (USA), the Bank of Ireland, and IPC (Germany).

The EBRD representatives give assistance to Russian lending officers by teaching the methods of financial analysis, project underwriting, lending portfolio management, and credit risk management. All essential decisions concerning small loans and micro loans are made by the Credit Committee, which is formed by the Russian bank according to the agreement with the EBRD. This Credit Committee consists of members of the bank's management of the Program, and if necessary they can exercise a veto at the meeting.

It is important to note that Russian commercial banks receive credit funds from the EBRD only in parts, as soon as local projects are ready for financing and as the funds are needed. This reduces the possibility of inappropriate fund utilization.

From 1994 to 1997, the Russian Small Business Fund Program proved its undoubted advantages and viability. Hundreds of small businesses, from various sectors of the economy throughout Russia, have used the European loans to finance their business activities. Thousands of new jobs have been created, and the number of real products and services in the market has grown significantly. It is important that the Program meets the interest of all parties, including the international financial lender, the EBRD which fulfills the tasks it was created for and gets its share of the margin, Russian banks which not only receive certain profit, but also get a chance to improve their lending culture and attract new clients, and finally, the small businesses. Russian businesses of any size, big or small, can also seek financing of $100,000 to $5 million directly from many privately owned financial institutions, without the EBRD as an intermediary, by using the guarantee of selected Russian banks to obtain credit from six months to five years.

The Russian Small Business Fund program was a touchstone, which proved the possibility of implementing international lending programs in Russia, and opened the way to others.

Other large credit programs being implemented in Russia by the International Bank for Reconstruction and Development and the EBRD are closely connected with the Financial Institution Development Projects (FIDP). Its objective is to assist Russian banks to reach the level of their work organization and reliability that is acceptable according to international standards. Each bank accredited in the FIDP carries out its own individual program of institutional development, automation and systems modernization using the funds received under the project.

The FIDP program is based on the Loan Agreements concluded by the Russian Government with IBRD and EBRD in 1994. Russian commercial banks accredited in the FIDP program receive funds through the Ministry of Finance in the form of loans and grants. The grants are provided by the official donors, which are mainly the governments of the Big Seven. The amount of the loan and of the grant is set for each Russian bank individually, as well as the purpose of their utilization. Both the loan amount and the grant amount are not to exceed $1.5 million USD per bank.

The Russian Ministry of Finance has concluded separate Subsidiary Loan Agreements with each of the banks accredited in the FIDP. In the Agreement, the loan amount, the use of funds, the loan security in the form of liquid bonds and marketable securities which the bank provides to the Ministry of Finance, the order and terms of repayment, and other conditions are stipulated. Funds are granted for the term up to 12 years, and the Ministry of Finance monitors their utilization.

The following credit programs are only implemented through the banks accredited in the Financial Institutions Development Program.

The EBRD, together with the IBRD, carries out the Enterprise Support Project. Their aim is to grant loans to the Russian businesses that have completed the privatization process and whose capital the percentage of ownership held by government entities does not exceed 25 percent. Loans may be utilized for increasing the working capital as well as for implementation of investment projects.

The EBRD and IBRD have granted the Russian Government a loan in the amount of $300 million USD, of which $200 million was provided by the IBRD and the remaining $100 million by the EBRD. The Ministry of Finance, acting on behalf of the Government, in turn, credits the authorized banks which carry out lending to the final business borrowers. The banks assume all the credit risks of the borrowers and the Ministry of Finance assumes the risk of insolvency of the banks. The IBRD and EBRD assume the risks of non-fulfillment of its obligations by the Russian Government.

Military projects, production of tobacco and alcohol items, real estate deals and others that are not eligible for financing out of the proceeds of the Small Business Fund program cannot be financed under the Enterprise Support Project either. The projects proposed for financing must undergo the Environment Impact Due Diligence procedures consistent with those established by the IBRD.

The amount of a loan granted to the final borrower business must not exceed $10 million USD, and this amount may be smaller depending on the size of the total share capital of the Russian bank granting the loan. The loans are granted for a term from one to nine years. The maximum grace period, which is the period before the first repayment on the loan, cannot exceed two years.

In order to receive a loan, the business must submit to the Russian bank a detailed business plan and financial projections for the project, its financial statements for the last reporting periods, information on its major shareholders, information on its procurement practices, and such other information as the bank reasonably requests. The bank reviews the financial position of the business and evaluates the proposed us of the money. The projects that have been approved by the bank are submitted for review to the coordinating bodies of the Enterprise Support Project, along with the above listed documentation, to which a copy of the document containing the description of the project analysis and a completed form of application for commitment and funding are appended.

In 1996, the IBRD began implementing a Housing Program in Russia. The World Bank has allotted $400 million for this purpose and additional funds in the amount of $360 million are provided by the Russian Government and private investors.

According to the conditions of the Program, a participating Russian bank can get credit funds for the term of a loan up to five years for the purposes of residential housing. The loan is granted only if the so called "zero cycle" of the construction works, the construction of the foundation and communications, have already been completed at the expense of some other sources of funding.

Housing projects financed are to meet certain technical and ecological requirements. In order to ensure responsiveness, the projects are subject to environmental due diligence and technical assessment inspections. For example, the projects connected with large-panel construction, which was once very popular in the Soviet Union, are not eligible for funding since large-panel houses do not meet the international standards of thermal insulation.

Implementation of a program of financing construction materials production has also been started. Its main terms are similar to those of the Housing Program. However, there is an additional condition on the availability of a qualified investor which must meet the criteria set by the IBRD, which is to be a Russian or international organization active in the construction sector or a capital venture fund, and to have audit reports prepared by established audit firms for a minimum of the last three years. Such investor is to finance not less than one third of the project cost.

Other international credit programs that are being carried out or are intended to be carried out in Russia are not yet well developed due to fear of corruption. However, private investors, especially the banks of Germany and other EC countries, are already taking the first steps in this direction. For instance, Stolichny Bank Sberezheniy (Capital Savings Bank) has entered into an agreement with a consortium of German banks to provide lending to the enterprises of the Ural region which conduct business with German companies.

Although international financing programs of the above type are developing in Russia, there is still unmet demand in these financial markets. The examples of IBRD and EBRD have shown that in the unstable Russia of today, financing can be provided from the budgets of Western governments which are not subject to the pragmatic requirements for safety and profit to which privately owned capital is subject. Such backing with public funds of other nations and the guarantee with such public funds of the guarantees of Russian banks, is making it possible for privately owned capital to provide credits as well, to some extent, based upon such Russian bank guarantees.

The credit Russian businesses receive, based upon the guarantees of other governments, whether direct or indirect through Russian banks, should not be confused with credit from privately owned capital extended purely on the basis of guarantees from Russian banks which is issued independently.

Chapter 3.4

Banking Credit for New Businesses

The Russian economy has suffered a deep economic crisis that has resulted in a majority of the working population to lose their jobs. Military, education, and cultural sectors of the economy were critically impacted. Workers from these sectors will face difficulty in finding alternative work in the foreseeable future. As of yet, new businesses lack the working capital to provide the wages and pay for the cost of raw materials to utilize this available labor to create an expanded production of goods. The market's demand for such goods and services cannot be met without such working capital. As a result, available labor remains unemployed even though its production is needed. New businesses are also hindered by political instability, unanticipated government actions, ambiguous tax codes, high inflation, lack of qualified consultants, lack of long-term business experience, and criminal and corruption factors. However, with proper organizational steps, new businesses and enterprises can be created, thereby generating new demand for workers. At a minimum, the following conditions must be met by a new enterprise so that it can begin to quickly and resolutely function:

- Effective leadership and management
- An economically viable business plan
- A solid financial base
- A resistance to crime

Of course, ideally, all four of these elements would be contained in an existing private business community. However, in Russia, there is simply not enough money circulating throughout the business sectors to finance new enterprises. Throughout the world business community, the problem of money shortage is addressed in different ways. The essence of solving the problem, however, remains the same. Some organizations with money, whether it's a private investment fund, a government organization, or a bank, agree to take the risk of investing in a new enterprise. In the private sector, this risk is taken in hopes of realizing profits from loan repayments or from an increase in the value of a business reflected in the price of its shares. A government organization may make a risky investment in order to provide employment or to fulfill a social goal. In a majority of developed countries, special laws and government organs exist to support the creation of new businesses. In Russia, these structures are still developing and are yet unable to offer full support.

Currently, basically the only generally accessible source for financial support comes from commercial banks. Although some Russian banks refuse to work with small or start-up firms, most banks will provide loans to such businesses if they present a sound project plan that appears profitable. When banks are presented with numerous sound and profitable opportunities, they will favor those which also promise to cultivate a long-term customer relationship. When stable Russian banks offer to guarantee repayment, Western financing companies will provide credits for the purchase and importing goods and machinery with which to operate and expand such businesses.

In Russia, an applicants credit worthiness cannot generally be evaluated along the terms of credit history or a firms reputation, because nearly all businesses are new creations and nearly all businesspeople have no previous business experiences. To evaluate the credit worthiness of applicants, Russian banks have come to rely on business plans as the basis for credit reviews.

Russian banks have come to expect the following information to be included in a business plan:
- details about the applicant
- goal of the business
- marketing plan
- economic environment and legal provisions
- geographic and seasonal factors
- project design and technological needs
- financial plans toward the realization of the project
- level of training and ability of the staff and management

Details About the Applicant

This part of the business plan is sometimes overlooked, although banks consider it to be very important. This information should be constituted by an overview of assets and financial resources of the applicant, a description of the directors and owners of the enterprise, and a description of past activities. Even if this information does not directly relate to the proposed project, it is needed for evaluating the credit worthiness of the applicant.

Goal of the Business

The applicant should clearly state how loaned money will be used, for what purpose it is required, and what the expected results will be.

Marketing Plan

This section should first prove that there is a market for the proposed good or service and then explain why the business believes it will be able to compete with others for this market and how it will accomplish that. Often, beginning business parties know well what they can produce and how they will produce it, but do not possess a conception of how and to whom this product will be sold. It would be worthwhile for them to remember one of the primary axioms of business:

It is not to sell what you produce, but to produce what they are buying!

The quality of the marketing section of the business plan can often serve as a litmus test for the quality of the business plan itself. Unfortunately, in many of the business plans presented to Russian banks, the marketing section has proven to be the weakest. Although lack of information and absence of trustworthy informational networks makes writing a coherent marketing plan difficult. However, new Russian businesses should, on the whole, be able to present a marketing strategy through information generated from the numerous new private business publications, business circles, and other sources. The bank experts who analyze the marketing plan want to be absolutely clear on how sales will be obtained, and be assured that the applicant has clearly assessed the situation and taken into account all risks. They will also want some proof that competent members of the application party will follow through on the sales and marketing.

Economic Environment and Legal Provisions
This section should explain the steps the business must take to be licensed to operate the business plan, and assure the bank that the business knows the legal documentation required and has knowledge of the laws that effect the business.

Geographic and Seasonal Factors
This section should inform about the geographic area covered by the business, as well as any technological, social, ecological or seasonal factors that the business might impact or require.

Project Design and Technological Needs
This section should describe the production or service process. In doing so, it should outline the technology, equipment, constructions, energy, and raw materials required. It should also indicate the expected cost of operating the business and producing the products or services, the predicted volume of sales, prices, margins of profit expected and the names of the primary and alternate suppliers as well as customers. All estimates in this section should be based on documentation that is also submitted to the bank.

Financial Plans Toward the Realization of the Project

This section should analyze expected revenue and expenditures, and present the applicants current ability to meet or not meet the financial requirements. This section will be meticulously examined by the bank which will wish to see and arrange a program that assures full and timely repayment of the loan at established intervals, whether intervals of months or quarters. The bank will also desire to see a proposal for alternate repayment plans in the case that unanticipated expenditures, unrealized revenue, or a sharp rise in costs threaten loan default or even bankruptcy. The experience of Russian banks has been that applicants frequently underestimate the amount of working capital required for a new project. In evaluating this section of the business plan, banks are careful to objectively analyze the financial prognosis, the strength of the alternate plans, and the applicants general credit worthiness. In this way, the bank protects itself so that it receives maximum profit from interest repaid on time and with little risk of default.

Level of Training and Ability of Staff and Management

This section should include information about the applicants staff and partners who will be working in the business. It should be proven to the bank that these people are adequately trained, educated, and licensed. This section should also provide information about the structure of the project leadership and about the qualifications of the leaders. It is very important for the bank that the business plan clarifies who will head the proposed business. In fact, the banks prefer to meet with the leadership so that they can personally assess them, establish a clear working relationship, and be assured that the leadership is qualified and able to adapt to the changing economic conditions. Finally, in this section, the bank will wish to see evidence that there will be an adequate number of managers to perform the necessary functions of the company which must be performed to achieve its sales projections.

After receiving the business plan, the bank will begin evaluation of its contents. Evaluation can be done either by the banks staff or by expert consultants contracted by the bank to analyze technical or specialized aspects of the plan. It is to the bank's advantage to leave no ambiguities in the business evaluation. After evaluation, the bank decides in principle if it will or will not work with the applicant. If the bank decides to work with the applicant, then it will begin defining the terms and conditions of the loan, although a realistic proposal for these conditions should be included in the initial plan. The bank should also arrange follow up meetings with the applicant to determine whether or not conditions have changed since the business plan was first submitted. In fact, follow up meetings and regular reviews become an essential component of a healthy working relationship between a bank and a new private business.

Chapter 3.5

Asset and Liability Operations

Profit asset operations in banks are diversifying as the Russian market slowly expands. Initially, short term loans were common (one week, one month, six months). Stability in the market has extended the terms to longer and more affordable loans, bringing returns in interest payments. Loans through credit cards are increasingly becoming available to the average worker, giving the banks steady income for additional investment. Investments are being made by the banks into the stock market, and directly into local businesses forming joint ventures with them. The default rate has made smaller banks suffer, however, good diversity has earned dividends on shares owned in the Russian market.

Great sources of income for the banks are the performance of services such as foreign currency exchange, cashier cheque cashing, and investment consultation and other related services. Satisfying liquidity requirements and rational risk diversification among a wide range of investments is required for a banks success. Finding qualified borrowers has become competitive, as the banks are finding it necessary to tighten their lending policies. The importance of qualified employees has been crucial to remaining competitive in the quickly changing economic environment that is Russia today. Learning and understanding the requirements of banking institutions and their lending policies has been a new process during this transition.

Asset operations in Russia consist of four distinct groups:

Lending :   the creation and sustaining management of the loan portfolio of a bank. It is the largest section of a bank's assets.

Investments: creation of diversified portfolio of financial instruments through ownership.

Clearing and Cashier Operations: banking services to individual clients and between financial organizations.

Other Asset Operations: intended to build an efficient infrastructure for diversified banking operations.

Figure 5.
Sample of Diversified Assets in 1994
(million rubles)

	Mosbusi-nessbank	%	Bank Saint Petersburg	%
Reserves at the Central Bank	483,600	11	200,747	19
Assets in other financial institutions	1,617,831	35	217,434	21
Investments in debts and equity	429,820	9	36,210	4
Personal and Business Loans	1,762,283	38	472,583	45
Material assets and intangibles	44,337	1	39,256	4
Other assets	274,840	6	71,475	7
Total	**4,612,711**	**100**	**1,037,705**	**100**

According to the data in Figure 5, the largest and most active operations in all three banks constitutes personal and business loans. This is true throughout Russia, as the demand for capital investment is high in this rebuilding and start-up period. A representative poll taken in Moscow and Saint Petersburg by the authors supports this fact.

The volumes and trends in credit and lending policies of the banks have been influenced by a number of factors. Each bank has been free to develop their own policies and make their own market driven decisions about political and macroeconomic developments. There have been many tough regulatory changes in the banking industry implemented by the Central Bank, working toward stability in concert with the commercial banks when possible.

The Central Bank and the governments anti-inflationary monetary policy, relatively low profitability in the industrial sector, combined with high profitability of financial markets operations, has had the most significant impact on lending. The following are various types of loans and the procedure of lending currently being used:

- stopping the use of Central Bank direct subsidies for budget deficit financing
- establishing new subsidies

- the Central Bank's decision to keep discount and Lombard rates higher or equal to interbank credit rates with compatible terms

In 1995, the government completely took over the system of subsidized industrial loans through Russia's commercial banks, including those granted to social services, and it became part of the government sponsored financing of the economy. The volume of such subsidies has been severely reduced. Usually, such subsidies were granted for financing of joint ventures at no more than 20% of its cost, or as a guarantee. Loans are granted based on tenders, and fast pay back, usually less than 24 months, which is an important criteria in the selection of recipients. The exceptions are granted only if investments are provided for remodeling or modernization of an existing business.

The main approach of the government to its anti-inflation policy is monetarist, seen as the restraint of the money supply. This is only possible with a tight credit policy. Money hunger and the low profitability of industry, combined with high income from purely financial transactions, were a strong disincentive for banks to lend to manufacturing firms. This in turn led the banks to confining themselves to activities in securities and in international currency exchange markets.

The two most common lending operations are direct commercial lending and bank guarantees for client obligations to third parties in the case of default. The latter method is beneficial for the banks, since its resources are not directly involved until the debtor defaults. The bank usually charges a fee for its guarantee. The aggregate of all fees is supposed to cover the obligations the bank will incur on the percentage of those guarantees in which the debtor defaults. The bank is fully responsible for payment in case of full or partial default.

Extension of credit and co-signing are two forms of guarantees. In the first situation, the bank issues to its clients the right to access money when it becomes needed. In the latter, the bank is responsible only if the client defaults. There is a high probability that both forms will be commonly used by the Russian banks in their lending activities.

Russian banks provide corporate loans under certain conditions, including the following:

- collaterization
- ability to repay
- term structure
- purpose

Collaterization

The loan should be guaranteed by the borrower's ownership of cash, securities, or liquid assets. Such assets may be direct collateral. For highest-graded borrowers, credit may be provided without collateral. However, in such cases, good financial position of the client presumes that it has some assets to repossess in case of default. The most common collateral is a lien on part of the borrowers property, which is usually related to the borrowed money.

Ability to Repay

The borrowers ability to pay both interest and principal in full, as well as early prepayment is his "ability to repay." It is impossible to determine this without a thorough check of what assets the borrower owns, as well as the purpose of the loan and the term for which the loan will be made.

Term Structure

The definition of the fixed period of the loan. The best method is to investigate the financial records and income reports of the borrower. In addition, the method and liquidity of collateral being used to guarantee the loan, must be satisfactory to equal the risk of the loan. The better the terms and amount of down payment, the better the conditions of the loan.

Purpose

With the current temporary unstable environment, banks are not confident enough to provide credit lines to firms and individuals, without liquid collateral as a guarantee. There must be a great demand for the products or services the business proposes to provide, and at a price which produces an adequate margin of profit. The primary objective is that the money be used for the intended purpose, and not for speculation in activities unrelated to the business. In Russia today, it is imprudent to provide general purpose lines of credit. The majority of loans are provided for an exact purpose, like the purchase of machinery or raw materials, or to pay wages until production of products is finished and delivered, and payment for them is collected. Even if the bank has known the borrower a long time, openness and accountability are demanded by the bank.

Methods of Lending

Before the re-establishment of commercial banks, there were two common methods of lending.
1. Loans guaranteed by a compensating balance as down payment.
2. Loans guaranteed by cash flow, or basically current contracts of the borrower generating income from sales of goods or services.

Such distinction is now totally irrelevant, because both an account balance and sales volume are related activities. Money flows cannot move without sufficient inventory and vise versa.

Today, each bank determines its own rules and policies for loans, which are based on accepted banking principles and conventions. Credit rules are approved by top bank management and banks usually adhere to them.

Depending on their technical capabilities, banks now ordinarily use one of two methods of lending.

1. Lending through open credit accounts
2. Lending through special credit accounts

The reality of the situation and the conditions of the loan are determined by each bank, which is more successful than extinct theories. The following are some average figures of the combined assets and liabilities of a Russian commercial bank.

Figure 6.
Average Ten Month Growth of a Russian Commercial Bank

(billion rubles)	1/01/96	1/04/96	1/07/96	1/10/96
Reserves	36,646	37,858	48,167	43,132
Assets	46,149	50,917	56,267	62,161
Government Claims	62,638	79,156	93,403	130,295
Additional Taxes	62,460	66,698	74,980	78,622
Demands of Private Sector	133,786	145,383	148,189	151,572
Claims of other Banks	525	1,471	1,473	2,738
Deposits	69,331	68,089	74,705	82,965
Fixed & Certificate Deposits	126,352	143,409	149,641	160,024
Foreign Currency Deposits	57,111	58,386	63,460	64,595
Securities	11,858	11,878	16,472	15,439
Foreign Liabilities	29,977	34,547	39,874	47,151
Government Deposits	9,741	11,452	11,768	12,346
Loans from Money Authorities	8,005	8,908	19,860	11,194
Capital Accounts	66,687	82,370	92,250	110,998
Other Balances	20,252	20,830	17,908	28,403

Chapter 3.6

Types of Loans and Procedures of Lending

Consumer Funds Loan

These loans are given to enterprises when they are temporarily short of financial resources for the payroll, bonuses and loan payments from the fund itself. In order to apply for the credit, the borrower submits an application to the bank accompanied by their balance sheet and required appendices. Information about other loans and financial obligations are necessary, as well as expense-revenue projections for the duration of the loan. Commercial banks also look at past records and copies of tax receipts showing proof of payments. The banks require a loan pay-back schedule and loan collateral documents.

The maturity of most loans is up to thirty days. This term is not extended beyond ten additional days, depending on the conditions. Each loan is arranged by a separate agreement against collateral on general conditions. An individual loan account is opened for each line of credit. The loan amount is placed either toward the customer's current account, transferred directly to meet cheques, tax payments, or consumer fund disbursements.

If the loan amount is placed on the customers current account, the bank accepts credit application for consumer fund support for the total amount requested. In such case, they may be given a credit line covering all overdue payments, including those obligations to the consumer fund itself.

In the case where the bank pays cheques or taxes directly, bypassing the customers current account, the bank undertakes additional risks of credit non-repayment. This type of loan schedule implies that the payroll is paid before other budgetary obligations due at the same time. The borrowers financial forecast and account are monitored by the bank throughout the life of the loan. The borrowers repay the credit by means of money transfer from their current account. At this time, actual disbursement of credit from the consumer fund is checked on-site.

Paper Credit

Commercial banks develop their own by-laws regarding the issue of paper loans. The most important aspect is a unified understanding of terminology, which is currently disordered. The lending procedure for paper credit is the same as with other loans. However, there are some peculiarities, such as when the notes are submitted for discounting they need to be checked in terms of legality and business viability. From a legal perspective, the paper submitted for financing is verified as to compliance with all legal procedures and for the authority of the companies chief executive officer who signed the paper.

From a business perspective, the paper loan is verified as to the actual real market value and its liquidity. The question is, will the loan be paid on-time? Developing creditworthiness and a respected position takes time, and those in Russia who are capable of honoring their responsibilities are producing greater paper value for their companies. Banks are looking for reliable and stable individuals that will take financial responsibility for loans. Once the credit standing of the client is accepted, confirmation of any related party's financial position is verified. Depending on the credit ranking of the client, various amounts of collateral for the loans are requested. Paper is not accepted from companies or individuals that have protested their papers in the past.

The development of banks for each level of the Russian economy, from the government to an individual entrepreneur, is growing to meet the demand. Regular guaranteed paper transactions between the many banks, the government, and certain established business persons is increasing. However, clearly the demand for credit still exceeds the supply available.

Paper loans are based upon the educated evaluation that the company will produce the projected income levels. Banks are looking for purchase orders and proven past transactions for paper loans. When the seller of the paper does not have sufficient liquid capital, guarantees can be accepted from established and future purchase orders in the form of a bill from the company or a third party. It is implied that this trade bill is guaranteed by future proceeds from the sale of commodities bought as a result of the bill. Because the trade bill appears in the bank after the deal is done, there is no need to make an analysis of the deal. One needs simply to trace back the origin of this note, for instance, to make sure that the bill reflects a real transaction. This may be accomplished by the thorough study of delivery agreements, acceptance notes, service contracts and transport documents. Financial paper of this type is based on a borrowing agreement, when one party borrows money from another and issues paper instead. Banks will discount paper notes only if the payer is a financially stable company with a proven reputation. Banks consider staying power and stability in the sales reports of the company when determining this reputation.

The banks insist that the financial paper is entered in the borrowers balance sheet or accounting books. Interest on the bills is calculated for each one separately, based on the data provided in the register, and then added for each register in order to assess the Central Bank's Discount Rate to determine how much is to be paid to the bearer of the paper loan. The Central Bank's Discount Rate is calculated as follows:

$$C = \frac{V \times M \times R}{100 \times 360}$$

V = Paper face value   **M** = Days to Maturity date   **R** = Bank interest rate

Paper Credit is a credit given by the bank to a company in the form of promissory notes. The face value of all notes is equal to the size of the loan, and the notes mature later than the loan itself. There may be several notes for one borrower, different in both value and the terms of maturity. With the notes, the borrower is able to pay for supplies, information, and services necessary to do business.

According to common credit agreements, the borrower must submit collateral equal to the size of the loan and pay a commission, interest, to the bank by a certain date. At maturity, the note bearer brings it to the bank and receives money instead. Paper credit is convenient for all related parties, because the bank does not need borrowed funds in order to finance a paper loan.

The borrower is able to receive a low rate loan that is several times less expensive than ordinary credit. The customers of the borrower are put into a position of obligation to make their payments on-time. Due to the short period of paper loan circulation, they have the same qualities as money. By means of the paper, the suppliers do not need to use their current account. This is important if there are claims to the supplier from other creditors or taxes due to the state.

On-Call Credit is a loan made to a company which turns the promissory notes into collateral. As opposed to the discounting of notes, the bank does not receive the ownership rights on the paper. They are put in pledge by the bearer to the bank for a certain period of time.

Credit Line Lending is a type of lending which implies that the borrower is promised by a bank, that a certain amount of funds will be made available to him for an agreed period of time. In this period of start-up and transformation, credit is being consumed by the borrower to meet payroll and necessary overhead. It is difficult to make serious internal investments by companies because of the high cost of money. Therefore, credit lines are used to keep the businesses afloat.

If the credit line is open, the borrower is able to get credit from the bank without separate negotiations. Still, the bank has the right to cut off the line and claim interest payments before the maturity if a loan is used improperly, if the collateral is insufficient or interfered with, if the accounting or warehouse bookkeeping is wrong, or if the borrower breaks other conditions of the credit agreement. Currently, credit lines are stopped if the payment is overdue past 30 days or if the company declares bankruptcy.

Revolving and Non-Revolving Credit Lines

A credit line is non-revolving after the expiration of a certain time period, or any consumption of the credit line. This is also called a purpose-oriented credit line, which is intended for only one contract.

A revolving credit line implies that the loan is to be consumed and automatically repaid up to a certain limit and term. The effective period of the credit line is fixed by the bank and the borrower in the credit agreement. If there is overdue principal and interest when the term of the line expires, these amounts are usually included into the new credit agreement.

While settling balances for executed work as accounts receivable, the size of the credit line may be extended by the amount of the trade deficit for goods shipped under normal terms, but no more than 30 days after the goods are shipped or after the work is performed.

Loans under the Open Credit Line are recommended to be issued to borrowers observing such requirements as the following:

- a stable financial position
- profitable business activities
- a minimum of three years experience
- insufficient working capital to increase production

It is wise to set up a special loan account which is combined with current accounts for open credit line lending. This access to additional funds can then serve all objects of the loan agreement.

Most Western banks offer such active-passive facilities, in the form of overdraft protection on special terms. Overdue sums should not exceed established financial limits. The interest rate charged on overdue amounts are usually higher than for other previously mentioned loans.

Lending to Customers and Construction Companies

If a construction company needs a loan, they submit to the bank a business plan which must be fully supported by a financial plan schedule. In the case when financing is guaranteed by the government, the business plan must be approved by the appropriate state bodies. If the financing is guaranteed by the private company at its own expense, the business plan must be authorized by the company's CEO.

The purpose of lending for construction can be for materials, wages, to pay contractors, or to purchase equipment. The size of the loan is limited by the amount necessary to complete the task or to satisfy a specific need. The maturity depends on when construction is scheduled to be finished, when the machinery begins full capacity operation, and when income can be realistically expected.

Credit can be issued in full or in phases, as the stages of the construction are completed or equipment and materials are needed. In the monitored disbursement of funds, arrangements are made to transfer the funds into the suppliers accounts with the terms of a promissory note.

Construction companies continuously benefit from this purposeful lending to recover insufficient working capital while construction takes place. Equipment and materials on construction sites are then used as the collateral for loans. To receive a loan, the client or subcontractor is obligated to submit a feasibility survey, construction contracts, and an assessment of the completed construction, costs and machinery to the bank. Credit is issued within 45 days, but the terms may differ from bank to bank. Conditions regarding collateral and interest rates are negotiated on general terms. Credit is issued in the form of a term promissory note.

Open Credit

Their security and guarantee is the trust and reputation of the client. Long-term relations with the bank, and stable creditworthiness of the client make it possible to issue such a loan. All terms and conditions are set and the credit line is available to the client when needed. These loans are usually short-term, up to three months, and used for working capital in production or in a service industry. In Russia, such an open credit is unique to the businesses which are solid, and they are an integral part of the economy, whether locally or nationally.

In order to receive a blank credit loan, the prospective borrower presents an application to the bank on their letterhead. Whether or not the loan is needed immediately is of no concern to the bank, as the purpose is to establish a financial relationship between the company and the bank. Money can be deposited directly into the company's account or it can be sent directly to a vendor for payment of an expense. Practice has shown that banks earn more on blank credits than on any other type of loan, due to the fact that they are associated with greater risk.

Current Account Credit

In today's world of Russian banking, a current account credit loan is rarely used. However, the more stable the economy becomes, and as the financial position of companies improve, a greater number of such loans will be issued by banks. This type of loan is used when the current account of a company is closed, and all transactions are recorded on one and the same asset-liability account. The prospective borrower submits cash flow projections to the bank, which indicates all its sources and disbursements of capital.

The difference between the need for and the sources of working capital is the limit for current account credit. A few versions of the required size of the loan, or loan limit, are stated in the credit agreement along with the respective term, whether it be quarterly or annually, and average gap forecast and maximum size of the loan. The decision on how to manage the loan is made after negotiations are completed between the bank and the borrower, and then fixed in the credit agreement.

Long-Term Lending

Long-term lending is associated with higher risk, therefore much more attention is paid to the business case evaluation by the banks. The terms of each long-term credit are very specific. A critical aspect to the success in long-term lending, and the pay-back of the loan, is how the bank implements the investment project. For these purposes, the bank opens, tenders and invites competition for the suppliers of equipment and materials. These contests are open to Russian companies as well as international ones, and usually the winners are those that offer a reliable bank guarantee or partial self financing. Common purposes for long-term lending are for capital investments in the following:

- industrial and social reconstruction, development, and improvement of equipment
- purchase of personal and business related real estate, vehicles, machinery, buildings
- scientific-technical production, intellectual ideas and other objects of property

In order to obtain long-term credit, the company must submit all required documents to the bank together with a feasibility survey of the business project. If a third party is to be contracted, then a construction contract and capital investment payback appraisal is required by the bank. A feasibility survey includes a study of the purpose of the loan, and cash flow projections with detailed descriptions of the most relevant articles. Additionally, any construction contract with a third party must also be included. All calculations and contracts must include prices, as per object or services required.

Profit from a financed project serves as the source of principal and interest reimbursement. If the project's profit is insufficient to cover these costs, the company's net profit should cover them.

The amount of the credit, depends upon the cost of labor and the borrower's personal capital resources. The cost of technical maintenance, designing and other costs paid from other sources are deducted from the total of the construction feasibility survey. Any company with less than one year of business history are not recommended for any lending above the excess of their charter capital.

Credit for long-term capital investment in Russia today is usually made for more than one year. Long-term credit interest rates are usually in observance of the bank's overall interest rate policy for the respective period, which may be changed in line with inflation rates.

All credits are served against collateral, such as by the opening of a ruble or hard currency deposit account with the bank. Also used are proceeds from the currency contracts with what the bank considers to be a reliable counterpart or a pledge of liquid property or property rights on unconditional and irrevocable guarantees served by companies able to repay the credit, providing insurance or reassurance. In certain cases, incompleted or finished construction may also be used as collateral, with the credit limit increasing in proportion to the level of completion.

Long-term credit may be issued in full or in part, according to the readiness of the construction stages, or the equipment and spare parts that are acquired. The funds are transferred to the supplier's accounts with arrangement of a term promissory note. When the construction is financed from long-term credit, the primary document that regulates cash, flows from the client to the contractor as stated in the construction agreement.

As soon as construction is completed and all acceptance notes are served, the schedule of monthly or quarterly installments for outstanding credit is prepared up to the date of credit maturity. The terms depend upon the cost of recovery, the creditworthiness and financial position of the borrower, various credit risks, credit capital turnover, and other credit related factors.

The maximum amount of risk per each borrower or group of related borrowers in respect to one another, dependent or principal and subsidiary, are established in percentage terms based upon the amount of internal funds in the credit organization. When determining the risk amount, the bank considers current debts of the given borrower or group of related borrowers. Also, the guarantees and warranties given by the commercial bank to the borrower or the group of related borrowers are accounted for by the bank. All loans and guarantees issued by the commercial banks are now being backed with collateral and assets. The necessity for guarantees and down payments for loans has been a difficult reality for Russian individuals and businesses in need of capital.

The maximum amount of high credit risk is established as a percentage ratio of the aggregate value of the high risks, and the internal funds of a credit organization or commercial bank. High credit risks are deemed to be the volume of the credits, guarantees and warranties in favor of one client, at a rate of over five percent of the internal funds of the bank.

The observance of compulsory and recommended performance standards is highly respected by the leading commercial bank's in Russia today. It is viewed as an indispensable condition for maintaining high liquidity and keeping active operations backed by an adequate resource base. Observance is also a factor in methods used to increase the Bank's capital and for changing its structure.

UNIT 4

Examples of Activities of Russian Banks

Introduction

Russian commercial banking practice varies significantly from common practices in other nations. In many aspects, Russian banking practices incorporate accounts receivable collection systems into a *checking account* structure, and it extends the equivalent of the American IRS collection privileges to other entities. These practices are described in this Unit.

On April 23-24, 1992, in the Bor Hotel, in the Moscow region, the Russian Banks Association, The Council on Foreign & Defense Policy, The New Policy Center for Humanitarian Relations & Business Cooperation, and Mezhekonomsberbank discussed the problems of Russia's financial settlements with neighboring states and the experience of commercial banks.

When Russia announced on July 1, 1992, that all ruble accounts beyond its borders would not be recognized, it in effect canceled all previous credits and past payments for goods which it had made, and basically created its own new currency. It also offered to sell its new currency and in some cases to continue to give credits in the new currency under certain conditions. In effect, it told the CIS that to be an independent country, they would have to have an independent currency.

The natural result was the issuance of new currencies by the countries of the *near abroad*, who soon discovered that currency is not *money* unless there is something behind it, which is of value and which makes it *convertible legal tender*. To be *money*, a currency must be accepted in payment and be *freely exchangeable* as property, without restriction.

The ruble has since become money, that is to say under certain conditions and restrictions it becomes convertible into *money*, such as dollars, yen, marks etc., and in this process it loses the restrictions and conditions formerly attached to the ruble.

When the entire domestic economy operates on real *money*, then all production of goods and services also becomes expressed in real money based upon world market prices. In the process of the evolution of the new Russian economy, Russian banking activities are achieving a greater recognition of the characteristics of money and are thereby facilitating the economic reconstruction of Russia.

Money is *canned human effort*, which is to say the current value of which is preserved without depreciation for future expenditure. It is savings. Such savings are also capital which can be invested. In the period from 1989 to 1995, rubles lacked the attributes of the definition of money and therefore was spent for goods as a means of preserving its value. It could not be invested because it could not be returned over time in an undepreciated value. At this point in 1997, that has changed, subject to some qualification.

A new respect has developed in Russia for money as a form of private property. After the great War, many European countries had laws prohibiting flight capital, so that *money* would remain within their borders and provide capital for reconstruction of their industries and economies. These laws were obeyed because people had confidence in the integrity and fairness of their governments. They believed the cost of government and its actions were reasonable, and that their capital would build industry and profits and increase their employment and wages. The believed that their money would be returned to them in an undepreciated form, equal in purchasing power, at a later date. Therefore, this limitation on their financial freedom was accepted by most people. Unpatriotic behavior was punished by a government, which itself did not participate in breaking such laws. In other words, government regulations worked because they were directed at achieving the welfare of the people.

Adopting a policy of real *money* as the currency of a country, always increases both domestic and international investment. These mechanisms are beginning to be evident in the activities of the Russian banks, who are now presented with the challenge of creating a coherent policy for harnessing the power of money as an investment medium.

The possibility of satisfying the needs of Russian industry for capital with which to create GDP and create employment, rests upon bringing the currency of Russia into compliance with the characteristics of the definition of money and not upon a shortage of money itself. As Russian banking explores new activities, it is discovering that barriers to economic progress are expressions of resistance to a *medium of exchange*, which is called *money* by semantic license, but lacks the characteristics of *money*.

There is a consistency in this activity compatible with international practices which is reflected in the activity of the Russian banks. The differences which superficially appear to be present, are nothing more than attempts bring local practices into compliance with universal truths of economics.

Chapter 4.1

Mosbusinessbank

Mosbusinessbank was established in 1990 from the basis of the large state bank Zhilsozbank. During its few years in business, the Bank has won a reputation for reliability and dynamism in Russia. Throughout that period the Bank has worked to faithfully fulfilled its commitments to all of its clients, shareholders, the budget, and to strictly observed the economic standards laid down by the Central Bank. In a recent article in Financial Izvestia, Mosbusinessbank was honored as a leader of all Russian banks, ranking in the top five.

In a situation where competition is growing ever stiffer from year to year, the Bank maintains its high rating and retains its credibility in the business community. In a number of its financial indices, the Bank is in a class with Russia's most respected credit institutions, enjoying their clients' absolute trust.

An introduction to the Bank's intensive development can be demonstrated by the following data:

Figure 7.
At the beginning of year (million rubles)

	Assets	Registered Capital
1992	28,563	800
1993	484,892	1800
1994	1,973,808	1800
1995	4,612,711	2800
1996	8,382,397	8000

Certainly, the above data reflects the influences of rapid inflation in Russia. But according to Russian practice, a commercial bank is not obligated to recount the annual report in accordance with the level of inflation. Nevertheless, the rate of inflation is decreasing and has approached a stable, controlled level in the last few years.

80

Figure 8.
At the beginning of the year.

	Individual Shareholders	Business Shareholders	Total Shareholders
1992	2,607	694	3,301
1993	6,109	1,032	7,139
1994	6,659	957	7,556
1995	7,900	932	8,832
1996	9,821	864	10,685

More than a half of the Bank's share capital is owned by 61 stockholders. The proportion of stockholders owning blocks of stock worth less than one million rubles, constitutes 94% of the total number of stockholders. At a recent general meeting of the Bank's stockholders, a decision was accepted to increase the amount of authorized capital to 100 billion rubles, increasing the per share value of the Bank's stock.

Mosbusinessbank has expanded its reach throughout Russia and the Commonwealth of Independent States, as a result of the development of branch offices and growing correspondent relations with other banks. By the beginning of 1994, the Bank had 38 branch offices throughout the CIS, and by the beginning of 1996 more than 56 had been opened.

As the Bank's network grows in scale, new branches are being opened and the volume and quality of operations steadily increases.

Figure 9.

Year	Number of Employees
1993	2626
1994	3260
1995	4446
1996	5235

Securities, Investments, and the Resources Policy
In conducting its credit operations, Mosbusinessbank seeks to contribute to the stabilization of Russia's economy, to support private business at home, and to expedite the financial recovery of the enterprises it serves.

Because of the Bank's steady and purposeful effort to reduce exposure, its diversified advances portfolio is secured by reliable and liquid collateral. In 1995, the Bank granted ruble and foreign currency loans in the amount of 54.4 trillion rubles, which was 2.2 times the amount of the previous year.

As of January 1, 1996, the Bank's outstanding loans totalled 3,236 billion rubles, which was an increase of 1.8 times over the preceding year. On the recommendations of the General Meeting of the Bank's Shareholders, nearly 60% of the aggregate loan investment went to the material production sphere, with top priority given to capital goods, and the manufactures that produce staple and popular consumer goods. Also, investment went to enterprises working in earnest to put their finances right and to improve their solvency. On the average, credit operations accounted for 43.4% of the Bank's assets, compared to 32.7% in 1994. Also, the Bank's advances portfolio is characterized by a greater proportion of long-term investments. By the end of 1995, they accounted for more than 16% of the total loan investments.

The Bank's borrowers included the country's leading state-owned and privatized industrial enterprises. Traditionally, large loans were granted to trading companies which met domestic consumer demands. For example, with the public demand for medicines steadily trending upwards, the Bank regularly grants credits to the leading pharmaceutical companies which supply their products throughout Russia.

Additionally, the Bank renders substantial credit support to medium and small businesses. As business risks are concentrating in the banking sphere, the Bank puts special emphasis on the quality of credit risk assessment. For all the pains it is taking to raise the standard of its credit programs, the Bank has failed to diminish the proportion of past due loan principal in its advances portfolio. The non-payment crisis in the industry, a reduction in the number of reliable borrowers, and the liquidation of small to medium size businesses have combined to create an adverse effects on Russia's banking system as a whole.

Under these circumstances, the Bank has concentrated on improving risk control procedures and techniques in an effort to optimize its risk management system. It's success depends on effective Asset and Liability Management by the Credit Committees responsible for the coordination, planning, and adjustment of the Bank's subdivisions' performance parameters.

The Bank maintains a reasonable and controllable level of risk by setting limits to individual balance sheet items, to the extent of open positions and allowable losses in response to set financial instruments. In setting these limits, the Bank seeks to diversify risk by properly reading instruments of the various markets, regions, branches and its clients.

In assessing credit risk and setting appropriate limits, the Bank goes by the credit ratings of leading Western companies, and by its own criteria of borrowers' solvency. In market risk management, open position and stop-loss limits are set for various financial instruments proceeding from the past record, and the likely prospects for price fluctuation intensity. Liquidity control calls for asset/liability pattern and gap analysis, which is essential for keeping the proportion of liquid assets large enough for the Bank to meet current liabilities.

Mosbusinessbank's risk management system spared it the adverse effects of the money market's instability in 1995. This was achieved through planning its operations and assessing their efficiency. The Bank has also attached special importance to the ratio of operating profit to possible losses in the closing of a position. The Bank is now busy building up the Automated Banking Risk Management System, intended as an extra means of monitoring the activities of the Bank's subdivisions.

New credit facilities, overdraft, paper, and factoring, have gained popularity quickly. The amount of loans on mortgages granted to the public continues to grow. In order to meet its clients' need for credit services, the Bank has stepped up the practice of providing guarantees in both rubles and foreign currencies.

By the beginning of 1996, Mosbusinessbank's investments grew 2.5 times compared with 1995. Securities trading transactions and investments accounted for 14.9% of the Bank's working assets. The Bank has invested the bulk of its funds in government debt securities. Also, ruble security transactions made up a substantial proportion of the total volume of government securities trading. Compared with the previous year's figures, the Bank's average investment in government treasury bills (short term - GKO) and federal loan bonds, grew 3.5 times to the amount of R393.6 billion rubles.

In a situation favorable to investment, the Bank has continually become more active in the corporate securities market, where it co-founded a number of promising industrial enterprises and financial companies. The network of subsidiaries pursuing courses of activity aside from the Bank's main line of business or functioning in the provision of various services, such as insurance, auditing, blue-printing and construction, have continued to take shape as part of the effort for the overall development and expansion of the Mosbusinessbank branch system.

The Bank has also developed its *trust* business. It invested most of the funds entrusted to it in government debt instruments. Clients were offered service packages and advised on the analysis and optimum conduct of financial and business transactions, such as trust property management.

Russia's fast-growing stock market infrastructure offers Mosbusiness-Bank ample investment opportunities. Therefore, the Bank plans to increase the share of investments in its working assets. As non-government securities trading is becoming more common-place, the Bank plans to do more business in the shares various commercial enterprises.

The Bank has sought to attract resources by issuing debt securities and by a rational redistribution of resources among the Bank's institutions. Following an improvement of the structure of the Bank's liabilities, borrowing against its finance bills and certificates of deposit has become common-practice. Throughout 1995, the daily turnover of borrowing against the Bank's debt securities grew 11 times, which was from 217 billion rubles to 2,384 billion rubles.

Mosbusinessbank continually seeks to expand its resource base amid stiff competition for all types of resources in the banking sector. This effort consists mainly in the promoting of funds transfer and settlement service, and the further diversification of funds supply sources. The latter assumes special importance under review, marked by the toughening of the Russian Government's monetary policy and the resultant instability of the Bank's main source of funds supply.

Being one of Russia's more reliable banks, Mosbusinessbank managed to increase the balances on its clients' accounts substantially, by encouraging its new clients to use its funds transfer and settlement services. These resources are traditionally considered to be of key importance for Mosbusinessbank, with its far-flung branch network, for all of its customers.

Instability of the main source of affordable monetary resources, foreign loans for short-terms, called for shifting the emphasis to more expensive but more predictable sources. The business plan of the Bank's development provided for an accelerated growth of corporate and private time deposits. Such a policy enabled the Bank to avoid a deficit of resources in difficult times.

Domestic and International Currency Markets

Mosbusinessbank consistently carries on currency trading and works to improve settlement procedures on the domestic and international foreign currency exchange markets. The Bank seeks to integrate itself into the international banking community as a first-rate credit and financial institution, having the reputation of a reliable business partner.

The Bank has broadened the scale of its correspondent relations, both inside and outside of Russia. Currently, the Bank's correspondent network, including Russian and international banks with and without accounts opened in them, is over 500 banks. Hard currency accounts were opened for 35 correspondent banks, bringing the total of correspondent banks having such accounts to 330 and growing. The Bank's correspondent network abroad comprises 245 banks, of which 37 operate NOSTRO accounts.

With a view to broaden the scale of soft currency trading, the Bank started making settlements in Byelorus rubles through its Minsk branch account. Now the Bank is also dealing in Ukrainian karbovantsi and the Kazakhstan tenge.

Mosbusinessbank's rising standing in the world banking community was evidenced by a dramatic increase in new credit, documentary or unsecured, deferred-payment, and foreign exchange credit lines granted to it by international banks. The Bank has received its first syndicated financial credit in the amount of $20 million USD, granted by a consortium of the leading banks of Switzerland, France, Austria, the United Kingdom, Germany, and the Czech Republic.

The Bank recently introduced state-of-the-art technology, which made automatic real-time processing of incoming and outgoing payments possible on the branch network scale.

In the sphere if international settlements, the Bank seeks to raise the standard of these services and to step up the efficiency of its banking controls over the influx of foreign currency receipts. While carrying on and improving conventional operations and services, including the placement of deposits in international banks, currency conversion, trading in foreign currency and in bonds of the Russian Finance Ministry, the Bank continues its efforts to build future business relationships.

The volume of trading done by Mosbusinessbank on the domestic foreign exchange market is steadily growing. It purchased foreign currency from international banks at wholesale, and then sold it to Russian banks, its branches and clients. In 1996, the Bank sold to its branches and to other Russian banks about $1.7 billion USD. Some of these clients and banks had purchased foreign currency cash on their own. Foreign currency is delivered to and from international banks literally door-to-door, to minimize transportation risk delivery costs and to simplify the transaction procedure. On the whole, in terms of dealing in imported foreign currency, Mosbusinessbank is among Russia's top five banks.

Mosbusinessbank continues to step up its plastic card operations. Specifically, it introduced ETN (European Travel Network) and IAPA discount cards, which entitle their holders to discounts on hotels and car rentals. In addition, the holders of Visa-Mosbusinessbank cards are entitled to policies of the Gesa Assistance French insurance company. The Bank issued 3,700 plastic cards in 1995, but including VISA-Mosbusinessbank and Mosbusinessbank-Union Cards, the total issued was 5,700. This amounts to a 2.7 time increase in plastic cards issued since 1994.

For its more reliable clients, the Bank has developed and implemented a Visa Mosbusinessbank business card program. The program provides for a short-term crediting of clients, rendering cardholders a supplementary set of services, including discount's on hotel bills, accident, medical, and loss of luggage insurance. Visa plastic cards processed by the Bank in 1995 totaled $110.6 million USD. Among the Russian banks who are members of the Visa payment system, Mosbusinessbank accounted for 21.8% of the total volume.

Additionally, the Bank continues to service Diners Club and Eurocard MasterCard holders.

For its clients, the Bank continues to cash traveller's cheques, including ETC-Thomas-Cook MasterCard, Visa, American Express, Bank of America, City Corp., Bank of Tokyo, Fuji Bank, Mitsui Bank, and Sumitomo Bank. The Bank also sells ETC-Thomas-Cook-MasterCard, Visa, and American Express traveller's cheques. The cash equivalents of the cheques accepted are entered into the clients' and Banks' accounts the day they are handed over to the cash department of the Bank's Head Office. In the Bank's exchange offices, private individuals can have their traveller's cheques cashed either in rubles or in foreign currency.

The Bank maintains active cooperation with foreign financial organizations, such as the World Bank, the ERBD, the IRBD, the International Finance Corporation, and other foreign banks, credit and financial institutions, with a view to drawing medium and long term loans from abroad for the funding of business ventures in Russia. Currently, the Bank is carrying out, in cooperation with the EBRD, five small and medium size business financing agreements.

Factoring Operations

With Mosbusinessbank's introduction to Russian banking state-of-the-art technology, which makes automatic real-time processing of incoming and outgoing payments possible on the branch network scale, the Bank has been accepted in the Factors Chain International (FCI) uniting it with the services of about 160 factoring organizations of over 45 countries. Using these services, the Bank has organized a factoring program for its clients within the framework of this international factoring system. This enables the Bank to credit exporters in the amount equalling the worth of the actually shipped goods for the period of its pay deferment. Such credits are secured by the Bank's correspondent factoring companies via the FCI network. The Bank may act as both a factorer for the exporter by crediting the client, or a factorer for the importer by extending guarantees on his behalf to other factoring companies, which then recovers his debt to the exporter in accordance with the pay deferment schedule.

Therefore, after preparing all the relevant materials and documents, the Bank introduces a system of communication between the factoring companies, called EDIFACToring, which permits information to exchange in real time. As a result, the factoring service agreements are signed with the Bank's clients, and the first invoices are financed within the framework of international factoring transactions. Such international factoring arrangements have been made with European, US and Japanese companies.

Achievements in the Banks Information Technology Systems

In the field of information technology, the emphasis has been on the need to develop an integrated banking data processing system. As clients insisted on ever higher standards of service, Mosbusinessbank has concentrated on raising the efficiency of its own internal information system.

The Bank gives top priority to projects intended to improve the technology of settlements in the national currency. Specifically, a method of entering intra-city receipts on the Head Office balance sheet, on the same day, has been introduced, raising the standard of correspondent business automation. The technique of making settlements between mutual correspondent accounts is now being developed jointly with other large banks. Meanwhile, Mosbusiness-Bank has completed the unification of an automated data processing system for the its branches.

A new deposit operations system has also been developed, and is now being implemented into the Bank's Head Office in Moscow. The system automates ruble and foreign currency operations, and has broaden the network of ATM's and further expanded their functions.

The Bank has put a great deal of energy in the further improvement of its Client-Bank electronic funds transfer system, using the RS-Mail and SFM systems. To ensure centralized control over its debt securities, the Bank also developed and introduced a stock version of SFM. Additionally, the Bank's automatic accounts processing system has been further upgraded, with a book keeping software support package in trial operation under Instruction No. 17 of the Central Bank.

In 1995, special attention was paid to the standardization of Mosbusinessbank's local and telecommunication networks. As a result, the inter-regional telecommunications system, which solves problems involved in the handling of data traffic within the Bank's nationwide branch network, is now functioning. Because of the continued effort to improve the Bank's network and information technologies, an increased profit has been realized.

Figure 10.

Annual Income (millions rubles)	1994	1995
Interest	802,557	1,493,655
Security Operations	246,909	712,374
Foreign Exchange	42,857	76,620
Other income	134,529	358,012
Total Income	**1,226,852**	**2,640,661**

Figure 11.

Annual Profit (millions rubles)	1993	1994	1995
Interest	93,568	477,021	1,075,603
Security Operations	587	142,994	262,770
Foreign Exchange	-	1706	1300
Other expenses	39,229	269,692	738,630
Total Expenses	**133,384**	**861,323**	**2,078,303**
Net Profit	**177,670**	**365,529**	**562,358**

Since Mosbusinessbank was established, it has continued to donate funds to culture, public health, sport, church restoration projects, children's homes, public organizations, low-income families, veterans, and the handicapped. In 1995, Mosbusinessbank allocated a total of over 4 billion rubles to these types of Russian charities.

Chapter 4.2

Bank "Saint Petersburg" PLC

Bank "Saint Petersburg" Public Limited Company, is a universal credit institution offering a full range of banking services to customers, with increasing assets and liability operations in balance. The Bank attracts monetary assets of enterprises, associations, organizations, institutions, co-operatives, and the general population. It carries out crediting and intermediary banking operations, provides financing of capital investments, performs settlements and cash services for the population, and conducts other banking operations for its customers, according to the regulations established by the Central Bank.

As with all Russian banks, international companies and individuals can be stockholders in Bank "Saint Petersburg" PLC. The following is a list of the Bank's major shareholders.
- Bolshevitchka Ltd.
- Monolitstroy Construction Agency
- Petrolesport PLC
- Elegant Furs Inc.
- Leningrad Regional Council for Tourism and Excursions PLC
- Moskovskiy Department Store
- Passage Trade Company
- Saint Petersburg Metro Administration
- Apraksin Dvor Department Store
- LenNIIproject

Bank "Saint Petersburg's" rational economic policy has enabled it to be among Russia's thirty largest, and most reliable banks in 1997. In 1995, the Bank was first in total assets among the banks of Saint Petersburg, and second in balance profit. It was the first bank in Russia to sign a cooperation agreement under the World Bank's program for development of Russia's financial institutions, beginning its work with the Union Bank of Ireland. The objective of this joint activity is to transform the Bank into a comprehensive financial institution, achieving international standards in customer service. In February, 1996, the Sixth Congress of the Association of Russian Banks unanimously elected Bank "Saint Petersburg" as a member of its Board.

In 1995, the Bank launched a new strategy to accelerate its formation of Authorized Capital. Without attracting any additional funds, the Bank has been able to increase its authorized capital by 8 billion rubles, through the use of a highly efficient instrument, convertible bonds. The Bank was the first Russian financial institution to use this method. Simultaneously, the Bank worked to increase its own capital, which consists of the Charter Capital, a reserve and other funds which belong to the Bank. The dynamics and evolution of the growth of authorized and ownership capital can be observed in the following:

Figure 12. (rubles)

Date	Authorized Capital	Ownership Capital
January 1, 1993	500,000,000	1,970,000,000
January 1, 1994	900,000,000	28,790,000,000
January 1, 1995	1,200,000,000	82,390,000,000
January 1, 1996	9,200,000,000	202,980,000,000

We can see from this information that during 1995, the authorized capital grew from 1,200 to 9,200 million rubles with no additional resources from the shareholders. The authorized capital was represented by 9,200,000 shares, at 1,000 rubles par value (7,190,000 of them being ordinary registered shares, while 2,010,000 are preferred registered shares).

History of Bank "Saint Petersburg" PLC

Bank "Saint Petersburg" was among the first Russian commercial bank to begin its activities before the Russian government passed its new banks and banking activities laws. Below are some of the most important events in the early development of Bank "Saint Petersburg."

1990
- Bank "Saint Petersburg" PLC is registered with the Central Bank on October 3, 1990, with authorized capital at 75 million rubles.

1991
- A license is granted for international and foreign currency operations
- A second issue of shares is undertaken, increasing authorized capital by 150 million rubles
- A third issue of shares is undertaken, raising its authorized capital to 500 million rubles
- A representative office is opened in Moscow

1992
- Becomes a member of the SWIFT system
- The Central Bank grants its General License No. 436
- A number of subsidiary undertakings are set up
- Participates as a founder of the Saint Petersburg Foreign Exchange

1993

- The fourth issue of shares is undertaken, increasing the authorized capital to 900 million rubles
- Private customer accounts are first offered, and corporate hard currency loans are offered
- Hedging operations are developed
- The fifth issue of shares increases the authorized capital to 1200 million rubles
- Dealing in the international currency and financial markets is begun
- Work begins in the market of state securities

1994

- Bank "Saint Petersburg's" plastic cards are first issued
- A new branch is opened in Moscow
- An agency for private customers' services is established
- The first issue of bonds, which are convertible into the shares of the sixth issue is made
- The Central Bank grants a license for transactions with precious metals

Credit and Investment Policy

One of Bank "Saint Petersburg's" main businesses is lending to enterprises, companies, and individuals. The lending policy was traditionally focused on socially important city industries. The Bank primarily made loans to trade, light and food industries, city utilities, smaller companies, and individuals. The following is a summary of its loan structure from 1991 on:

- 42% Short Term Loans totaling 347 billion rubles
- 17% Foreign Currency Loans totaling 142 billion rubles
- 14% Long Term Loans totaling 112 billion rubles
- 10% Credit loans to other banks totaling 89 billion rubles
- 17% Discounted Notes in the Bank Portfolio totaling 141 billion rubles

In 1995 Bank "Saint Petersburg" increased its lending to the private sector by 30%, capturing a 7% share of the Saint Petersburg market. Loans were made against Bank shares as collateral, but also against the shares of other issuers. In 1995, the Bank had stakes in 98 companies of different forms of ownership, and carried out joint business with 4 other companies. The 1995 volume of investments in non-government securities increased five times over 1994. The Bank's representatives were elected to the Boards of a number of joint-stock companies, allowing the Bank to follow the main principle of investing - to invest in those companies whose financial operations are manageable. With its experience of representation in joint-stock companies,

Management Boards have enabled the Bank to work out a general concept of managing the elective bodies of other companies. This concept is backed up by a comprehensive database.

In carrying out its investment policy, Bank "Saint Petersburg's" primary concern is to further support those companies that would make an efficient use of their capital. The Bank has increased their authorized capital by the reinvestment of dividends and the making of additional investments. The Bank has also promoted seven new companies. Apart from earning good income, these investments enabled the Bank to take part in some purpose-oriented projects, including the State Privatization Program. Special attention was also paid to the consolidation of holdings in the privatized enterprises, which the Bank had acquired earlier.

In 1995, the Bank continued to actively work with its subsidiary undertakings, through nonstandard financing mechanisms of various financial instruments. Also, new subsidiaries were set up in those markets where the Bank's presence had been previously limited. Priority was also given to investments in residential and industrial construction, light industry, consumer goods production, and the hotel and tourist industries. The 1995 volume of direct investments more than doubled 1994's. An even stronger growth of 700% was experienced in residential investments.

The Bank has continued to further diversify all of its services, which include the valuation of both the financial condition and the development projects of companies, and assistance in the preparation, and the execution of business plans. The Bank also acts as an agent in large scale international investment projects.

Bank "Saint Petersburg" in March of 1995, became a fiscal agent to the Russian-American Government Project, "Dwelling for Russian service men retired on the territory of the Baltic countries." Within three months, 438 Russian servicemen were provided with privately owned apartments in Saint Petersburg. The Bank's successful work on this project was confirmed by the inspection of the US Agency for International Development Commission.

Participation in the Securities Market

Bank "Saint Petersburg" has issued their own stock six times, and it is actively traded in Russian securities markets. The price of the stock has continually increased. However, the Bank does not confine itself to the issue of its own shares. Investors, both private and corporate, are offered a wide range of other securities. The Bank issues certificates of deposit, using interest at maturity, compound interest, and interim interest. The different terms of certificates with circulation from 16 to 180 days, attract additional investors.

Throughout 1995, the certificates were offered at the interest rates comparable to the average rates in the north-western region of Russia. Their volume in this market in 1995 was 92,000 million rubles. There also existed a steady demand for the Bank's promissory notes, which were used in crediting customers. During that year, the Bank discounted bills of major Russian banks and other reliable issuers. These operations yielded an average of 115% per annum.

Bank "Saint Petersburg" also maintains an active position in the stock market by dealing in most current Government securities:

- Government Short Term Bonds (**GKO**)
- City Government Coupon Bonds (**GGKO**)
- Federal Loan Bonds with Variable Coupon Rate (**OFZ-PK**)
- Government Savings Bonds (**OGSZ**)
- Government Internal Currency Bonds (**OVGVZ**)

The major share of the Bank's and its customers 1995 investments were in Government Short Term Bonds, and Federal Loan Bonds with Floating Coupons. The annual turnover of its consolidated investment portfolio reached 164.3 billion rubles for GKO's, and 19 .9 billion rubles for GGKO's. The income generated by trading state securities exceeded 51 billion rubles in 1995, with brokerage fees reaching to 3.8 billion rubles.

In response to investor activity, Bank "Saint Petersburg" mobilized all of its branches to trade in Government Short Term Bonds. They delivered an excellent performance, with Bank's share in the total value of transactions at 30%. The Bank also carried out an active policy in respect to corporate securities. The most significant results were achieved with the shares of large companies. It should be noted, that due to the instability of the Russian corporate stock market, short term speculations prevailed.

Bank "Saint Petersburg" continues to develop its services as a paying agent, depositary, and broker. There was also considerable growth in the volume of information and consulting services performed in 1996, with the Bank specialists advising customers on the condition and trends of the stock market, and providing a thorough analysis of their investment portfolios.

Information Technology

High competitiveness and a wide range of banking products could hardly be provided without state-of-the-art technology and perpetual improvement of the Bank's information systems. Much attention is paid to these advanced banking technologies, with their high quality hardware and the latest software.

In 1996, there were 73 local networks in operations based on the 3COM equipment, a leader in the banking field. Implementation has begun in a corporate bank network based upon fiber optic communication channels. Software packages developed by the Bank's own programmers automate the main banking operations, operational data processing and timely money transfers.

To improve the quality of its banking services the Bank has introduced the "Bank Customer" electronic payment system, which allows customers to check on or make abstracts of their accounts and to effect payments without a time-consuming visit to the Bank.

The Bank has joined the interbank electronic payments system, "The Bank Cards Union," which was established in 1994. Together with other banks in Russia, the Bank took part in the foundation of a smart card-based payment system which will cover the entire country.

The Bank has become an active member of Visa International and obtained a license for all the operations requested. The chip card based electronic payment system encompassing the Bank's staff and more than 30 geographically neighboring enterprises , is also in place.

Because a large part of settlements in Russia are realized in cash, for the purpose of cash flow automation old machinery is constantly being replaced with newer. De La Rue banknote counters and TCD electronic tellers have been purchased and installed. A lot of effort is devoted to information protection and the prevention of unauthorized access and destruction. The Bank's information systems store back-up copies of all major information and, in case of emergency, it enables the Bank to recover the core of the central information system. The Bank's information technology strategy supports a high level of banking services and opens new skylines for cooperation with national and international banks and companies.

Customer Service

Bank "Saint Petersburg" is committed to the development and continued improvement of its customer service. In 1995, the number of corporate and private customers increased by 50%, exceeding 30,000. The majority of these customers represent areas of business where the Bank's influence has always been strong. Light industry enterprises, trading companies, municipal organizations, communications companies, cultural, scientific and medical institutions make up the core of these customers.

The 1995 crisis in the banking system resulted in many bankruptcies and eventually led to an active migration of customers to more reliable banks. Last years total of new customers was doubled those who closed their accounts. This strong growth in customer base can be credited to the Bank's stable financial position and the expertise of its staff. It is also noteworthy that a comprehensive rating of every new customer provides a good basis for their individual treatment. Consequently, the opening of business accounts has consistently increased, as shown by the following data:

Figure 13. (Million rubles)

	Business Deposits in Bank
January 1, 1995	503,338
April 1, 1995	481,966
July 1, 1995	624,592
October 1, 1995	687,727
January 1, 1996	711,487

As a diversified financial services institution, Bank "Saint Petersburg" attaches great importance to the further development of its wide network of branches. The Bank's goal is to turn every branch into a financial institution, providing a full range of services to meet all customer demands. In the meantime, Bank "Saint Petersburg" continues to actively serve its private customers. The Bank's reliability, reputation, and excellent service record enable it to increase as well as maintain the volume of its transactions with private customers. Simply put, long-term stability and reliability pay off.

The Bank's main operational objective in services to individual customers, is to raise private funds. In this area the Bank offers a variety of agreements which can only be provided by the leading banks of Moscow and Saint Petersburg. In 1995, the volume of funds placed in the Bank by private customers rose by 51.5 billion rubles, totalling 73.3 billion rubles on January 1, 1996. Large deposits equaled 64% of the total volume of private customer monies. The following data indicates the Bank's increase in personal accounts:

Figure 14. (Million rubles)

	Individual Deposits
January 1, 1995	21,799
April 1, 1995	34,556
July 1, 1995	60,286
October 1, 1995	57,126
January 1, 1996	73,303

The Bank has accepted demand deposits, and time deposits capable of prolongation for a period equal to the initial one, with the income paid every month or on the expiration of the agreement. 1995 also saw a new kind of agreement providing a demand deposit with an unlimited term of validity. To stimulate customer base stability, the Bank introduced a special kind of deposit unique for their customers.

Another promising activity for the Bank is its lending to individuals. The types of credits available for these customers include those issued against the Banks' customers' guarantee, collateral of stocks, and term deposits with the Bank. The Bank has also maintained an active policy of extending loans to the general public. The volume of such loans in 1995 totaled more than 9 billion rubles.

Correspondent Relations and Operations with Foreign Currencies

The Bank's main goal in its correspondent relations is to optimize their network. High quality and promptness of interbank ruble and hard currency settlements at a minimum payment risk, were achieved due to advancing technologies and a financially stable network of correspondent banks.

Bank "Saint Petersburg" is one of the major clearing centers in Saint Petersburg. To date it has established correspondent relations with over 130 banks. More than 600 banks from different countries also avail themselves of this vast network to settle their payments. In developing their network, the guiding factor has been the geography of the business connections of their customers, whose 30,000 plus accounts provide a substantial part of the Bank's resources.

The Bank maintains correspondent relations with these western banks:
1. Bankers Trust Company, New York (USA)
2. Bank of New York, New York (USA)
3. Republic National Bank of New York, New York (USA)
4. Banker Trust International PLC, Frankfurt/Main (Germany)
5. Dresdner Bank AG, Frankfurt/Main (Germany)
6. Deutsche Bank, Frankfurt/Main (Germany)
7. National Westminster Bank, Overseas Branch (England)
8. Midland Bank, London (England)
9. Banque Rivaud, Paris (France)
10. Svenska Handelsbanken, Stockholm (Sweden)
11. Postipakki, Helsinki (Finland)
12. Meespierson, Amsterdam (Holland)
13. Creditanstalt, Vienna (Austria)
14. Generale de Banque, Brussels (Belgium)
15. Den Danske Bank, Copenhagen (Denmark)
16. Den Norske Bank, Oslo, (Norway)
17. Credit Suisse, Zurich (Switzerland)
18. Banca di Roma (Italy)

19. Bank of Tokyo, Tokyo (Japan)
20. Standard Chartered Bank, Singapore
21. Banco de Sabadell, Sabadell (Spain)
22. Royal Bank of Canada, Toronto (Canada)
23. Unibank, Copenhagen (Denmark)

As many customers of these Western banks have business activities in the north-western region, they give priority to establishing correspondent relations with Saint Petersburg banks. International bank relations account for 100 billion rubles in the daily volume of interbank settlements, which amounts to not less than 50% of the total ruble payment turnover. Bank "Saint Petersburg" is one of the major banks having counterparts in the Baltic countries. For many years they have maintained correspondent relations with such large banks as Rigas Kommerzbank and Baltiysky Transit Bank.

The Bank has achieved a healthy growth in its volume of operations with banks from the CIS and the Baltic states, with settlement being effected in their national currencies. Also evident was a remarkable increase in transactions through the correspondent accounts opened with Ukrainian, Byelorussian and Kazakh banks. Correspondent relations with several banks in Latvia, Lithuania and Estonia are also strengthening. Negotiations are under way with Uzbekistan and Moldova to open accounts in their national currencies.

With a view to the customers' business priorities, the Bank has opened Indian Rupee (INR), Dollar for Settlements with India (XDI), Spanish Peseta (Banco Sabadell, Banco Exterior De Espana) and Kazakh Tenge (KAB "Kramds-Bank) correspondent accounts.

By 1995, there was additional signs of the Bank "Saint Petersburg's" rising reputation in international markets. Bank of New York, Commerzbank AG, Deutsche Genossenschaftsbank, and Deutsche Bank AG reduced their commission rate for Bank "Saint Petersburg," while a number of correspondent banks chose the Bank as their trustee in the settlement of payments. Exchange, conversion and documentary operations were strongly backed up with clean new credit lines.

To justify this trust, the Bank did its best to deliver high maintenance on the correspondent accounts of both Russian and international banks. Positive prospects are evident in the extensive use of on-line payments through the electronic communications system. As a result, 85% of the total number of banks with *Loro* correspondent accounts have their payments settled through the *SPRINT* and *SWIFT* electronic systems. The Bank remains the most active SWIFT user in the North-Western Region and it has become a member of the Committee of the Association of Russian SWIFT Users.

Bank "Saint Petersburg" constantly develops and upgrades its information services such as the latest exchange quotations, currency exchange rates by phone, fax, and the telex SPRINT system. The Bank issues weekly reports on international financial markets and holds seminars to explain the Central Bank's regulations wherever the Bank acts as its agent.

On short notice, the Bank's customers may also have their currency converted into practically any currency on the international money market. To provide these services, the Bank maintains strong positions on the largest foreign exchanges in Russia. As in all cases, flexible tariffs for currency buy-sell transactions depend on the volumes and terms of the money's transfer into customer accounts.

Bank "Saint Petersburg" is a leading dealer in the currencies of the CIS countries and other former Soviet Republics as well as those currencies which are not quoted by the Central Bank. As this segment of the financial market is only gaining strength, such operations are performed with the Bank acting solely as an agent for its customers.

Because of these growing involvements, the Bank has established a special division for international transactions. They have prepared an informational brochure which includes the following information about the services they provide:

Over 700 enterprises, companies and organizations of all legal forms, including those with international capital, together with about 1000 individual customers maintain their foreign currency accounts with the International Banking Division of Bank "Saint Petersburg's" Commercial Banking Department.

Highly professional staff, state-of-the-art technologies, such as REUTER, SWIFT, SPRINT, ect., enable the Bank to operate profitably in the highly competitive foreign currency market. The range and quality of services provided by the Bank are in accord with the level provided by all leading Russian banks.

Correspondent relations have been established with most banks of Russia, countries of the former Soviet Union, and all over the world. Customers can, free of charge, make a transfer to one of the 50 largest banks of Russia, as well as to some non-resident banks such as: Kredyt Bank (Poland), Lithuanian Innovation Bank, Privatbank (Ukraine), Latvian Deposit Bank, Belbusinessbank (Belorussia), New Georgian Bank, and so on. Subject to current trends of demand, customer needs and industry preferences, correspondent relations could also be set up with other international banks.

Bank "Saint Petersburg" is able to offer unbeatable conditions to buy and sell at one of Russia's three largest currency exchanges; Moscow Interbank, Saint-Petersburg, and the Siberian International Interbank Foreign Currency Exchanges, as well as in the over-the-counter market.

In the meantime, the International Banking Division offers the following major services to its existing and potential customers:

- Opening and maintenance of resident and non-resident corporate client currency accounts. Interests accure monthly on the credit account balance.
- Foreign currency transfers to any international bank, with free of charge transfers between the Bank's branches and customs fees payments.
- Soft currency operations, with the countries of the former Soviet Union.
- Open currency time deposits for:
  - one day to two months, at a mean European interbank rate
  - three months or more at an interbank rate
- Conversion of "hard currency into hard currency" on the customer currency account:
  - up to $30,000 USD, or equivalent in any other hard currency, shall be carried out at the exchange rate of the Central Bank, plus a 2% commission charge.
  - over $30,000 USD, or equivalent in any other hard currency, shall be carried out without any commission at the world market rate on a real time basis.
- Foreign currency guarantees
- A full range of customer services including consultation and information on:
  - currency exchange rates
  - soft currency settlements
  - export-import operations
  - legal advice on the Russian currency control laws

At the request of its customers, the Bank may buy or sell foreign currency at an exchange or interbank currency market, including the futures contract market. Bank customers have the opportunity to run the following deals according to applicable law:

- Buy and sell USD, Deutsche Marks, or French Francs at the Saint Petersburg Currency Exchange Rate, provided the procuration contract with the Bank has been concluded.
- Establish long-term service relations with the Bank concerning:
  - buying and selling hard currency for rubles
  - buying and selling soft currency for rubles
  - soft to hard currency conversion
- Through existing correspondent relations, the Bank may open a Letter of Credit on behalf of its clients, advise, confirm and execute an export L/C drawn by an international bank in favor of Bank "Saint Petersburg" and other banks' customers. Owing to the SWIFT

interbank communication system, an L/C opened at the customer's request will be delivered to counterpart with maximum possible promptness.

- Opening and maintaining a resident or nonresident individual customer's personal foreign currency account with a $10 USD fee and 2% accrued annually on the account balance.
- Opening foreign currency deposits for individuals for a period of 3,6,9, or 12 months bearing 5% to 10% per annum, depending on the account terms and amount of deposit.
- Individual remittances from overseas
- Cash transfer operations through the Western Union System.
- A full range of operations with International VISA, EUROCARD-MASTERCARD, and Diners Club International Smart Cards.
- Cheque handling through the:
  - cashing of traveller's cheques
  - registered cheques collection with further payment after obtaining foreign currency at the Bank's exchange offices
- Buying and selling foreign currency at the Bank's exchange offices.
- Exchange of unfit foreign banknotes for valid ones.
- Account transfers, including those through the SWIFT system.
- Foreign banknote verification.

Bank "Saint Petersburg" took an active part in a number of projects of various international financial institutions, including both, the World Bank and European Bank for Reconstruction and Development, foreign government agencies, investment funds and other commercial banks. All these projects were designed to attract international investments to Saint Petersburg.

The Bank was included in a "core group" of six Russian banks accredited to participate in the Russian Financial Institutions Development Project. In accordance with this project, the Bank's institutional development is to be secured by a twinning program with a leading western bank.

Also, under this project, Bank "Saint Petersburg" has improved its structure, introduced modern management techniques and procedures which could meet the high international standards of banking and promote advanced know-how. To implement this the Bank was provided with $3 million - of which $1.5 million is a European Union grant and $1.5 million a long-term loan extended by the World Bank and the European Bank for Reconstruction and Development. Another long-term loan extended by these banks was $3.1 million which is being used to finance the upgrading of the Bank "Saint Petersburg's" information system. The Bank was the first among Russian commercial banks to enter into a Twinning Agreement with Ireland's Allied Irish Bank.

The growing prestige of Bank "Saint Petersburg" is winning recognition on the international market. The European Center for Market Research awarded the Bank with a Gold Prize for its impressive growth, high-quality services and contribution in revitalization of the city and the region.

The result of the Bank "Saint Petersburg's" assets and liabilities operations showed an increase in profit in 1995 as illustrated by the following:

Figure 15.
Profit and Loss Statement (million rubles)

Income	1/1/96	1/1/95	Variation +/-
Loan interest income	325,816	198,439	127,377+
Brokerage income	87,324	31,773	55,551+
Currency income	44,466	2,861	41,605+
Other income	91,490	62,112	29,378+
Total income	**549,096**	**295,185**	**253,911+**
Expense			
Loans, accounts, and deposits interest expenses	197,248	72,354	124,894+
Brokerage expenses	39,820	31,754	8,066+
Currency expenses	6,683	49	6,634+
Other expenses	179,449	83,608	95,841+
Total expenses	**423,200**	**187,765**	**235,435+**
Profit	**125,896**	**107,420**	**18,476+**

Bank "Saint Petersburg's" sponsorship and charity contributions in 1995 totalled 3300 million rubles, which is considerably higher than in 1994. Based upon the best charity traditions of Russia's progressive entrepreneurs, the Bank gives priority to preserving and developing the rich cultural heritage of Saint-Petersburg. On the whole, in 1995 the Bank sponsored or rendered charitable assistance to more than 150 cultural organizations and institutions, artistic unions and companies.

Chapter 4.3

Industry and Construction Bank

Industry and Construction Bank (Promstroibank) was originally founded as the northwest regional arm of the State Industrial Construction Bank, whose statute was registered by the State Bank of the USSR on October 3, 1990. In May, 1992, the Bank was converted into an Open-Type Joint Stock Company, changing its status to an Open Joint Stock Company in June 1996, when it renewed its banking license.

At the beginning of 1997, Industry and Construction Bank had 18 branches in Saint Petersburg, with a further 15 branches in the northwest Leningrad Region, one in Moscow, eight in other parts of Russia, plus 37 agencies and three representative offices, including one in Berlin. Branches in Smolensk and Vyborg were opened during 1996.

Involvement in Russian and International Government Programs

Industry and Construction Bank is authorized:
- as a "second category" bank for holding federal government accounts
- to provide services for holding the tax funds of the Leningrad Region
- as a primary dealer in the GKO and OFZ markets (Federal government bonds and savings bonds), to effect repo deals and also to operate non-resident accounts for operations in this market
- by the Russian Federal Property Fund to provide money transfer services connected to the sale of state-owned enterprises under the privatization program

Industry and Construction Bank is accredited by The World Bank and EBRD for participation in:
- the Financial Institution Development Program
- the Small Business Program
- the Enterprise Support Project
- the Housing Project in Russia

The Bank is also accredited to the GSM-102 program of the United States Department of Agriculture, as a guarantor for payments in relation to food contracts. Industry and Construction Bank is a member of the National Association of Stock Market Participants (NAUFOR). JSC Petersburg

Bankaudit is the auditor for Russian Statutory audit. Price Waterhouse has been the Bank's international auditor for the past four years.

Economic Situation in Russia During 1996

During 1996, the economic situation in Russia remained difficult and macroeconomic trends were unpredictable. As a result of the government's consistent application of a tight policy aimed at restricting the growth in the money supply, inflation decreased significantly to the lowest levels since 1992, with consumer price inflation falling to an annual rate of 23%. The rubles exchange rate essentially stabilized, helping to reduce inflation expectations.

Activity in the financial markets during the year was dominated by the declining level of interest rates and falling yields on government bonds. These factors in turn allowed a more even distribution of monetary flows between different sectors of the economy, and an increased investment into the manufacturing sector.

The victory of Boris Yeltsin in the Presidential elections was an additional stabilizing factor which provided a boost to the reform process, and also helped to increase the confidence of international investors investing in Russia. However, the effective measures taken by the Russian government and the Central Bank in the sphere of monetary policy were not accompanied by similar positive developments in the budgetary and tax policies, and in the restructuring industrial sector. In this environment, short-term lending to and longer-term investment in the manufacturing sector remained high risk. Resulting high interest rates limited the demand for credit. The flow of capital into the manufacturing sector failed to increase with few stimulants to investment.

The experience of 1996, indicate that in order to reverse these negative trends in manufacturing production and investment, a coherent range of policy instruments needs to be employed which incorporates measures to overcome the structural problems in both the industrial sector and government financing. In particular, the taxation system must be improved along with the competitiveness of domestic producers.

Developments in the Banking Sector

Political and economic developments of 1996 naturally had an effect on the banking system. The most significant developments to be noted were the falling yields on the main financial instruments, which are primarily government bonds. A sharp increase in competition in this sector was seen and consequently there was a realignment of influence between the largest banks.

Significant changes took place in the regulatory sphere. At the beginning of April, the Central Bank introduced new reserve requirements. As a result, the deposit reserve requirements for ruble deposits decreased. However, the reserve requirement for foreign currency liabilities increased. Non-resident investors were allowed to operate on the GKO (Federal government bonds) and OFZ (Federal loan bonds with a variable coupon) markets, increasing the number of market players. The foreign exchange policy was adjusted, resulting in the continuing stability of the ruble. The Central Bank's refinancing rate fell significantly from 160% to 48%.

These developments had a significant impact on the banking sector as a whole. During 1996, 289 Russian commercial banks had their licenses revoked (an increase of 20% over the previous year). This represented approximately 15% of the registered banks at the beginning of the year. The decline in the number of small banks, particularly in outlying regions, was a result of the combination of the revoking of licenses and also the conversion of some banks into branches of larger, more stable banks. This suggests that the consolidation of the banking sector is proceeding.

These developments were reflective of the situation in the banking sector in the northwest region, and in the city of Saint Petersburg in particular. In the city, eleven banks stopped operating, along with a further thirteen in the northwest region. According to the Saint Petersburg Regional Office of the Central Bank, at the beginning of October 1996, 57 local banks and 61 from other cities outside the region were operating in Saint Petersburg. In general, however, the consequences of change in this sector for the banking systems of Saint Petersburg and the Leningrad Region have been more positive than in other region of the country.

Credit resources in the region had increased by the end of the year by 7.3 billion rubles over the previous year, totalling 24.8 billion rubles. Saint Petersburg banks accounted for 55% of this amount, 28% was accounted for by the Saint Petersburg arm of the Savings Bank of the Russian Federation, and the remainder by branches of banks based in other cities. Total profits for this sector in Saint Petersburg increased by 40% to 1.865 billion rubles, using Russian accounting standards.

The Bank's Strategy

Developments during 1996, closely followed the strategic plan established by Industry and Construction Bank for the period 1996-98. The strategy was and is marked by an emphasis on improving customer service, the further expansion of the range of services, improvements in the organizational structure, increased use of informational technology to improve efficiency, an increasing level of investment lending, and entry into new geographical markets in both the northwestern region and elsewhere in Russia.

The organizational changes were directed at implementing a more flexible and market-oriented structure resulting in the following:

- the clear separation of direct income-generating activities, from the accounting and analytical functions
- the development of business units responsible for corporate customers, private individuals and financial institutions
- the implementation of new approaches to customers account management
- the establishment of a single Back Office
- the integration of ruble and foreign currency operations
- the definition of reporting lines, allowing tougher control over the branch network

General Overview

According to the "Rating" agency, Industry and Construction Bank is one of the leading Russian banks based on a set of performance indices. It is number 20 in terms of total assets, number 19 in terms of capital size, and number 13 in terms of profit.

Data obtained from the Saint Petersburg Association of Commercial Banks in October 1996, describes Industry and Construction Bank, in the context of Saint Petersburg, as:

- the largest holder of corporate current accounts (both rubles and foreign currency)
- the largest holder of vostro accounts of correspondent banks
- the second largest holder of individuals' deposits, after the Savings Bank of Russia
- the largest bank in terms of lending to corporations
- the largest investor in shares of joint stock companies

Figure 16.

Key Performance Indicators	1996	1995
Interest margin	52%	61%
Profit after tax to interest income	19%	48%
Operating expenses to operating income	72%	50%
Return on average equity	18%	79%
Return on average total assets	3%	12%
Effective tax charge	13%	16%
Dividend cover	5 times	11 times

In these circumstances and taking into account the expenditures on the dealing function, strategic investments, and increase of the branch network, the 1996 profit figure of 97 billion rubles remains a creditable performance. Industry and Construction Bank continues to generate steady income levels despite the difficulties prevailing in the market, and maintains a cautious risk strategy, largely reflecting effective liquidity and funds management.

Capital Base

The Shareholders decided to increase the Bank's equity in 1996, with a 7th issue of ordinary shares consisting of 700,000 shares with a nominal value of 1,000 rubles. The increase in share capital was the result of the capitalization of a portion of the fixed asset revaluation reserve. The new shares are fully paid. However, no additional funds were received. All shares were distributed to existing shareholders. Industry and Construction Bank's authorized share capital in December 1996 was 2 billion rubles.

The ownership structure of share capital has remained virtually unchanged, with 64.2% of the equity being owned by 343 corporations, and 35.8% by 22,248 private individuals as of January 1, 1997. The shares are actively traded on the secondary market and the demand has been reflected by the share value exhibiting a steady increase.

During 1996, the Bank's equity and reserves increased by 72%, from 402 billion rubles in 1995, to 692 billion rubles. Retained profits of 403 billion rubles and the fixed asset revaluation reserve of 274 billion rubles, represented the major part of reserves at the year end.

Dividends are declared on a quarterly basis throughout the year. The dividends declared for 1996 totalled 22 billion rubles, up from declared dividends of 20 billion rubles in 1995. During 1996, 12 billion rubles was paid to shareholders and the remaining 10 billion rubles was retained in reserves and not distributed.

Figure 17.

Bank Equity (billion rubles)	1994	1995	1996
Issued Share Capital	1	1	2
Share Capital Premium	7	11	14
Fixed Assets Revaluation	15	71	273
Retained Earnings	122	319	403

Risk Management

Risk management systems continue to be actively developed, with the Bank's risk strategy being more closely defined. Industry and Construction Bank has established a special division whose main functions are risk assessment, compliance monitoring and capital adequacy issues. The risk management system is founded on the basic principles of market and credit risk limits, and detailed operating policies relating to dealing operations. An accompanying system of close compliance monitoring has supported this establishment of an effective risk management system. However, the Bank recognizes the danger of complacency and continues to strive to ensure that its risk management systems develop in line with its business.

Credit risk management is constantly being improved through the continued development of loan portfolio quality monitoring and control, a comprehensive limit structure and detailed lending policies. The loan loss provision decreased for both commercial loans and loans to other banks from 14% and 15% in 1995, to 11% and 5% in 1996, respectively. One of the reasons for the decrease was that the portion of overdue loans fell from 7% of the total portfolio in 1995, to 4% in 1996.

Industry and Construction Bank continues to follow a policy of maintaining high liquidity levels, in order to take into account continuing uncertainties in the economy and banking sector. Liquid assets represent 35% of the total assets, with cash and dealing securities representing 19% and 16% of total assets respectively. Liquidity ratios of the Bank have consistently been between five and ten times higher than those required by the Central Bank. A summary of Industry and Construction Bank's performance, compared with the Central Bank economic ratio requirements, is presented in Figure 18.

Asset and Liability Management

Industry and Construction Bank continues to focus on efficient usage of funds, increasing the capital base and optimal management of the balance sheet structure. To this end, it continues to actively develop its Asset and Liability Management systems. This has been achieved through the automation and development of an integrated funds management system, allowing the reallocation of manpower to analysis and risk management.

In addition, improved coordination between the Bank's Head Office divisions and the branches, encouraged improved asset and liability management. The system is designed to be flexible to allow an approach which takes into account conditions in different locations and varying customer needs, while reacting quickly to market condition.

Figure 18.
Compliance with Central Bank's Regulations (January 1, 1997)

Economic Ratio	Central Bank Requirements	Industry and Construction Bank Position
Capital /Risk Weighted Assets Ratio	>0.05	0.34
Current Liquidity Ratio	>0.20	0.63
Quick Ratio	>0.10	2.70
Long-Term Liquidity Ratio	>1.20	0.26
Liquidity Assets/Total Assets	>0.10	0.42
Maximum exposure to a single borrower or group of related borrowers	<0.60	0.14
Maximum Single Large Exposure	<12	1.03
Maximum Deposit Concentration (single depositor)	<0.60	0.18
Maximum Exposure to a single Shareholder	<0.20	0.16
Aggregate Amount of Loans to Shareholders	<0.50 by January 1, 1998	0.38
Maximum Amount of Loans, Guarantees and Warranties to a Single Party	<0.10	0.004
Maximum Amount of Loans, Guarantees and Warranties to Parties	<0.30 from July 1, 1997	0.023
Maximum Amount of Individuals' Deposits	<1.00	0.53
Use of Equity for Acquiring Shares of Other Corporate Entities	<0.25	0.11
Maximum Investments for Acquiring Shares of one Corporate entity	<0.10	0.038
Risk Requirements for own Bills	<2.00	0.21

Figure 19.

(million rubles)	%	End of 1995	%	End of 1996
Cash and Short Term Funds	28	634,213	20	703,901
Loans to Customers	23	522,347	24	837,655
Loans to Banks	3	74,028	7	230,006
Investments	11	234,172	12	431,862
Fixed Assets	14	316,341	15	545,180
Other Assets	7	138,112	6	216,535
Dealing Securities	14	315,795	16	564,434
Total Assets	**100**	**2,235,008**	**100**	**3,529,573**

During 1996, interest rates on loans and deposits were reduced steadily, as policy was adapted to take into account falls in Central Bank rates and the level of inflation. The new approach to fund management allowed the Bank to implement these reductions in a smooth manner.

Through an effective system of liquidity and cash flow forecasting on a short to long-term basis, Industry and Construction Bank has been able to make sure that it is always in a position to meet its obligations to customers, while ensuring that it is generating sufficient returns from its funds. It is determined to continue to recognize the prime importance of maintaining sufficient liquidity at all times. During 1996, total liabilities increased by 1.004 billion rubles and funds on customers accounts grew by 766 billion rubles. On a Russian accounting basis, the deposits of corporate customers represented 18.7% of the total corporate deposits of the member-banks of the Saint Petersburg Association Commercial Banks as of October 1, 1996.

During the year, Industry and Construction Bank started operating as a regional clearing center, and this resulted in the further development of settlement services and an increase in correspondent bank vostro balances. Increased funding from credit facilities obtained from international institutions, allowed growth in the foreign currency component of the balance sheet. The Bank has made significant efforts to decrease the proportion of non-income generating assets with the income-generating proportion having been increased by 2% to 68% over the year. A second priority was to take advantage of profit opportunities in the government bond market, a highly profitable but low-risk area.

Figure 20.

1997 Loan Portfolio	%	Million Rubles
Industrial Enterprises	49	582,536
Trade	12	146,718
Interbank	21	242,665
Other	18	211,408
Total	**100**	**1,183,327**

Credit Portfolio

The Industry and Construction Bank credit strategy is aimed at increasing the number of medium to large corporate borrowers, improving information on borrowers, and supporting the industrial development of the northwest region. In addition, despite the difficult economic environment, the Bank retains its belief in the successful longer-term development of the regional economy and has not changed orientation. The Bank continues to make investment loans to the industrial and service sectors. While maintaining this orientation, Industry and Construction Bank has tightened credit policy by taking a stricter approach to collateral and loan classification.

During 1996, Industry and Construction Bank continued to lend to public utilities, which are key to the functioning of the city of Saint Petersburg. The departments taking advantage of these loans include metro construction, bridge construction, bus transportation, transport, electricity supply, and water and sewerage. Loans to these sectors totalled 32 billion rubles in 1996.

Active lending to the construction sector continued, including assistance in providing guarantees to Inzhstroi Saint Petersburg, in relation to contracts from the City Administration funded by credits from the IBRD and the Mayor's Office. In cooperation with Industry and Construction Bank, the Admiralty Shipyard continues to construct ships for both Russian and international customers. A loan of 60 billion rubles was granted for the construction of tankers for export.

Industry and Construction Bank continues to recognize its responsibilities in helping the social problems prevailing in Saint Petersburg. Loans to the sum of 131 billion rubles were extended to the Finance Committee of the Saint Petersburg City Administration, and a further 51 billion rubles were granted to the Finance Committee of the Leningrad Region. At the end of 1996, outstanding loans net of provisions totalled 1,068 billion rubles. Loans to retail customers and other banks increased by 315 billion rubles and 156 billion rubles respectively. During 1996, the average maturity of loans was 66 days.

Securities Portfolio

As in previous years, a significant part of the Bank's securities holdings has consisted of state bonds. This is reflected by the status Industry and Construction Bank reached as the Primary Dealer of the Central Bank in the OFZ bond market at the end of October 1996.

With the goal of ensuring effective management of the securities portfolio, Industry and Construction Bank founded a subsidiary, entitled Lenstroi-Invest-Management. A significant part of the Bank's securities portfolio was transferred to this company. Those stocks remaining in the Bank's portfolio mainly relate to investments made with long-term strategic aims, and these are actively and carefully managed by the Bank itself.

The investment portfolio consists of shares in over 50 enterprises, most of which are in the City of Saint Petersburg and Leningrad Region. Investments include holdings in a number of companies with significant positions in the Russian economy as a whole, such as Kirovsky Zavod, Baltisky Zavod, Syktivkarsky Timber Processing Plant and Kotlass Pulp. While a conservative approach was taken to making investments and maintaining the high quality of the investment portfolio, returns remained at an acceptably high level.

Dealing Operations

The Dealing Division of the Bank operates in the money, foreign exchange, and securities markets. Industry and Construction Bank obtained the status of the primary dealer in state securities in October 1996. This requires the purchase by the Bank of 1% of the issue of state securities at auctions, and gives the Bank the right to provide quotations on NAUFOR. This in turn allows Industry and Construction Bank to deal in corporate securities.

The fall in profitability of government bonds towards the end of the year necessitated improvements in operating methodologies in this area of work, in order to service customers more effectively and to generate additional income. To this end, a new dealing room was established, which enables customers to operate on a real time basis and information services were developed to assist customers in analyzing market developments. The system was extended to the branches enabling customers to operate on a live basis in the State and Municipal securities markets.

The permission granted by the Central Bank for non-residents to invest in State bonds, enabled the expansion of the Bank's customer base in this area. To accommodate this situation, the Bank received permission to operate "C" accounts (ruble accounts for non-residents) which are designed to enable the receipt of funds from non-residents for operations in the government bond market.

In addition to these developments, a decision was taken with the objective of diversification to invest more actively in corporate securities. The attractiveness of such investments from the point of view of liquidity and profitability increased significantly during the year. To this end, an agreement was signed with NAUFOR, to allow Industry and Construction Bank to carry out operations in the stocks of privatized enterprises.

Interbank operations have also changed significantly in nature. The high level of activity in the interbank loan market during the first half of 1995 declined significantly, as trust evaporated during the second-half of the year following the interbank crisis. The market picked up however, during the first half of 1996, as banks became more conservative in choosing counter-parties and opening credit lines. Industry and Construction Bank succeeded in opening a series of credit lines with targeted counter-parties despite the continuing difficulties in the market.

During the second half of 1996, the situation changed significantly, reflecting the stability of the ruble, particularly during August. At the same time, an increase in government bond rates followed by a steep decline led to increased entry by banks into the interbank market, with the result of the Dealing Division being able to double the volume of the Bank's interbank operations.

International Operations

Significant progress was made in implementing the Bank's strategy of operating more actively in international markets, and enhancing Industry and Construction Bank's image in this area. The main development related to the obtaining of relatively cheap resources in order to assist the development of a longer-maturity deposit base, and the provision of trade-related services to customers.

The name of Industry and Construction Bank is becoming increasingly well-known in international banking markets. The Bank has striven to remain open in providing information to the international banking community. In addition to continuing, for the third year, with an audit to international standards performed by Price Waterhouse, Industry and Construction Bank obtained a 1996 rating of IC-D/LC-3 from Thomson BankWatch. This rating testifies to the capability of the Bank to meet short-term and medium-term obligations.

This increasing reputation for reliability allowed Industry and Construction Bank to obtain unsecured international credits on favorable terms with the goal of financing industry. The results of this development include:

- A syndicated loan from 12 large Western banks of $25 million USD, the lead banks in this syndicate being Union Bank of Switzerland, Citibank NA, Dresdner Bank Luxembourg alongside Bayerische Vereinsbank AG.
- The EBRD granted a credit line to Industry and Construction Bank of $30 million USD.

- Participation in projects of the IBRD and EBRD. The funds available from these sources, depending on demand for resources from industrial enterprises total $140 million USD.
- Guarantees of Industry and Construction Bank are accepted by leading international financial institutions. The volume of guarantees granted by the Bank increased six-fold and now exceeds $50 million USD.
- Since the beginning of 1996, Industry and Construction Bank has participated in trade financing arrangements for the export of pulp and paper and the import of food-stuffs.
- Industry and Construction Bank was one of the first Russian banks, and the only one in the northwest region, to obtain accreditation from the Trade Credit Corporation of the US Ministry of Agriculture under the Export Credit Guarantee plan for the Export of Agricultural Products to Russia (GSM-102). The Bank received a line of $5 million from a line of $30 million granted to Russia in 1996.
- It was possible to increase dealing limits due to the increase in lines from correspondents for currency transactions.
- Documentary operations increased significantly during the year, encouraged by the opening of lines from international banks for trade operations to the tune of $60 million.
- Export Letters of Credit totalling $24.6 million were granted to customers during the year, with turnover on Import Letters of Credit totalling 5.4 million rubles. More than 30% of the Letters of Credit's were accepted without calling on the guarantee of the Bank.
- Purchase of foreign currency at the request of customers increased two-fold, while sales of currency increased by 10%. Turnover in foreign currency cash increased 600%.
- Currency exchange offices sold American Express traveller's cheques to the sum of $3.4 million. Some 90,000 traveller's cheques were cashed with turnover on these operations increasing by 8% and totalling $7.7 million. Turnover doubled over 1995, and the Bank holds the leading position amongst Saint Petersburg banks in this area.

Credit Operations Under Projects of the IBRD and EBRD

Participation in programs of The World Bank and the European Bank for Reconstruction and Development expanded during 1996. The total of funds granted to the Bank under the Development of Small Business Program, the Financial Institutions Development Program, the Enterprise Support Program and the Housing Program, amounted to over $60 million compared to only $7.7 million in 1995. An agreement between Industry and Construction Bank and the EBRD, was signed on February 1, 1996. At the beginning of 1997, all funds available had been lent to companies, including those involved in construction and renovation, furniture, medical products, food production and film production. Funds have also been granted for the following:

- medium and long-term financing of projects and investment programs connected with the construction, modernization, expansion and diversification of manufacturing enterprises
- increasing working capital for manufacturing companies
- venture capital for entrepreneurs
- export financing

Prior to the granting of the credit line, Price Waterhouse performed an extensive due diligence review of the borrowing enterprises.

Under the IBRD housing program, funds are lent by Industry and Construction Bank to companies involved in housing construction and the production of construction materials. The objective is the financing of construction and the completion of new homes, and also the funding of investment projects to promote the manufacture and sale of construction-related materials. The program has given the Bank extensive experience in assessing and managing long-term investment projects.

Participation in the Programs of the ERBD and IBRD allow Industry and Construction Bank to:

- grant relatively low cost loans for medium to long-term investment project
- apply, along with the borrowing companies, project-financing techniques meeting the   requirements of international financial institutions
- promote the expansion of production of competitive products by Saint Petersburg enterprises and others in the region, as well as the up-grading of technical equipment in these enterprises.

"Twinning" under the
Financial Institutions Development Program

At the end of 1995, Industry and Construction Bank signed a "Twinning" agreement with one of the biggest European banks, ABN AMRO, with the objective of obtaining consultancy advice in areas key to the Bank's strategic development. The agreement is part of the Financial Institutions Development Program of the Russian Ministry of Finance, which has accredited a number of the largest Russian banks under this program. The project is focused on such key areas as strategic planning, organizational structure, credit risk management, financial management and human resource management.

During the first year of the project, the emphasis was on developing a strategic plan and defining an appropriate organizational structure, this being key to the successful implementation of the strategy. Considerable progress has been made in this area, with a detailed strategic plan having been developed and approved. The next step has been to draw up a detailed approach to implementing the strategy based on detailed planning for operations in different market segments. A new Head Office organizational structure has been implemented, and progress has been made in revising the branch organizational structures.

Services to Corporations and Individuals

In an environment of falling interest rates and increasing competition, only those banks which offer customers a broad range of services and high quality customer service in both domestic and international markets will be able to retain their position. With this in mind, Industry and Construction Bank is placing considerable emphasis on the customer.

The Bank's primary orientation is toward its traditional customers - the major enterprises in the shipbuilding, timber and paper pulp, machine building and defense industries. The use of the Customer Budget system has enhanced the monitoring and analysis of cash flows through customers accounts. This has helped the Bank from a risk management and customer service perspective, and it also helps customers understand their cash flows.

A Client Manager system is being introduced, which allows more dedicated service aimed at increasing customer satisfaction and monitoring customer needs. The key to meeting customer needs remains the extension of loans to meet their financial needs, and the Bank endeavors to meet these needs as far as possible, and within risk levels acceptable to the Bank. The obtaining of relatively cheap longer-term financial resources on international markets has been important in enabling this to happen.

Financial Industrial Grouping

An encouraging development in the financial system has been the creation of Financial Industrial Groups, within which settlements between group members are processed through the lead bank as the principal settlement center, main lender and financial advisor to the group. Industry and Construction Bank is in the process of building up its own Financial Industrial Grouping, aimed at expanding and improving its services to the group companies. The structuring of the group enables Industry and Construction Bank to act in a financial-adviser role, being close to the customer, understanding his business and financial needs and assisting in the structuring of complex projects. Companies involved includes those from the shipbuilding, generator/turbine, timber, pulp and paper, and metallurgical industries.

In cooperation with the Administrations of the City of Saint Petersburg and the Leningrad Region, the Bank is also drawing up programs for the regeneration of the industrial potential of the region.

Services to Individuals

The main services offered are still individual savings and time deposits accounts in rubles and foreign currency. Deposits totalled 409.8 billion rubles at year end in 1996, with over 70,000 individual depositors.

Services are developing in the area of receiving payments from customers on behalf of public utilities and companies, such as Delta Telecom and FORA Communication. A program to assist local companies to meet payroll needs through Industry and Construction Bank cards has also been developed.

Settlement Systems and Technology

Industry and Construction Bank remains active in developing payment systems. Its extensive network of branches in the northwest region and in other parts of Russia, place it in a good position for making settlements between customers. Around 80 banks from Russia and neighboring countries have ruble accounts with Industry and Construction Bank, enabling payments to be made to customers of those banks on a same day basis with repaid payments to Moscow accounts being made through the Moscow branch.

Due to the switch by the Bank to the electronic inter-city payment system operated by the Head Cash Settlement Center of the Saint Petersburg branch of the Central Bank, the time required for settlement through the Center has been reduced by one day. This is not an insignificant amount of time, especially bearing in mind that a large proportion of inter-city payments are made to the City and Federal treasury.

Bank Securities

In 1996, Industry and Construction Bank issued promissory notes, certificates of deposit for corporations, and savings certificates for individuals. Sales significantly increased from 1995 to 1996 the issue of the following:
- promissory notes from 21 billion rubles to 1,300 billion rubles
- certificates of deposit from 44 billion rubles to 133 billion rubles
- savings certificates from 0.9 billion rubles to 11 billion rubles

Personnel Management

The Bank has approximately four thousand employees, most of them having a higher education and genuine work experience in the banking sector. Despite the growth in the number of clients, range of services offered and the improvements in customer service, an increase in staff numbers was avoided. In fact, staff numbers fell as technological improvements reduced manpower requirements.

Considerable attention is being paid to training needs of all employees. During 1996, over 1000 employees participated in seminars, training courses or conferences. Emphasis was also placed on improving the quality and relevance of training with the addition of and through inter-active training and testing. Part of the customer service development program has been the implementation of comprehensive training aimed at improving staff customer service inter-action.

Industry and Construction Bank has continued its active cooperation with the institutes of higher education in Saint Petersburg. Students receiving grants numbered 88 in 1996, with 83 students undertaking practical internship work experience at the Bank. Toward the end 1996, a Management Development Committee was formed to oversee the development of management skills and resources.

Charitable Donations and Sponsorship

Charitable activity continued during the year, with the implementation of programs developed in collaboration with the Saint Petersburg regional division of the Peace Fund. This involvement has become a tradition for Industry and Construction Bank and related activities included child care, culture, and many other social outreaches in the Saint Petersburg area.

Chapter 4.4

Petrovskiy Commercial Bank

The group of middle level banks in Russia are those which possess authorized capital between 500 million and 5 billion rubles. One of the most stable and reliable of these banks is Petrovskiy Commercial Bank. There are also other classifications of size used for commercial banks, the foundation of the amount of assets. If we use this methodology, we can confirm that Petrovskiy Bank belongs among Russia's fifty largest banks.

Petrovskiy Commercial Bank was established in November 1992, and since that time has intensively accumulated authorized capital and increased its asset - liability operations. The range of services rendered by the Bank, both in rubles and hard currency, are the following:

- attraction of free monetary funds of companies and individuals, keeping them on settlement, current, deposit and other accounts
- lending
- keeping the accounts of clients and bank-correspondents
- settlements on instructions of clients and bank-correspondents, including any necessary cash services required
- financing of capital investment
- all operations with securities not prohibited by law, including those as a dealer for Municipal Short-Term Bonds
- issue of warranties, guarantees and other obligations for third persons foreseeing fulfillment in monetary form
- forfeiting and factoring
- trust operations
- brokerage and consulting
- leasing operations
- documentary operations in foreign currency
- acceptance and sale of travellers cheques in foreign currency
- operations for purchase and sale of foreign currency both in cash and by check
- currency conversion's both in cash and by check
- wide spectrum of services for private customers, including holding current pension accounts and the payment of pensions

The rapid expansion of Petrovskiy Commercial Bank's range of services, its advent into new markets, and its tactical flexibility, enabling it to keep abreast of a changing economic environment, make it possible to speak of Petrovskiy Commercial Bank as a rapidly growing bank. Over the years that have elapsed since its incorporation, the Bank has grown into one of the largest financial institutions in Saint Petersburg, and is well-known both in and outside of Russia.

This growth can be confirmed by the increase in the Bank's registered capital and the amount of assets held by it throughout its development.

Figure 21.

(Million rubles)	Registered Capital	Assets
January 1993	255	8,041
January 1994	1,361	149,066
January 1995	2,590	409,356
January 1996	3,660	728,759

From Figure 21, one can see the consistent growth in the Bank's level of authorized capital and assets, even while including the factor of inflation.

Petrovskiy Commercial Bank has had success in all spheres of its activities, but the greatest has been in its services to individual customers and small businesses. Research among Saint Petersburger's, carried out by GALLUP in October 1993, consistently rated "Petrovskiy" second only to Sberbank in terms of reliability and prominence.

Banking Operations for Senior Citizens

Petrovskiy Commercial Bank's operations consist of three interconnected parts. Since 1993, the Bank and the Saint Petersburg Department of Federal Mail Service have joined forces in the consistent implementation of a banking services program for improved social security. This program was fully accomplished in 1995. From 1994 through 1995, 246 bank subbranches, fully equipped with computers and office hardware, were opened at Saint Petersburg's local post offices. The offices now pay out pensions to some 1,000,000 pensioners, using a new technology developed jointly by the Bank and the Saint Petersburg Department of Federal Mail Service.

This new technology for pension payment from current retirement accounts has given Saint Petersburg's pensioners, for the first time in Russian history, an opportunity to receive their monthly pension on any office day of the month starting from the date when the amount is credited. Pensioners can receive their pension payment during business hours. They can also draw on their pension accounts bit by bit, leaving the balance to earn a supplementary income in the form of interest. They are also free to use all the advantages of a bank account, such as, deposit or withdraw, dividends or other forms of revenue accrue on their account, or payment for purchases without the use of cash.

This program signified the beginning of a series of joint projects aimed at supporting the city's under-privileged. Since it was first launched, social tension has decreased noticeably within the city.

Among the system's other benefits are lower inflationary tendencies due to less cash in circulation, automated pension reporting, reduced paperwork, higher precision and speed of data transfer because of modem communications, automated updating and identification checks in retiree databases, uninterrupted cash supply, and the creation of new workplaces.

Over the course of its work under this program, Petrovskiy Commercial Bank has acquired invaluable hands-on experience in the development, implementation and operation of a comprehensive individual customer service system. The following data illustrates the growth of this service:

Figure 22.
Subbranches in Saint Petersburg's local post offices

	Subbranches
January 1995	122
March 1995	160
June 1995	217
September 1995	246

Rent and Utilities Payments

Recently, the Bank and the Saint Petersburg Department of Federal Mail Service launched an additional phase in their joint program for the development of residential banking services. In this phase, the Bank's branches and subbranches can now accept rent and utility payments. Payment is accepted in cash or by transfer, either on a long-term, or a lump-sum basis. From June to December 1995, the total number of payers increased 1300%. Long-term payment by transfer, which is by far the most convenient for customers, increased 1000%. All a customer needs to do is open a current account and instruct the Bank to pay the incoming bills. The customer is thus relieved of making monthly payments in person, insuring that payment is made on time. However, if the customer prefers to pay in person or one month at a time, this option is also available.

Plans currently call for the acceptance of payments for national telephone calls and for building society membership dues. The feasibility of accepting other forms of mandatory payments is also being studied. Petrovskiy Commercial Bank's customers are free to choose the payment methods which suit them best, which is the chief advantage in dealing with this Bank.

Social Programs

Zabota is a Russian word that means, "care for elders." The Zabota Central Consumer Society was founded in 1995 with the participation of the Department of Federal Mail Service and Petrovskiy Commercial Bank. The idea behind it is to create, in Saint Petersburg, a system for providing pensioners and other underprivileged community groups with food at discounted prices, using the existing network of pension-paying subbranches in the post offices.

Zabota CCS caters to pensioners by accepting, forming, and issuing pre-ordered "food baskets." At the initial stage pensioners were able to purchase a fairly wide selection of long-storage groceries at their nearest post office. The prices are, on average, 10% below regular retail prices.

Pensioners place their orders at their nearest post office. The ordered groceries should be made available in one day, and pensioners are then welcome to pick them up at the package section of the post office.

Payment is made by writing off the value of an order from the relevant pension account after the order has been fulfilled. In the future, payment will be made by plastic card. Zabota and Petrovskiy Bank's Card Center are jointly carrying on a detailed design for this technology.

Zabota's long-term plans call for further proliferation of this service extending it to other socially disadvantaged community groups. Special attention is also being paid to the possible provision of tailored food packages for sugar diabetics. A system for taking orders by phone with front-door delivery of food to bed-ridden or home-bound pensioners, and the seriously ill, is also in development.

Petrocard Payment System - Plastic Credit Cards

To improve their customer service, Petrovskiy Commercial Bank launched its own system for non-cash payments using plastic credit cards called the PetroCard. There are two types of credit cards for the individual customers, a Social and a Classic "Petrovskiy" card. The Social Card is mainly for pensioners and the underprivileged, while the Classic Card targets customers in the average income group.

Practically all pensioners in the Frunzensky District of Saint Petersburg were offered an opportunity to obtain free Social Cards at their nearest bank subbranch. The Bank does not charge Social Card holders for card maintenance. Because this group of customers has little experience in banking, the new payment system is unprecedented in its simplicity and proof against customer error, as well as forgery and misuse.

Five of the Bank's branches joined the PetroCard system in 1995, as well as 9 subbranches and 3 major retail outlets. Approximately 4,000 of the Bank's customers became cardholders. Six bank-o-mats now operate with the PetroCard system. In its first full year, the monthly turnover on card accounts was 2 billion rubles, as the number of monthly card transactions reached 5,000. The system serves its customers from 8 a.m. to midnight, seven days a week.

The Bank is continuing to work on further improvements of its PetroCard system. As part of its further development, the system will incorporate all of the Bank's branches and subbranches. It will also support the issuance of plastic wage cards to corporate employees. This card will, at some point, be accepted by retail stores and restaurants, with cash machines installed in well-visited public places.

Individual Customer Service

Petrovskiy Commercial Bank is continuing to enhance its spectrum of services available through the use of current pension accounts. A "Petrovskiy" customer holding such an account is now able to:

- transfer funds from the current pension account to a time deposit as directed by the customer
- subscribe to periodicals in installments, with monthly payment made by bank transfer
- pay, by bank transfer, for national and international telephone services
- pay building society membership fees by bank transfer
- purchase durable goods with payments in installments, loans will be repaid with funds from the current account, requiring no acceptance
- pay for insurance services
- transfer funds to other regions of Russia

Finally, retired customers of the Bank will soon be offered soft short-term loans.

Policy of Loans and Security Market

The lending policy is the Bank's top priority in terms of active loan transactions. The following illustrates the rapid growth in loans given throughout 1995.

Figure 23.

1995	Loan (million rubles)
January	258,409
March	355,162
July	407,119
October	415,522

By January, 1996, the total amount of loans issued by Petrovskiy Commercial Bank in the previous year was 4,540,929 million rubles. During 1995, the Bank provided a total of 51 billion rubles in loans to the city of Saint Petersburg. The Bank has provided other sizable loans to the Saint Petersburg and Leningrad Regional offices of the Russian Federation State Pension Funds to ensure the timely payment of retirement pensions. Also, the Bank provided a number of soft loans to medical institutions, including approximately 2 billion rubles intended for the payment of wages, and 2.3 billion rubles for the purchase of medicines.

The Bank's branches carried out their lending to businesses and organizations under the centralized administration of the Business Analysis, Lending and Investment Division. All lending activities were carried out within the framework of a consolidated credit policy, aimed to reduce the risk of loan non-payment.

The Bank has been actively and consistently cooperating with Saint Petersburg's industrial entities, the leading sector of the region's economy. Since 1992, the Bank has participated in the Federal program for the conversion of the Military-Industrial Complex by providing loans to 14 of the city's leading enterprises. The amount of budgetary credit resources made available by the Bank exceeded 8.25 billion rubles. Most enterprises have already repaid these loans.

Industrial lending is one of the Bank's top priorities. Recently the Bank provided loans to entities operating in the power, machine-building, consumer goods, and food sectors. Loans were provided to some of the city's leading manufacturers, including Samson, the Krupskaya Candy Factory, a baking plant, the Saint Petersburg Pasta Factory, and the Saint Petersburg Seaport.

Since 1995, a successful project is in progress to create a baking industry group in Saint Petersburg, centered around the Bank's Birzhevoy Branch. Over the course of the project, many businesses became customers of the Bank. Of course, the Bank continues its mutually beneficial cooperation with its long-standing customers.

Paying a great deal of attention to industrial entities, Petrovskiy Commercial Bank offers its customers a range of services which, apart from cash and settlement support, also includes the establishment of Bank offices right on the premises of large industrial facilities, ensuring encashment, short-term lending, investment lending, provision of bank guarantees, and the payment of employee wages into current accounts.

The Bank made its eighth and ninth share issues in 1995, boosting "Petrovskiy" Bank's authorized capital by 1.63 billion rubles. The market value of the Banks' shares has always remained stable.

The Bank has noticeably strengthened its foothold in the marketing of state and municipal securities. As an authorized dealer of municipal bonds, the Bank has, from the beginning, played a leading role in stock exchange sessions, with a turnover in local bonds totaling over 70 billion rubles in 1995.

When a new regional Government short-term securities sale opened in 1995, Petrovskiy Commercial Bank became an authorized dealer, which considerably expanded the range of opportunities available to the Bank in this market. The Bank's short-term bond turnover totaled over 400 billion rubles in that first year.

The Bank then launched its own drafts program, targeting companies with overdue accounts payable to suppliers or contractors, as well as creditor companies with heavy overdue accounts receivable from contractors. In other words, this program is designed to make drafts available to companies experiencing a working capital deficit. Relying on its extensive database for mutual debts in industry, the Bank is helping build ideal draft chains leading to the repurchase of existing debts, and enabling the companies concerned to use drafts to further their mutual settlement. Moreover, the Bank offers companies the opportunity to use its drafts as a tender for debt payment, as it simplifies settlement procedures and drastically reduces the time the funds remain in current accounts. In spite of the fact that the draft program was launched only in the fourth quarter of 1995, by year-end the Bank had already issued 16.5 billion rubles worth of drafts. The amount of drafts issued since that time have only increased.

Petrovskiy Commercial Bank further improved its work with clients in the stock market through contracts authorizing the Bank to manage customers' funds. Under such a contract, a customer transfers funds into the Bank for a certain period of time, while the Bank, acting on behalf of the Customer, proceeds to build and manage a securities portfolio with guaranteed returns on the customer's investment upon the contract's expiration. Being an authorized short-term government bond dealer, the Bank is in a position to form ideal and reliable state and municipal securities portfolios.

International Operations

Consistently, the development and expansion of Petrovskiy Commercial Bank's correspondence network continues. The network now includes approximately 35 of the world's leading banks, who also have sprawling correspondent links of their own.The Bank includes these Western banks among it correspondent relations:

1. Bankers Trust Company, New York (USA)
2. Bank of New York (USA)
3. Republic National Bank of New York (USA)
4. Banker Trust International PLC, Frankfurt/Main (Germany)
5. Dresdner Bank AG, Frankfurt/Main (Germany)
6. Deutsche Bank, Frankfurt/Main (Germany)
7. National Westminster Bank, Overseas Branch (England)
8. Midland Bank, London (England)
9. Banque Rivaud, Paris (France)
10. Svenska Handelsbanken, Stockholm (Sweden)
11. Postipakki, Helsinki (Finland)
12. Meespierson, Amsterdam (Holland)
13. Creditanstalt, Vienna (Austria)
14. Generale de Banque, Brussels (Belgium)
15. Den Danske Bank, Copenhagen (Denmark)
16. Den Norske Bank, Oslo (Norway)
17. Credit Suisse, Zurich (Switzerland)
18. Banca di Roma (Italy)
19. Bank of Tokyo (Japan)
20. Standard Chartered Bank, Singapore (Malaysia)
21. Banco de Sabadell, Sabadell (Spain)
22. Royal Bank of Canada, Toronto (Canada)
23. Unibank, Copenhagen (Denmark)

Correspondent relations were also established with banks in the CIS, including Latvia, Estonia, and the Ukraine. The Bank now accepts payments in Kazakh Tenges, Uzbek Soms, and other currencies as quoted by the Central Bank.

Recently Petrovskiy Commercial Bank considerably expanded its range of international services available to individuals. Among the services offered by the Bank's branches to private customers are: hard-currency deposits, cash for foreign currency conversion, and acceptance and issuance of traveler's cheques. The Bank's branches across the city also open and maintain hard-currency accounts for local businesses.

In order to further improve its documentary transactions on behalf of its customers, the Bank has been talking extensively to its leading correspondent banks seeking to establish letter-of-credit cover facilities. Such transactions are already performed with Dresdner Bank and Postipankki Oy.

Petrovskiy Commercial Bank was invited by the European Bank for Reconstruction and Development to participate in its Trade Facility Program. This program is aimed at bolstering the trade turnover between Russia and the European Community.

The Bank is still among the city's leading bankers in terms of banknote transactions, offering the most competitive terms on cash transactions involving 26 world currencies. As part of its activities as a foreign currency flow control agency, the Bank monitors foreign currency revenues on its customers export contracts registered with the Bank in accordance with applicable and current law. The Bank ensures the steady monitoring of hard-currency payments made by customers, in order to control their compliance with applicable regulations, and to quickly notify the Central Bank of any instances when imported goods fail to arrive in Russia, or in any case of capital flight abroad.

The Electronic Data Processing Division of the Bank is designed to support and maintain transaction automation software for transactions carried out by the Bank's International Transaction Division. This includes the Bank's Foreign-Currency Operating Day, Private Deposits, Export Operations Monitoring, and others. In line with the State Customs Committee's requirements, a range of programs has been implemented ensuring effective controls over imports and interaction with their Computer Center.

Those Russian bank's which have reached a level of development high enough to become full fledged members of the international banking community, need to upgrade their information technology first. In so doing they can substantially expand their services range, boost operating efficiency, add promptness to customer service, and ensure the secure functioning of their banking information systems at a higher level. Petrovskiy Commercial Bank continues to offer a range of additional solutions for management and the control of the activities of all divisions of the Bank, ensuring its secure placement in the international banking system.

The Bank has already begun implementation of a new quality automated information system. The system's selection was carried out in the form of an international tender involving over 20 Russian and overseas hard- and software vendors, including Digital Equipment Corporation, Price Waterhouse, IBM, Bull, and others. The Bank has carefully prepared a list of requirements for their new system, having formulated its information technology strategy years ahead. Petrovskiy Commercial Bank was assisted in the preparation and running of its tender by Great Britain's PA Consulting Group, a world leader in the selection, creation, and implementation of international information systems. The participation of these highly experienced consultants made the project's successful progress a certainty.

International Credit Cards

In mid-1995, the Bank joined the Europay International payment system as a Principal Member, becoming entitled to issue the Eurocard MasterCard Standard and Gold, as well as the Cirrus Maestro Pictogram credit card. Eurocard/MasterCard Standard and Eurocard/MasterCard Gold can be used to obtain cash or to pay for services worldwide and any Russian citizen or company may qualify to become a card holder. The target market for both of these cards is mainly the high-income and stable customer. Cirrus/Maestro/edc/ec Pictogram is a debit card, primarily for medium-income customers, and costing less to maintain. This card can be used at cash machines bearing the Cirrus or Eurocheque Pictogram logo, or to pay for goods or services at venues bearing the edc or Maestro logo. As the card also bears the PetroCard logo, it can be used within the PetroCard service network.

Petrovskiy Commercial Bank has plans for the quick development of its system for international card payments. Facilities are being implemented for cash advancing on international cards. It will then become possible to pay for goods and services on behalf of those customers who hold international cards issued by other banks. The Bank's plans also envisage improved interaction with other Russian and international payment systems.

The total balance of profits by 1994 was 935.4 million rubles. During 1995 the total of profits increased to reach 4,092 million rubles, an increase of more than 400%!

Petrovskiy Commercial Bank has always regarded assistance to art, culture, science, sports, healthcare and education as an integral part of its operations. Over one billion rubles were donated to charity and various sponsorships in 1995.

UNIT 5

Arrangements of Cash Payments in Russia

Introduction

In 1992, Russian bankers and their clients started to acquire the realization that a market economy implies individual control over decisions affecting private property. Bank Account owners were given the right to determine when and to whom money should be paid from their accounts. Indebtedness ceased to automatically convey to the creditor signature rights on the debtors bank account. The principle that every creditor had an equal right to the deposit balance in an account and in some established order of preference, while strange to most other countries, had been firmly established in Russia for decades. The significance of placing upon the individual, responsibility for determining how, when and where to deal with obligations cannot be underestimated in the current evolution in developing Russian society.

The elimination of a system of satisfaction of contractual obligations of the individual, by others who are not direct parties to the transaction, through regulation rather than due process of law, gave recognition to the new principle that credit extension involves risks and therefore has consequences for the creditor as well as the borrower. One party cannot create certainty at the expense of the demise of the other, without an unacceptable cost to society. Granting the freedom to the involved parties to resolve these consequences independently is important. Other economies have come to recognize that the risks involved in ill-advised credit must include the potential consequence of non-payment, in order for a market economy to self-regulate as it should.

Due process of law implies that the verdict of the court should determine not only the return of funds withdrawn in an unwarranted fashion, but should equally protect against the abuse of taking without consent as well. Western nations call this the presumption of innocence. The entire economy of Western nations would be disrupted if the accounts of companies who had accounts payable over 30 days old, were seized by banks on behalf of creditors, without due process of law.

Excusing banks from the requirement to withdraw penalties for late payments to creditors from their client's accounts is another sign of progress in establishing private property rights. Very few American companies could remain in business if subjected to an interest penalty of 0.5% per day. Banks are recognizing that late payment at an affordable interest rate imposed by adjudication is better than an interest rate that imposes bankruptcy.

In reading this chapter concerning common practices in the Russian banking industry and their evolution many, seemingly trivial, characteristics provide insight into the direction the banking system is taking in providing for self-management by individuals of their own business affairs and the restoration of respect in the Russian banking law for private property rights.

Chapter 5.1

Concept and Terms of Non-Cash Payments

Unlike cash circulation, when money is handed over from the cash desk of the payer to the cash desk of the payee, the concept of noncash payments means that payments are made by transfer of money from the payer's to the payee's account in the bank. The banks maintain savings funds of businesses on their accounts, and deposit funds coming into these accounts. They also implement orders of the businesses to remit and withdraw these funds from their accounts as well as to perform other banking operations envisioned in the banking rules and agreements.

Non-cash payments are effected upon meeting the following conditions:

- The payer has the right to refuse to pay for the submitted document in full or in part in those cases foreseen in the law or the agreement.
- As a rule, it is not allowed to withdraw from an account without the payer's consent or order.
- Payments are effected with the payer's own funds, or in some cases, with the bank's loan or other borrowed resources.
- The funds are debited to the payee's account only when they are written off from the payer's account.
- Compliance with the rules of document circulation, developed by the Central Bank, which determine the flow of money and financial documents.
- The overall term of the non-cash payments shall not exceed two operational days within Russia and five operational days internationally.
- Financial documents for noncash payments by companies have to meet the requirements of the Central Bank's standards. Payment documents are accepted by the bank for execution, if the first copy has the two authorized signatures to dispose the account and the legal stamp that has been registered with the bank.
- If payments are effected by an entrepreneur without the status of a legal company, the bank will accept payment documents with one signature and no stamp.
- Mutual claims to payments by both the payer and the payee of the disputed funds are considered for the parties via the courts, without the participation of the banking institution.

When there is a shortage or absence of funds on the payer's account, the question of order of payments arises. The selective order of payments on documents had been in practice until 1989. In this system, payments were made depending on the economic nature of the transactions.   All payments were grouped into five situations, with different terms for each. That approach didn't help to strengthen the payment discipline, and it weakened the interest of companies in making timely payments. It was presupposed that the selective order of payments protected the interest of the working people and the government, and it dictated that the first course of payments be for salary and taxes. However, it failed to take into consideration the many other costs of doing business and overhead required to stay productive.

In 1990, the selective order of payments was replaced by the calendar order, which envisioned a strict turn of payments, irrespective of the nature of those payments. It meant that the cash that had been debited to the account could be used for the payment of salaries after the claims of all suppliers had been met, material and services paid, and any arrears to the bank recovered, if the maturity of these invoices came before the scheduled salary payment.

In the middle of 1992 the calendar order of payments was canceled and payers were given the right to determine for themselves the order of payment made from their accounts.

At first sight, giving such a right to payers meets most market relationships, for unlike the selective or the calendar order of payment, it gives them broader independence. However, in practice this may entail violations to the principle of equality for the creditors, for at his own discretion the payer can give preference to one company over another to whom he may have a long-term account payable.

In the course of 1992-1995 the Russian government began to take different decisions, regulating the order of payments. Then, in 1995, they stated that the first priority for payments would be based upon urgent needs, taxes and non-tax payments to the state. All remaining payments were affected according to the order of calendar maturity dates of the invoices presented to the bank.

Payments are made with the consent or acceptance of the account holder, although in some cases it is allowed to exercise a nonaccepted drawing of the cash from the payer's account.   Such withdrawal is used as a form of payment between the parties under agreement, and these cases, are permitted by Russian law. In particular, the right to nonaccepted drawing of the funds is granted to the supplier of delivered electrical and heating power, water supply (except for public municipal and state-owned organizations), as well as for electric power delivered by nuclear power stations, and for the post, telegraph and telephone services provided by the communication companies. The condition of payments in the form of the nonaccepted drawing of the funds may also be included in an agreement to cover other cases.

The right to the nonaccepted drawing of the cash from a borrower's account for repayment of loans whose terms have matured, is widely used by banks in their loan agreements. If the nonaccepted drawing is not mandatory by law, then the right to decide whether to include it or not in the agreement belongs to the payer. By giving his counterpart the right to withdraw the funds from his account in this manner, the payer still exercises his authority to dispose of his own account and the funds within it.

When the payee is given the right to the nonaccepted drawing of the funds, this puts the payer in a disadvantageous position. An unscrupulous withdrawer has the opportunity to charge amounts against the account without due reason. Furthermore, at the stage when the agreement is implemented there could arise some circumstances which, in an ordinary situation, give the right to the payer to refuse to pay for the demand, whether for a shipment of goods not foreseen in the contract, or defective goods, etc. However, it is impossible to suspend the drawing of funds on the demand because of an unacceptable withdrawal. When the payee does not consent to the return of the unduly withdrawn funds, such return can only be carried out by verdict of the courts.

If the payer and his creditor have agreed to the conditions giving the creditor the right of nonaccepted drawing of the due amounts, the payer must then arrange a corresponding agreement with his bank. Only when there is such an agreement, can this mechanism of payments be implemented. Therefore, in a letter to the bank, or in the text of the bank account agreement, it shall be noted which creditor has the right to withdraw nonacceptedly an amount from the payers account and for what products, whether they goods, services, labor, etc.

In taking a decision related to the right of the creditor to withdraw the funds from the account of the payer in the nonaccepted manner, the bank must follow the said letter of the payer or the agreement previously concluded with the bank. The right to an indisputable withdrawal of funds from a bank account can also be ascribed to the nonaccepted drawing of funds. This right is given to tax and financial bodies for the arrears payment of taxes and corresponding fines. These government bodies also have the right to withdraw the funds in the indisputable manner from the accounts of payers who are scheduled to make payments to them. The state authorities of pension security, medical insurance, pricing regulation, etc., also have the right to extract their due money in this enforced manner.

In addition, the regulations dealing with the supply of manufactured products, technical equipment and public consumer goods, dictates that the value of a defective shipment and a corresponding penalty fee can be withdrawn from the manufacturer in the indisputable manner. This provision allows a long-lasting way to perform such operations. Claims to the bank related to the implementation of payment are delivered directly to the bank which has allowed the violation. It is considered to be an untimely withdrawal by the bank if it takes place later than the next day after the bank's receipt of the due document. If the bank performs in an untimely manner, if there is an incorrect withdrawal of the funds from the holder's account, or if the amount due the holder is deposited late, he is entitled to demand that the bank pay, in his favor, a 5% fee of the untimely debited amount for every day of delay. The agreement between the bank and the holder of the settlement account can determine another rate if the fee and procedure for violation is made in payments.

In 1992 the banks accrued and extracted penalty fees from their customers' accounts for defaulted payments to suppliers. Since July 1992, the banks have been released from the obligation to calculate and extract such penalty fees. The Buyer now pays a basic penalty fee for such payment defaults, according to the procedure determined in the purchasing agreement between him and his supplier. Penalty fees for every day of default is now 5% per day, unless otherwise defined in the agreement between the parties.

Companies, organizations and institutions, together with their creditors, choose the form of noncash payment to be made and state this in their purchase agreements. In the noncash payments, it is allowed to use a remittance order, check, letter of credit, or a payment demand-order. The payment demands were the principal form of payment before 1992. Today, this form is not recommended, however, given the historical relationships between suppliers and buyers, the banks are entitled to accept the payment demands in accordance with any concluded agreements.

Chapter 5.2

Settlements with Remittance Orders

The remittance order is an instruction from the account holder to the servicing bank to remit a definite amount of his funds to the account of another company, in either the same or another bank. The order is completed through a form which contains data about both the payer and payee necessary to effect the payment. The order is accepted by the bank for execution within 10 days from the date of its issue, based upon the availability of sufficient funds in the account. Let's review the flow of the remittance order as a document and the remitted money in payments through a bank in another town.

Figure 24. Flow of the remittance order in payments with banks from other towns.

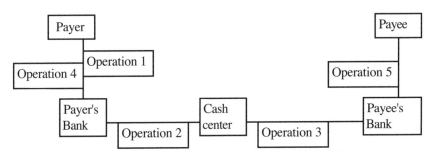

With the remittance order the cash will flow in the following manner:

Operation 1. The Bank has accepted the remittance order from the payer company.

Operation 2. The Bank has withdrawn the amount from the payer's account and transferred it, together with the order, to the Cash Center. Having drawn the money from the payer's account, the Bank has instructed the Cash Center to transfer it from its correspondent account to the correspondent account of the bank who serves the payee.

Operation 3. The Bank of the payee deposits the money to the payee's account through its corresponding account.

Operation 4. The payer receives a statement of his account confirming that the money has been remitted.

Operation 5. The bank confirms to the payee, in a statement of settlement, that his due money has been received.

Implementation of this operation is accompanied by a copy of the remittance order as a payment document, which is completed in five copies. From the point of the terms of payment, under the agreements, the payments executed by means of remittance orders, can be either term, pre-term or deferred.

Term payments are advance payments, and are effected before shipment of the products, upon acceptance of the goods, or as partial payments in the cases of large deliveries. Pre-term and deferred payments may take place within the frame of the agreed relationship, with no financial harm to the parties.

Scheduled payments are settlements with remittance orders, which are executed on delivery of products or services, including transportation. The idea is that on agreement with the supplier, the buyer remits the money to him on a periodic basis. At the end of the agreed period they specify the amount of payments and deliveries. These specified conditions are regulated through regular scheduled payments.

To transfer settlements with scheduled payments, the payer company submits to the servicing bank, copies of the agreements or a list of the companies with which it has concluded agreements on scheduled payments. These must indicate the duration of the payment period, the dates to remit payments, what account the payment is remitted from, and what account it is to be credited to. They must also include the terms for reconciliation of the payments and a procedure to make them complete.

The scheduled payments may be effected on a daily basis or periodically on the dates agreed upon by the supplier and buyer. The amounts of every scheduled payment are defined by the parties for the forthcoming month or quarter, based upon the needed frequency of payment, volume of delivery, or services rendered.

Suppose, there is an expected delivery of products valued at 180 million rubles in a quarter. Under the agreement between the parties, the frequency of the scheduled payment would be set at once a week. The amount of each weekly payment, made on Wednesday, would be 15 million rubles, or 180 million rubles over a 12 week period. An individual remittance order must be submitted to the bank for every scheduled payment. These scheduled payments can be executed with either the remittance or payment demand-orders.

The parties must periodically, at least once per a month, specify their settlements on the basis of actual delivery of goods and services for a reporting period, and make a recalculation in accordance with the procedure provided in the agreement. The difference may then be transferred with a separate order, or be taken into consideration in the next payment. It is expedient that the specification of settlements is timed to coincide with the last payment of the month, so that any delays are kept to a minimum on the reporting date.

Payments with the accepted orders are paid through the post office and are based upon the idea that the bank guarantees payment of such an order. It is accepted by the bank, on condition that the amount of the order is logged on the individual balance sheet account, "Accepted payment orders and settlement checks." This is account No. 723 on the balance sheet of the bank. The orders accepted by the bank are used in the following settlements:

- in payments by tax supported organizations for received goods and rendered services, and in return of the tax income via the post office.
- as remittance for goods and services, via the post office
- with the post office, for orders fulfilled via the post, for delivery of parcels and in payment of cash on delivery
- onetime payments to transport organizations for transportation of goods, passengers and their baggage

Accepted orders are widely used in payment made via the post office. The payers have the right to send postal orders with no amount limit in the name of:

- some individuals expecting payments for pensions, alimony, salary, traveling allowances, royalties, etc.
- some companies, as well as their authorized persons
- postal orders may also be used to pay out salary and to pay for procurement of agricultural products in places where there is no bank.

The bank takes for acceptance the orders issued to the nearest post office which has an account for the transfer of funds in the same or another bank. The bank office hands over samples of the signatures of the authorized officials and a pattern of its stamp, which are used to arrange acceptance of the order, at a relative post office. It is necessary to indicate in the order a purpose of the transferred amount, such as "in payment for the pay out of pensions, salary, alimony etc." If the cash is remitted for different purposes then the individual amounts of those specific purposes are noted. The remittance orders for every payee of the money are attached to the accepted order, and are to be left with the post office.

Chapter 5.3

Settlements with Payment Demand-Orders

The payment demand-order is a demand of the supplier to the buyer to pay the value of the delivered products, implemented works, or rendered services against these payment and shipment documents sent to the buyer's servicing bank.

Payment demand-orders are issued by the supplier and together with the shipping documents are sent in triplicate to the bank of the buyer, which transfers the demand-order to the buyer, and keeps the shipment papers in the file of documents awaiting the decision of the buyer. The payment demand is completed in a standard form. Upon receipt of the document, the payer is given three days to make a decision on payment. The payer must either accept the payment demand-order, or partially or completely refuse its acceptance. The payer must notify his servicing bank within three days, of his refusal to pay the payment demand-order in full or in part. In this case, a negative form of acceptance is submitted to notify the bank in writing, of the payee's refusal to accept. The payer's consent doesn't require a written confirmation, as silence is considered a token of consent. With the positive form of acceptance either consent or refusal require written notification to the bank. Under the consent to pay the payment demand-order in full or in part, the payer certifies it with the signatures of all authorized persons placing the company stamp on all the copies, and leaving them with the servicing bank which will remit the money to the supplier. One copy of the demand-order is then passed over to the payer, together with papers certifying the shipment of goods, implementation of works or provision of services.

If the payer totally refuses to accept, the demand-order and the shipment documents have to be returned to the supplier or contractor.

Figure 25. The flow of cash with payment demand-orders are as follows:

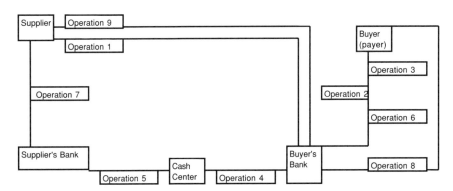

With the payment demand-order, the cash flows in the following way:

Operation 1. The completed package of the payment demand-order, in triplicate, and the shipping documents are delivered by the supplier to the bank of the buyer.

Operation 2. The shipping documents are taken as a record with the bank of the buyer, and the complete package is given to the buyer.

Operation 3. The payer accepts the demand-order and returns it to his bank.

Operation 4. Against the first copy of the demand-order, the cash is withdrawn from the settlement account and transferred together with the second copy to the corresponding Cash Center. The Cash Center withdraws the cash from the corresponding account of the bank servicing the buyer, and remits it to the corresponding account of the bank, servicing the supplier.

Operation 5. The cash, coming to the corresponding account of the supplier's bank in the Cash Center, is credited to the supplier's account.

Operation 6. The payer is given the third copy of the demand-order with the complete package of shipping documents attached.

Operation 7. The supplier receives a statement of his settlement account, confirming receipt of the cash. The second copy from the complete package is attached to that statement.

Operation 8. This operation takes place only when the buyer declares his refusal of acceptance, specifying the reason.

Operation 9. Having received the buyer's completed refusal of acceptance, his servicing bank sends back to the supplier the complete package of the demand-order and the shipping documents.

The reasons, giving the right to the payer to refuse acceptance in full or in part, are provided in the agreement between them. The bank doesn't consider any payment disputes between the parties. It can only check the consistency of the reason for refusal taken by the payer with the provisions of the agreement. The bank doesn't consider a complete refusal of the payer to pay for the payment demand-order, if it qualified to be paid in part.

Chapter 5.4

Settlements with Checks

A *check* is a security of standard form, giving the right to receive the amount noted on it. There are checks to receive cash money and checks to effect settlements with noncash payments.

As a rule, four legal entities or individuals take part in the arrangement of non-cash payment with checks and, therefore, exercise certain operations:

- *the bank of the check issuer* - the bank which gives blank forms of the check to its depositor and ensures payment of the issued and duly completed checks presented by the bank of the check bearer
- *the check issuer* - the person who issues a check as the document ensuring the receipt of money by his bank for payment of delivered goods, implemented works, or rendered services
- *the check bearer* - the person who holds a formal check, giving him the right to receive money from the check issuer
- *the bank of the check bearer* - the bank which pays the check presented by the check bearer from those funds which have been received from the bank of the check issuer

Payment by checks between individuals is not yet allowed in Russia. In some cases, both the check issuer and the check bearer are served by the same bank which plays the functions of both the first and the forth party. In the future, upon the elimination of the difference between cash and payment checks, personal checks will be taken for payment in any bank, as it now happens in other developed countries. The blank forms of the checks are the same for all banks, and before their issue the banks have to provide the following required data without which the check is considered invalid:

- Name of the head office of the bank and its location and its logo may be placed next to the name of the head office in the top left part of the check. If the check is issued by the branch, the name of the branch and its location must be shown in the top right part of the check along with the identification number of the bank issued by the network of the cash centers under the Central Bank.
- name and number of the account of the check issuer
- cash limit for the check noted on its back side

To complete settlements with checks, the bank-issuer of the check must have the cash to immediately recover the due amount to the bank that has paid the bearer for the check. This task is accomplished in two ways. The first, when the amount equal to the amount of the check is withdrawn from the account of the check issuer and logged into an individual account (account No. 722 in the balance sheet of the commercial bank). The second, presumes the presence of necessary cash in the account of the check issuer, permitting the bank to guarantee payment of the check to the issuer of the check from the funds of the bank, if there is temporarily no money on his account.

In order to get checks, the business submits to the bank an application in a standard form, signed by the officials who have the right to do settlement transactions.

The business-bearer of the check, has to verify the proper completeness of the check, in particular that the amount of the check doesn't exceed the limit noted on the back side and on file, that the number of the check issuer's account noted on the check is consistent with the one on the file, the passport data of the check issuer is consistent with the data noted in the check card; the signature of the check issuer put on the check when it was completed and the signature on the check card are identical.

The business-bearer puts its stamp on the back side of the check, accepting payment for the goods or services, and ascribes the signature of the authorized person. The check, taken by the check bearer, are grouped in the registers of the standard form and left with the bearer's bank within 10 days, with the date of issue not counted. Checks provided to the bank after this term become invalid.

The flow of payments with checks when the banks are served with cash centers is as follows:

Figure 26. Flow of settlements with checks with servicing the banks in cash centers.

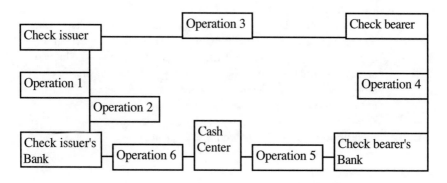

Operation 1. The check issuer provides an application to issue checks to him and at the same time gives a payment order, on the basis of which the bank debits the cash to pay for the checks.

Operation 2. The bank completes the necessary data in the checks and passes them over to the check issuer together with an identification card.

Operation 3. The check issuer issues a check to the check bearer.

Operation 4. The check bearer makes up the register of the checks in four copies and passes them over to his bank, which pays for them from the funds of the check issuer's bank and credits the money on the check bearer's account. The bank returns the fourth copy of the register to the check bearer.

Operation 5. The check bearer's bank transfers the check and the third copy of the register to its cash center which credits the money to the correspondent account of the check bearer's bank, having them withdrawn from the correspondent account of the check issuer's bank. The third copy of the register and the check are left with the cash center, and the first and the second copies are delivered to the cash center servicing the check issuer's bank.

Operation 6. On the basis of the received registers, the check issuer's bank debits the check issuer's account and reflects the use of the money on its correspondent account in the cash center.

Chapter 5.5

Settlements with Letters of Credit

The letter of credit, or L/C, is a conditional monetary obligation of a bank, issued by it on a customer's order in favor of his supplier. In so doing, the bank that has issued the letter of credit can effect a payment to the supplier or to delegated authorities through another bank. Payment is made against the submission of these documents provided in the letter of credit, along with the compliance of its other terms and conditions.

The decision on application of the L/C form of settlement is taken on the signing an agreement between the buyer, or payer, and the supplier. With the L/C form of payment, the agreement has to indicate:

- the term of validity for the L/C
- the name of the issuing bank
- the type of L/C and its method of execution
- the method of notifying the supplier of the opening of the L/C
- a full list, including the exact characteristics of those documents submitted by the supplier to receive funds against the L/C
- the terms for providing documents after shipment of the goods, and the requirements for their completion
- other conditions which are necessary for compliance to receive money against the L/C

There are two types of Letter of Credit's (L/C) in relation to the buyer with its termination before the term, the irrevocable and the revocable. The irrevocable L/C can't be changed or canceled without consent of the supplier, in whose favor it is opened. However, the supplier may refuse the use of the L/C before its term, if it is provided with these conditions. The revocable Letter of Credit can be changed or canceled by the issuing bank with no preliminary agreement with the supplier, if there is a default of the conditions provided in the agreement, or the refusal of the issuing bank, before the term, to guarantee payment against the L/C. All directives to change the terms and conditions of the revocable L/C are provided by the payer to the supplier only via the issuing bank which notifies the bank of the supplier, which then notifies the supplier. But the supplier's executive bank must pay for all documents, consistent with the conditions of the L/C, which have been submitted by the supplier and accepted by the bank before the latter receives any notification of change or cancellation of the L/C. The L/C should specifically indicate that it is irrevocable, otherwise it is considered to be revocable.

In terms of the very cover with the cash to effect payments against the L/C, they are divided in two types, covered (lodged) and uncovered (guaranteed). In opening a covered L/C, the issuing bank transfers funds of the payer, or its loan, in disposal of the supplier's executive bank. The account No. 720 "L/Cs" is open with this bank to account for the received cash. The uncovered L/C is opened in the correspondent bank of the issuing bank. The correspondent plays the role of the executive bank and is given the right to withdraw a full amount of the L/C from the account of the issuing bank. With the secured L/C, the buyer transfers money from his account to the account of the supplier's bank opened in the issuing bank.

To open an L/C, the buyer submits an application for L/C. To receive money against the L/C, the supplier provides the executive bank with the documents that prove implementation of all conditions stated in the L/C. If any conditions are broken, no payments are made against the L/C.

If the terms of the L/C require acceptance by the authorized buyer, then he must submit to the executive bank:
- passport or other substituting document
- sample of his signature , if there is none in the bank
- traveling certificate or a letter of authority given by the organization that has issued the L/C

The note of acceptance, confirmed by a signature of the authorized person, should be placed on the account register or shipping documents which are accepted for payment of the L/C. The closing of the L/C in the supplier's bank is done when:
- the term of L/C is expired.The executive bank notifies the issuing bank of the L/C's closing
- the supplier provides an application with refusal to use the L/C before the term is over. The non-used amount is transferred by order of the payer back to the bank account where the money was originally withdrawn
- the buyer provides an application to revoke the L/C in part or in full.

The L/C is closed or reduced on the day the notification arrives from the issuing bank. This is only possible without the consent of the supplier if the L/C is revocable.

144

Figure 27. Documentation flow in settlements with L/C.

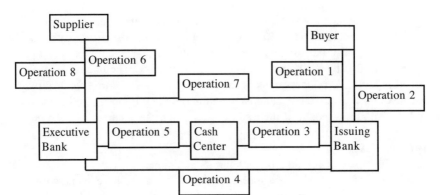

Operation 1. The buyer submits to the issuing bank a complete package of applications in six copies. The first one is signed and stamped, and is left with the bank as the reason to withdraw money from the buyer's account with the aim to lodge them in the executive bank.

Operation 2. One copy (the sixth) is returned to the buyers as a receipt of the application, and another (the fifth) is used by the bank for an off-balance sheet accounting of the issued L/C.

Operation 3. A copy of the application, functioning as a letter of advice, is delivered to the Cash Center to reflect the lodged amount on the correspondent accounts of each bank.

Operation 4. Two copies (the third and the forth) of the application are sent by the issuing bank to the executive bank which uses one copy for accounting the received L/C and gives the other to the supplier.

Operation 5. The executive bank receives a statement of its correspondent account from the cash center and fixes in its balance sheet as the amount of the received L/C.

Operation 6. The supplier submits to the executive bank the account register in three copies with a supplement of the shipping documents. The first copy of the register serves as a reason for the remittance of money from the L/C to the settlement account of the supplier.

Operation 7. The second copy of the account register with the supplement of the shipping documents, is delivered to the issuing bank by the executive bank.

Operation 8. The third copy of the register is returned to the supplier and serves as a receipt of the acceptance of all documents.

The issuing bank does not accept the account registers for payment without an indication of the date of shipment, the numbers of shipment documents, postal receipts when the goods are delivered via the post office, an act of acceptance and a listing of the type of transport on which the goods were shipped to receive their acceptance by a representative of the buyer.

UNIT 6

International Money Settlements

Introduction

Economist-philosopher Marx's most powerful idea was that economic and social organization of a nation is fundamentally driven by technology. Since the 1970's technology has been driving the world down a new road which was not foreseen. We have never been down this road before, global connection. Nearly all the key resources of the modern world are embodied in free, educated people - not hidden in the ground. Possession of resources is not longer necessary. Advanced countries no longer need to carve out new cheap resources. Technology is drying up the need for resources or concerns about scarcity. Technology creates resources. The entire U.S. economy has expanded nearly 50% since 1978, with virtually no increase in energy consumption. Technological efficiency has provided the resources. The modern economy derives an increasing proportion of its wealth from the production and consumption of information, which is not a scarce resource. It can be duplicated and transported with little use of physical resources. There is too much. We are going to poison ourselves, and die - not of starvation, but of worldwide gluttony. Call it Eco-Marxism, if you will. Central Government control of the economy, which Marx said was necessary to make things more productive, is now being called upon to limit production. For the Russian banking industry, this means redefining the entire nature of money settlements.

The tools of a modern economy breed individual economic initiative. If you try to run a modern enterprise from the top, nobody will understand it by the time a question gets to the top, and by the time the answer comes down, it will usually be too late and the wrong answer.

World War III, the Cold War, is over. But a new conflict, World War IV has already started. The nature of conflict among developed nations has fundamentally changed. Weapons War between highly developed countries is technically obsolete. Nuclear power is no longer the basis for claiming super-power status. The chief conflict of the next decade, World War IV, is economic. The new measure of super-power status will be the level of material prosperity provided to the population. Weapons use will be limited to policing the globe against regional fanatics. The contest of coming decades will be among competing economic variants of enabling individual creativity and productivity. Countries willing to participate in the global economy - to let goods, capital, technology, people and ideas flow FREELY across their borders - will share in the worldwide advance in knowledge and prosperity. This is the best hope for improving a national economy. It also requires letting go of obsolete concepts of national sovereignty. Nations are being replaced by trading blocks.

Tiny Taiwan's foreign-exchange reserves dwarf those of the United States. Knowledge and nations can be conquered economically - and at a relatively modest cost. Economic mistakes are the equivalent of losing Leningrad or Stalingrad to invading Nazi forces. World War IV will be without bullets. No one has to die. But geographic borders will not offer protection against such modern economic skirmishes or the depredations of international commerce. The interweaving of the world's markets subjects weak national economies to the rule of the financially strongest, even as it blurs national boundaries. We have found the enemy, and it is ourselves.

Russia, as all other nations, will re-stabilize by participating in a universal set of economic, political and social rules. To ignore these is to court a process of economic, political, social, and environmental collapse from which there are few escapes. The nations of the world lie on a continuum. The questions are, which ones will integrate smoothly into the new global system? Which will delay so long they collapse?

Economic well-being does not depend on physical resources, but on how efficiently these resources are used and how efficiently manpower is used. It is within this context that the Russian banking industry is adopting the new technology of world banking.

Using modern technology effectively requires the following of some very specific economic, social, and political rules. All attempts at independent isolationist development have failed. A decentralized, open, capitalist economy is needed, open to free international flow of trade, capital, people and technology. The function of governments will become to deny mobs and private armies access to physical force and protect the lives, welfare, individual freedom and property of it's citizens, without infringing upon their economic freedom to be productive and creative.

Most nations face a simple choice: trade or starve. Global specialization adds to efficiency. The pressures of international competition are a superb antidote to the reluctance of monopolies. The more a country opens its borders to global competition, the more it benefits its domestic consumers. Citizens will be hard-pressed to develop a reasonable standard of living, until they engage in international trade. The most valuable cargo of all is a human being.

Today's international financial transactions dwarf the volume of goods and services. In ruble value, more capital crosses national borders in two weeks time than internationally traded goods do in an entire year. Finance, not weapons, is one of the world's great equalizers. Within 30 years this equilibration process will be largely complete among the nations choosing to play by international rules. Well run Western financial systems will preferentially invest money in Russia, which has a larger potential for the expansion of output and, therefore, a larger potential for profits.

The ultimate products of an information age can be sent around the world at speeds approaching that of light. Automatic translation of text via telephone will greatly accelerate global integration and is here now. Electronic voice translation will be here soon. By 2020, translating telephones will be available for all major languages. Global television dishes will soon be available for less than R600,000. These developments will accelerate Russian integration into the global community. Direct global broadcasting will unify cultures.

As standards become increasingly universal, maintaining a diversity of cultural traditions will grow difficult. In the long run, what is now viewed as vital may change dramatically. The changes of the next 50 years will be far more astounding than the changes of the past 50. Limitations will be imposed only to the extent of our lack of vision.

Chapter 6.1

State Guarantees for International Transactions

State guarantees for the protection of international investment in Russia consist of the following provisions:
- International investors in Russia may be an international business, which may include companies, institutions and associations established and legally authorized to carry out investment activity in their country of origin
- Non-resident citizens, stateless persons, Russian citizens permanently residing abroad, in event that they are registered to engage in commerce in their country of citizenship or permanent residence
- International states
- International organizations

International investment means all types of material assets and intellectual property invested by non-Russian investors, into objects of entrepreneurial and other types of activity with the aim of making an income or profit. International investment within Russia may be affected by way of:
- Shares in enterprises established jointly with Russian businesses or individuals, or people or businesses from other countries.
- The establishment of enterprises fully owned by international investors, as well as of subsidiaries of international legal residents.
- The acquisition of enterprises, assets, buildings, stocks, bonds and other securities, as well as other property, which in accordance with the legislation existing in Russia, may belong to international investors.
- The acquisition of rights to use land and other natural resources.
- The acquisition of other property rights.
- Other types of investment activity not prohibited by Russian Law, including the extension of loans, property and property rights.

International investments in Russia shall enjoy the full and unconditional legal protection which shall be provided by Law, other legislation, and international treaties. The legal status of international investments and of the activity of international investors owning them shall not be less favorable than that provided for the property, property rights and investment activity of citizens and businesses of Russia.

International investment in Russia shall not be nationalized and shall not be sequestrated or confiscated, except for exceptional cases when such measures may be taken in the public interest. In the event of nationalization or confiscation, an appropriate and effective compensation shall be promptly paid to the international investor.

International investors shall have the right to compensation for their losses, including lost profits, if caused by unresponsible state action. The compensation paid to an international investor shall be equal to the actual value of the nationalized or confiscated investment, prior to the official announcement concerning the defacto or impending nationalization or confiscation. The compensation shall be payable without any ungrounded delay, in the original currency of the investment or in any other foreign currency acceptable to the international investor. Prior to the payment of the compensation, interest shall be paid on it according to the interest rate currently existing in Russia.

Following the payment of corresponding taxes and duties, international investors shall be guaranteed the unhindered transfer of payments abroad in connection with the effected investments, provided such payments were obtained in foreign currencies. Such payments may include:

- Incomes from investments, including profits, a share of the profits, dividends, interest, license or commission fees, payments for technical assistance and maintenance, and other fees.
- Amounts payable on the grounds of the rights arising from monetary claims and claims arising in connection with the execution of contractual duties which have an economic value.
- Amounts received by investors in connection with the partial or full liquidation or sale of investments.
- Compensation stipulated by the Laws of Russia.

International investors may utilize monies in rubles in their accounts, to acquire foreign currency on the foreign exchange domestic market. All hard currency expenses of enterprises involved in international investment arising from the conducting of different types of economic activity within Russia, including the reparation of part of an international investor's profits, shall be covered by the enterprises' hard currency incomes from such activity. These expenses shall also be covered by other legitimate sources of foreign currency. Enterprises with the involvement of international investment shall conduct transactions with foreign currencies according to the procedure established by the existing legislation of Russia and the Central Bank.

Chapter 6.2

International Participation in the Securities Markets

International investors shall have the right to acquire share-holdings, shares, holdings and other securities of enterprises located in the territory of Russia. International investors may acquire share-holdings in enterprises with Russian currency. In this case, the foreign currencies are converted into rubles according to the exchange rate established by the Central Bank at the time of purchase. Should an international investor pay in foreign currency for share-holdings of an enterprise, it is regarded as an enterprise with the involvement of international investment. International investors shall have the right to participate in the privatization of state and municipal enterprises, as well as of incomplete projects in Russia. The terms of their participation in tenders and auctions, concerning the privatization of state and municipal enterprises, are determined by the existing legislation of Russia. All such transactions must be in Russian rubles. International investors may exchange their currency into rubles at the exchange rate established by the Central Bank, for any legal foreign trade operations, and place them on special accounts at duly authorized banks.

Non-residents shall have the right to place their funds in government securities, unless the Russian Ministry of Finance introduces restrictions on their potential holders, such as non-residents of Russia, when it makes a decision on the issue of relevant bonds. In this case the non-resident shall be obliged to open an S-type account in Russian rubles with an Authorized Bank, which has permits from the Central Bank for opening and keeping special accounts in rubles. They shall have the right to buy these government securities at the expense of their balances of rubles.

Business dealings of non-residents involving the purchase and sale of government securities and incomes from these securities, shall be conducted according to the rules introduced for the relevant markets. Non-residents have the right to carry out only special conversion transactions. These transactions are of the purchase and sale of foreign currency for Russian currency, concluded between a non-resident and the Authorized Bank or between a non-resident and the Central Bank acting in their own name and for their own account.

Special accounts may be opened for non-residents and companies, including those which have no branch or representative office in Russia, for non-residents, natural persons, and those who are not business oriented.

Acceptable conditions for S-Type Accounts are as follows:

- Special accounts of non-residents only holding hard currency which is designated for the purchase of government bonds.
- Currency received as a result of the cancellation or sale of government treasury notes and federal loan bonds. In this case, it is the income from the sale of such notes or bonds, which were bought earlier by a non-resident and paid for from his account.

For the following reasons, amounts in rubles may be transmitted by a non-resident from the special account:

- to pay for foreign currency acquired by a non-resident in transactions on the securities market
- to pay the settlement in the market of government treasury notes and federal loan bonds and the subsequent acquisition of these securities
- to pay the expenses associated with transactions in government treasury notes and federal loan bonds
- to pay taxes associated with the receipt of income from government treasury notes and federal loan bonds

In the Russian newspaper, "Economics and Zhizhn (Life)," Number 5, February, 1997, it was reported that during the first six months of 1996, foreign firms and individuals invested $887 million USD in Russian securities with depositary receipts.

Russia is re-entering the European bond market. This method of attracting foreign capital has not been used by Russia since 1917, and a goal of $2 billion USD's in bond issues is now set by the Central Bank. It is now possible for Russia to enter these Western markets because they have finally assumed the debt of the former Soviet Union, and Westerners are now showing a willingness to buy Russian bonds.

Chapter 6.3

International Settlements

The first step for international settlements in Russia, is to open an account in a Russian bank. To open an account, a corporation must render the following information:
- Document of Legal Status and Registration
- Assurance Card with the signatures of its officers
- State Registration, whether Russian or International

Additionally, the corporation must conclude an agreement with the bank. Following is a sample of such an agreement that is used by Bank "Saint Petersburg" PLC:

FOREIGN CURRENCY BANK ACCOUNT AGREEMENT

Bank "Saint Petersburg" PLC, represented by _____
acting in accordance with _____
hereinafter referred to as the Bank, on the one part, and _____
represented by _____
acting in accordance with _____
hereinafter referred to as the Client, on the other part, both being legal entities and at full mutual consent have agreed on the following:

I. SUBJECT OF THE AGREEMENT

1.1 Bank opens and maintains current and transit foreign currency accounts in _____ (name of foreign currency) and undertakes obligations stipulated by the Agreement: keep cash funds on the Client's accounts, credit these accounts with the amounts received in their favor, transfer amounts and effect cash payments from the account in accordance with the Client's order. Operations, which are not directly connected with the aforementioned, are effected under the separate agreements.

II. RIGHTS AND OBLIGATIONS OF THE PARTIES

In their activities hereunder the Parties will be governed by the existing legislation, normative acts issued by the Central Bank of the Russian Federation, rules and other Bank's internal regulations.

2.1. Bank undertakes to:

2.1.1. Open Client's accounts within 5 days from the day of submitting all required documents to the Bank and provided they comply with the existing legislation.

2.1.2. Keep information on Client's operations and account confidential.

2.1.3. Provide Client with cash services and ensure safety of Client's funds in the bank's account.

2.1.4. Ensure prompt - not later than on the following day after the receipt by the Bank of duly settlement document - crediting Client's account with the funds.

2.1.5. Effect debiting Client's account, within the limits of the account's balance, not later than the following day after receipt by the Bank of duly issued settlement document. In case of required non-acceptable and non-disputable debiting the account, the Bank has no responsibility for reasonableness of claim.

2.1.6. Provide Client with account reports on the following day after debit or credit operations in the account.

2.1.7. Deposit to the account Client's bank notes in cases stipulated by instructions of the Central Bank of the Russian Federation, effect encashment from the account (with consideration of cash resources in stock) for the purposes not contradicting Russian legislation and instructions of the Central Bank of the Russian Federation, and provided internal Bank regulations are met.

2.1.8. Bank pays interest on the Client's account balance for the right to use Client's funds.

2.1.9. Interest rate for using Client's funds is set in accordance with Terms and Conditions of Bank "Saint Petersburg" PLC, and subject to change unilaterally by the Bank at the decision of the Bank's management following changes in the "Bank's Interest Policy on Credit and Deposit Operations."

2.1.10. In case the submitted payment document does not comply with bank rules, the Bank returns such payment document to Client with reference to the reasons of such return and request for their removal.

2.2. Client undertakes to:

2.2.1. Keep all funds, own and borrowed, with the Bank, except for the amounts allowed to spend by the relevant normative acts.

2.2.2. Deliver to Bank's cash department bank notes assorted for dilapidated and fit ones in accordance with the established rules and not later than 12.00 o'clock.

2.2.3. Place cash funds to other credit institutions and lend them to other companies or to participate in foundation of other commercial banks only provided there is no outstanding amounts on loans received in the Bank.

2.2.4. Follow the rules for operations on this particular account and make orders in relation to such account according to the established norms of settlements and rules for making documents.

2.2.5. Advise the bank on amounts credited or debited to the account by mistake within 20 days after receipt of account reports.

2.2.6. Promptly pay for the Bank's services in case of providing chargeable services by the Bank.

2.2.7. Follow the service hours established by the Bank and security rules inside the Bank.

2.2.8. Submit within a 3-day period, at the request of the Bank, accounting and other required documentation, necessary for control over compliance with cash discipline and in other cases stipulated by the existing legislation and internal regulations.

2.2.9. In case of receipt of foreign currency bank notes for the purposes stipulated by the regulatory acts of CB of RF, promptly submit to the Bank cash plans according to the established form.

2.2.10. When opening an account, present to the Bank the following documents certifying the right for authorized persons to manage funds in the Client's account:
  • two copies of list of authorized signatures and seal sample, certified by the superior Organization or notarized;
  • notarized decision of Client's authorized managerial body on the appointment of its Director;
  • order of the Director on the appointment of chief accountant.

2.2.11. Present to the Bank information on changes of name, legal and Organization form, location, management and other persons authorized for signing payment documents and other changes within a 10-day period from the date of approval of such changes

2.2.12. One month in advance advise the Bank in writing of the intended closing of account (termination of agreement). At the request of the client, accounts may be closed only after the final settlement in relation to all payment documents, invoices and all kinds of borrowings from the Bank.

2.2.13. Present to the Bank before January 10 of the next fiscal year an acknowledged balance of all accounts.

2.2.14. Lack of transactions on the Client's accounts excluding interest accrual should not be longer than 6 months.

156

2.3. **Bank has the right to:**

2.3.1. Control the Client's observance of settlement-cash discipline, report to tax agencies on all appearing violations, so that penalties could be imposed which are stipulated by the RF Presidential Order of May 23, 1994 N 1006.

2.3.2. Provide to Client additional banking services under supplementary agreements.

2.3.3. Unilaterally debit Client's accounts with amounts which were placed into such accounts without appropriate and duly reasons.

2.3.4. Unilaterally debit Client's accounts for fulfillment of obligations under agreements concluded with Bank "Saint Petersburg."

2.3.5. When closing such accounts and transferring funds to another bank, Bank "Saint Petersburg" reserves the right stipulated by Clause 2.3.4. hereof.

2.4. Client has the right to:

2.4.1. Manage its funds in the account, except for the cases stipulated by legislation and this agreement.

2.4.2. Entrust the Bank with the right to manage Client's funds (under bilateral agreement with the Bank).

2.4.3. Avail oneself of services under the present agreement.

2.4.4. Terminate the present agreement (close the account).

III. SETTLEMENT PROCEDURE.

3.1. Payment for the Bank's services in compliance with Bank "Saint Petersburg" Terms and Conditions and Bank-Client contracts and agreements shall be in the form of nonacceptable debiting the account if not otherwise stipulated by the agreement (contract).

3.2. Payment for additional services is effected according to the procedures established by the Bank and in compliance with the concluded agreements.

IV. RESPONSIBILITY OF THE PARTIES

4.1. For delayed (more than two days after submission of the properly compiled payment document to the Bank) crediting the Client's account through the Bank's fault, the Bank shall pay to the Client a fine as to 0.05% of the payment amount for each day of delay. The Bank shall not be responsible for delayed incorrect crediting of the account happened through no fault of it as well as for actions taken by other banking organizations or third parties.

4.2. The Parties shall not be responsible under obligations and losses of each other unless it is stipulated by the relevant agreements.

V. SETTLEMENT OF DISPUTES

    5.1.   Considering the advantages of the Arbitration tribunal settlement, the Parties hereto have agreed to submit all disputes and differences which may arise from performing, amending or terminating the Agreement or in connection therewith to the constantly acting Arbitration tribunal at Bank Saint Petersburg.

VI. MAKING ALTERATIONS AND AMENDMENTS

    6.1.   The present Agreement can be altered or amended in the form of a written agreement between the Parties hereto.

    6.2.   It is the Bank's own discretion to set and change the, amount of fees and commissions for operations.

VII. VALIDITY OF THE AGREEMENT

    7.1.   The present Agreement comes in force from the moment of its singing by the Parties hereto and shall remain in force within unlimited period of time.

VIII. TERMINATION PROCEDURE

    8.1. Termination of the Agreement shall be documented in the form of an agreement signed by authorized representatives of the Parties. Termination of the Agreement is considered to be sufficient reason for closing the Client's account.

    8.2. The Bank hereby undertakes to transfer the balance from the Client's account to the account advised to the Bank by the Client beforehand. In the event the Bank is not informed of the account number, the amount shall be transferred to non-interest-bearing Bank deposit.

X. LEGAL ADDRESSES OF THE PARTIES

BANK: **CLIENT:**

Bank "Saint Petersburg" PLC   _____

191011 Saint Petersburg   _____

7 Ostrovsky Square   _____

MFO 044030732   _____

correspondent account # 700161932   _____

sub-correspondent account # 732911401

Settlement account in TSRKTS of the Head Office of the   #_____

Central Bank for Saint Petersburg

In Bank "Saint Petersburg" PLC

"_____" _____ 1997   "_____" _____1997

        Seal   Seal

For settlements with foreign customers, the following rules of instruction are used:

- Uniform Customs and Practice for Documentary Credits, commonly referred to as a Standby Letter of Credit, a Letter of Credit or simply an LC, which was published by the International Commercial Chamber, No. 500 in 1993.
- Uniform Rules for Collections, which was issued by the International Commercial Chamber in 1995 and enforced in 1996.

A L/C is an agreement between a corporation, or Applicant and an Issuing Bank, who acts on either its own behalf or of the applicants to:

- make a payment to the order of a third party or Beneficiary, or to accept and pay bills of exchange drawn by the Beneficiary
- authorize another bank to effect such payment, or to accept and pay such bills of exchange
- authorize another bank to negotiate against the stipulated document, provided that the terms and conditions of the LC are complied with.

LC's can be revocable or irrevocable. A revocable LC may be changed or canceled, where the irrevocable LC cannot. Early in the transformation of the Russian economy, Letter's of Credit were rarely used because they were very complicated and, for the buyers, part of the money was needed in advance. Originally, the most widespread form of payment in Russia was the payment settlement known as collection.

Collection Instructions

All documents sent for collection must be accompanied by a collection instruction, which indicates that the collection is subject to URC 522 and is giving complete and precise instructions. Banks are only permitted to act upon the instructions given in such collection instruction. Bank's will not examine documents in order to obtain instructions. Unless otherwise authorized in the collection instruction, banks will disregard any instructions from any party or bank other than those from whom they received the collection. This collection instruction should contain the following items of information, as appropriate:

- Details of the bank from which the collection was received including full name, postal and SWIFT addresses, telex, telephone, facsimile numbers and reference.
- Details of the principal or benefactor including full name, postal address, and if applicable telex, telephone and facsimile numbers.
- Details of the drawee or payor, including full name, postal address, or the domicile at which presentation is to be made and if applicable telex, telephone and facsimile numbers.

- Details of the presenting bank, if any, including full name, postal address, and if applicable telex, telephone and facsimile numbers.
- Amount(s) and currency(ies) to be collected.
- List of documents enclosed and the numerical count of each document.
- Terms and conditions upon which payment and/or acceptance is to be obtained.
- Terms of delivery of documents against:
    - a. payment or acceptance
    - b. other terms and conditions
- Charges to be collected, indicating whether they may be waived or not.
- Interest to be collected, if applicable, indicating whether it may be waived or not, including:
    - a. rate of interest
    - b. interest period
- basis of calculation (for example, 360 or 365 days in a year) as applicable.
- Method of payment and form of payment advice.
- Instructions in case of non-payment, non-acceptance or the non-compliance with other instructions.

If the address of the drawee is incomplete or incorrect, the collecting bank may, without any liability and responsibility on its part, endeavor to ascertain the proper address and will not be liable for any ensuing delay.

Presentation

Presentation is the procedure whereby the presenting bank makes the documents available to the drawee as instructed. The collection instructions should state the exact period of time within which any action is to be taken by the drawee. The documents are to be presented to the drawee in the form in which they are received with the banks authorized notary stamp. This is done at the expense of the party from whom the collection is received, unless otherwise instructed.

For the purpose of giving effect to the instructions of the principal, the remitting bank will utilize the bank nominated by the principal as the collecting bank. In the absence of such nomination, the remitting bank will utilize any bank of its own, or another bank's choice in the country of payment or acceptance. This can be in another country where other terms and conditions have to be complied with as stated in the documents.

The documents and collection instructions may be sent directly by the remitting bank to the collecting bank, or through another bank as an intermediary. If the remitting bank does not nominate a specific presenting bank, the collecting bank may utilize a presenting bank of its own choice.

Sight/Acceptance

In the case when documents are payable at sight, the presenting bank must make presentation for payment without delay. In the case when documents are payable at a tenor other than sight, the presenting bank must, where acceptance is called for, make presentation for acceptance without delay, and where payment is called for, make presentation for payment not later than the appropriate maturity date.

Release of Commercial Documents
Against Acceptance (D/A) and Against Payment (D/P)

Collections should not contain bills of exchange payable at a future date, with instructions that commercial documents are to be delivered against the payment. If a collection contains a bill of exchange payable at a future date, the collection instruction should state whether the commercial documents are to be released to the drawee against acceptance (D/A), or against payment (D/P). In the absence of such statement, the commercial documents will be released only against payment.

If a collection contains a bill of exchange payable at a future date, and the collection instruction indicates that commercial documents are to be released against payment, the documents will be released only against such payment.

Where the remitting bank instructs that either the collecting bank or the drawee is to create documents, whether bills of exchange, promissory notes, trust receipts, letters of undertaking or other documents that were not included in the collection, the form and wording of such documents shall be provided by the remitting bank. Otherwise, the collecting bank shall not be liable or responsible for the form and wording of any such document provided by the collecting bank or the drawee.

Documents vs. Goods/Services/Performances

Goods should not be despatched directly to the address of a bank, or consigned to or to the order of a bank, without prior agreement on the part of that bank. When the bank agrees to have goods despatched directly to the address of a bank or consigned to or to the order of a bank, for release to a drawee against payment or acceptance, all aspects must be written with prior agreement on the part of that bank. Such bank shall have no obligation to take delivery of the goods. The goods in this case, remain at the risk and responsibility of the party despatching the goods.

The banks have no obligation to take any action in respect of the goods, which a documentary collection relates, including storage and insurance.

This applies even when specific instructions are given to do so. Nevertheless, in the case that banks take action for the protection of the goods, whether instructed or not, they assume no liability or responsibility with regarded to the fate or condition of the goods. Also, the banks are not responsible for any acts or omissions on the part of any third parties entrusted with the custody or protection of the goods. However, the collecting bank must advise without delay to the bank from which the collection instructions were received, of any such action taken.

Any charges or expenses incurred by the banks in connection with any action taken to protect the goods, will be received from the account of the party from whom they received the collection.

Responsibility for Acts of an Instructed Party
Banks utilizing the services of another bank or other banks, for the purpose of giving effect to the instructions of the principal, do so for the account and at the risk of that principal. Banks assume no liability or responsibility should the instructions they transmit not be carried out, even if they have themselves taken the initiative in making the choice of the other bank(s).

Responsibility on Documents Received
Banks must determine that the documents received appear to be as listed in the collection instruction and must advise by telecommunication or, if that is not possible, by other expeditious means without delay, the party from whom the collection instruction was received of any thing missing or additional items not listed. Banks have no further obligations in this respect.

Payment
Amounts collected, less charges, disbursements, and expenses where applicable, must be made available without delay to the party from whom the collection instruction was received in accordance with the terms and conditions of the collection instructions.

Payment with rubles
Payment by the presenting bank must, unless otherwise instructed in the collection instruction, release the documents to the drawee against payment in rubles. This is only if enough rubles are immediately available for disposal in the manner specified in the collection instructions.

Payment with Foreign Currency
In the case of documents payable in a currency other than that of Russia, the presenting bank must, unless otherwise instructed in the collection instruction, release the documents to the drawee against payment in the

162

designated foreign currency only if such foreign currency can immediately be remitted as required.

Partial Payments
In respect to clean collections, partial payments may be accepted on the conditions on which partial payments are authorized by the law. The financial documents will be released to the drawee only when full payment thereof has been received. In respect to documentary collections, partial payments will only be accepted if specifically authorized in the collection instructions. However, unless otherwise instructed, the presenting bank will release the documents to the drawee only after full payment has been received.

Interest
If the collection instructions specify that interest is to be collected and the drawee refuses to pay such interest, the presenting bank may deliver the documents against payment or acceptance, or on other terms and conditions as the case may be without collecting such interest. This applies except when the collection instructions expressly states that interest payment may not be waived. If the drawee refuses to pay in this case, the presenting bank will not deliver the documents and will not be responsible for any consequences arising out of any delay in the delivery of the documents. When payment of interest has been refused, the presenting bank must inform by telecommunication or by other expedient means the bank from which the collection instructions were received. Where interest is to be collected, the collection instructions must specify the rate of interest, the interest period, and the basis of calculation.

Charges and Expenses
If the collection instructions specify that collection charges or expenses are to be charged to the account of the drawee, and the drawee refuses to pay them, the presenting bank may deliver the documents against payment or acceptance or on other terms and conditions as the case may be. Unless, where the collection instructions expressly state that the charges or expenses may not be waived, and if the drawee refuses to pay the charges, the presenting bank will not deliver the documents and will not be responsible for any consequences arising out of any delay in their delivery. When payment of collection charges or expenses has been refused, the presenting bank must inform the bank from which the collection instructions were received.

Whenever collection charges or expenses are waived, they will be charged to the account of the party from whom the collection was received and may be deducted from the proceeds.

In all cases where in the express terms of a collection instruction or under the Rules, disbursements, expenses and collection charges are to be borne by the principal, the collection bank(s) are entitled to recover promptly outlays in respect to disbursements, expenses and charges from the bank from which the collection instructions were received. Also, the remitting bank is entitled to recover promptly from the principal any amount so paid out by it, together with its own disbursements, expenses and charges, regardless of the fate of the collection.

Banks reserve the right to demand payment of charges and expenses in advance from the party from whom the collection instructions are received. This payment is used to cover costs in attempting to carry out any instructions. Pending receipt of the payment also entitles the banks to not carry out collection instructions.

UNIT 7

Securities Markets in Russia

Introduction

This unit describes the Russian securities market in the words of Russian bankers, from a Russian perspective, so that readers with an international vocabulary can understand and identify the references being made to concepts they are familiar with in their country, but which are being described in terms unfamiliar to them. Therein lies its usefulness.

Three blind men described an elephant by touching it. One felt the tail and said and elephant is like a rope. One felt the trunk and said an elephant is like a tree. One felt the body and said an elephant is like a wall. It requires vision to see the same thing in the same way, as it is in its entirety.

While the market may be more an activity than an object, there is no confusion about its objectives. While we may pursue cultural variations of "creative accounting," it is no coincidence that our differing languages and alphabets utilize the same Arabic numerals.

Nevertheless, it is important to understand the semantic meaning of what we are saying to each other, so our interpretation and conclusions remain consistent and compatible. This unit contributes to that objective by presenting the thought process behind the development of Russia's securities markets and the terminology employed in describing financial functions. To the careful reader it makes clear that the functions which are described, are identical to their economies and that only the designations vary according to local custom. Our objectives and methods remain uniform. In our own way we are all talking about the same thing. There is nothing to correct. There is only something to grasp and understand.

When we do that:

"debt receivables" become "account receivables"
"records the right" turns into "grants the right"
"determination of mutual obligations," becomes "settling accounts"
"special funds" become "sinking fund reserves"
"keeping" becomes "maintaining"
"constituent documents" become "articles of incorporation"

"self-government body" becomes "a privately owned business"
"professional securities market-maker" becomes "an NASD broker-dealer firm"
"civil-law transactions" becomes "brokerage"
"debt" becomes "deficit"
"civilized manner" becomes "plan of action"
"Control of" becomes "Management of"
"Orientation" becomes "viewpoint"
"controlling body" becomes "the organization"
"demands" become "regulations" or "by-laws"
"lay down the rules" becomes "agree on procedures"
"broken into" becomes "subdivided into"
"on the Investor's possessing no right" becomes " limiting the Dealer's right"
"day of redemption" becomes "maturity"
"non-competitive bids" become "a firm offer"
"the amount of the basic debt" become "face value"
"hierarchy" becomes "management chart"
"higher controlling bodies" become "levels of authority"
"bear obligations" becomes "exercise authority"
"a scheme" becomes "a loophole for tax avoidance"
"profitability of the shares" becomes "rising stock market"
"problem of non-payments" becomes "overdue accounts receivable"
"redeem loans" becomes "repay debts"
"turnover" becomes "trading volume"
"benefit from inflation" becomes "avoid inflation"
"avoided losses" or "previous non-payment is made comparatively easy"
becomes "recover losses with other earnings"
"serious projects" becomes "positive cash flow"
"convenient" becomes "logical"
"capital" becomes "a loan"
"foreign currency corridor" becomes "fixed schedule of declining FOREX value"

Russian command of the English language is not the culprit in these seemingly differing interpretations of fact. Any economy which has not possessed a market for 70 years does not possess an equivalent vocabulary for market concepts. In a real sense Russians must *adopt* English vocabularies of concepts for which the Russian language will not have a corresponding concept. In a real sense a Russian language is being developed for market concepts. This new Russian vocabulary has no choice but to search for English language vocabulary that seems to correspond, without access to the historical development of English language as it was ultimately applied to the development of securities markets.

This book and particularly this unit demonstrates that we all mean the same thing even when we are saying it differently, and that there is no difference in ideology. Rather the difference lies in semantics which can be cured by definitions. They do not require changes in economic mechanisms.

In that sense, this book will be an eye-opener for international investment bankers as they visit with Russian bankers on these pages. If it serves this function, it should shorten the length of negotiating time for all parties.

Chapter 7.1

Overview of the Securities Markets in Russia

The securities markets performs two functions. The first, to provide flexible conditions for allocation of capital and the mobilization of investors money for the development of profitable industries, creating competition through choices in supply sources. The second, the mobilization of private money for temporary use by the state and privately owned companies.

Before the 1917 October Revolution, the securities market in Russia was very diversified. The Bolshevik government, led by Lenin, in February, 1918, abolished all securities. There were 87 different Russian bonds and 13 different foreign bonds. Today, the Russian government has begun to pay for many of those which were confiscated. For example, in Russia many of the bonds were issued to pay for the railway. The old debts of the Russia government are slowly beginning to be repaid by the present government, a sign of integrity.

Around 1921, "Lenin's New Economic Policy" introduced the issuance of government bonds for bread and sugar. During the 1922-1957 period, the Russian government issued 60 different types of bonds. The general population was not interested in buying these bonds, and the government sold them by means of a mandatory decree. In 1957, the government, led by Khrushchev, declared a 20 years moratorium on the repayment of these bonds. But, not until 1991, nearly 34 years later, did the government repay these obligations. Considering inflation the amount paid was a fraction of the original value of the bonds when originally issued.

In December 1990, the government passed a law defining the concepts of securities circulation in Russia, thereby recognizing the public's right to buy and sell securities, and conduct other related activities, and establishing the basis for a free exchange of securities by owners. During the period from 1991-1995, the securities market in Russia functioned without regulation, but the Ministry of Finance and the Central Bank recognized that the public interest required regulation of securities transactions. Not until early 1996, did the Duma and Federal Council pass laws regulating the securities industry. The following excerpts from these laws are provided with some explanation.

The law declared the structure of regulator jurisdiction of the securities market in Russia, which is very similar to that in Western countries and corresponds to prevailing international customary practices. The Federal Commission of the Russian Securities Market (FCRSM), was established as the legislative and executive regulatory commission of the securities market.

The FCRSM is a federal agency which regulates the securities industry, and establishes standards of conduct for the activities of brokers, traders and over market-makers. and sets guidelines for the issuance of securities and related disclosures. The head of the FCRSM reports to the Ministry of Finance. The FCRSM is called upon to establish administrative agencies to perform its functions throughout the territory of its jurisdictions. The authority of the FCRSM does not extend to issuance of debt instruments of the Russian Government or of securities of the Russian people.

The Federal Commission shall make administrative decisions about the regulation of the securities market, the activity of those engaged in the industry, of self-regulating professional organizations, and about conformity to the regulations of the Russian legislature and their administrative actions relating to securities. The FCRSM also adopts its decisions in the form of resolutions.

The securities market consists of different types of instruments. A "share" is a security that establishes certain property rights of its owner (shareholder) to the receipt of a part of the profit of a joint-stock company, when declared and distributed in the form of dividends, in participation in the management of the joint stock company, by means of a shareholder vote, and to a pro-rated share of the property that is distributed at the time of liquidation. The issuance of shares to the bearer is permitted in a definite ratio to the amount of the paid-up authorized capital of the issuer in conformity with the norm fixed by the Federal Commission for the Securities Market.

A "bond" is a security that evidences the right of its holder to receive payment of its designated face/par value at the date of maturity provided for therein, together with the payment of interest as stipulated. A bond may provide any additional property rights to its holder that is not specifically prohibited by law.

"Clearing" means the determination and resolution of the obligations of buyer and seller such as payment collection and disbursement, review and correction of information relating to securities transactions and the preparation of accounting records relating to them, and the physical delivery of securities and payments for them. The clearing organization which makes payments for securities transactions shall be obliged to form special accounts and reserves to reduce the risk of co-mingling of funds and non-fulfillment relating to securities transactions.

Persons engaged in maintaining the stock register of securities owners are called "registrars" of securities. The keeping of the register of securities owners shall include the collection, establishment, processing, storage and preservation of all data comprising the record of the maintaining the register of securities owners. Only legal companies have the right to maintain the register of securities owners. A legal company that maintains the register of securities owners, recorded in the register of the issuer, shall have no right to engage in securities transactions.

A Stock Exchange is a trading organization for the marketing of stocks which, in order to be recognized as such, may not combine the function of marketing any other kinds of commodity, with the exception of acting as a stock depository and defining activity transactions settlement procedures. A stock exchange shall be set up in the form of a non-commercial partnership. The stock exchange shall limit trading activity to the trading transactions conducted between the members of the stock exchange. Other participants in the securities market may conduct transaction on the stock exchange exclusively through the mediation of the members of the stock exchange only.

Securities may be issued in one of the following forms:
• Registered securities of documentary issue
• Registered securities of non-documentary issue
• Securities to bearer of documentary issue

The form of securities chosen by the issuer shall be unambiguously determined in its articles of incorporation or by its decision on the issue of securities and by its issue prospectus. An issuer is a corporation or an instrumentality of government that assumes obligations, on its own behalf, to the owners of securities. The brokerage of securities implies the completion of civil-law transactions with securities by the broker as agent, acting on the basis of a contract or commission, and also on the strength of a power of attorney for the consummation of such transactions.

A dealer is the professional securities seller or purchase whose activity is the completion of contracts on one's own behalf and at one's own expense, by announcing to the public the prices at which he is prepared to make purchases or sale of securities.

A depository is a professional securities custodian engaged in the business of rendering securities certificates and the record-keeping for securities and the transfer of ownership rights to them. Only a corporation may be a depositary. The contract, concluded between the depositary and the depositor, which regulates their relations in the conduct of depositary custodianship activity, is called a depositary contract which is concluded in written form. The depositary is obliged to endorse the terms and conditions of the depositary activity, which becomes an integral part of the concluded depositary contract.

170

Chapter 7.2

Government Short-Term Bonds

Before 1992, the Russian budget contained a very large deficit. The deficit was covered by printing money, which was the cause of run-away inflation. Beginning in 1993, the Russian government began their first attempt to cover the deficit through the sales of debt securities in a manner similar to the past practices of other nations. The Russian government, at that time, began to issue short-term bonds to obtain financing to cover their budget deficit.

When the first government short-term bonds where issued, several goals were achieved, including the following:
- Utilization of idle money in the hands of Russian banks, businesses, and individuals.
- Modification of the rate of inflation through reduction in the amount of cash emissions placed in circulation by the government's printing of bank-notes.
- Stabilization and support of the ruble.
- Finance the deficit of the annual budget with loans obtained by selling securities as a substitute for emissions.
- Provide those engaged in investing money in securities with an investment instrument offering a rate of return competitive with other available options.
- Formally recognize politically the basic right to earn interest on privately owned capital.
- Establish and promote the development of an infrastructure and framework for a national securities market.

Government bonds are issued by the Ministry of Finance on behalf of Russia. The maturity dates of the bonds were Initially three months, but were later extended to six months and ultimately to one year.

In this segment of the securities industry in Russia there are several participants which interact. The most important participant is the Central Bank. The functions of the Central Bank on the Bond Market are as follows:
- as an Agent of the Ministry of Finance, involved in servicing Bond issues
- as the Dealer
- as the regulatory commission
- as the paymaster for cash settlements on the bonds

In performing the functions of the Agent of the Ministry of Finance, in servicing of the Bond issues, the Central Bank shall:

- Define the rules and regulations to be promulgated to the Trade System, Settlements Centers of the Securities Market and the Depositary System
- Sign agreements with organizations for the performance of the functions of those systems
- Define the regulations applicable to the Dealers, as well as the criteria for selecting the Dealers (usually commercial banks) and for their numerical composition.
- Sign contracts with organizations for performing the functions of the Dealers
- Establish the rules for the holding auctions and actually holding the auctions to sell Bonds on the primary market
- Effect, on the orders of the Ministry of Finance, additional sales of Bonds on the secondary market, those which have not been sold during the initial offering
- Effect, the redemption of the Bonds, in accordance with the instructions of the Ministry of Finance, on the day of redemption.

While performing the functions of the Dealer, the Central Bank shall:

- Possess the rights of the Dealer and the right to sign the corresponding contracts through the Chief Boards (the National Banks)
- Effect the sale of the Bonds on the secondary market by announcing the bids for the purchase and for the sale of the Bonds during the bidding
- Collect the bids of the bidders for the purchase of, or for the sale of, Bonds on the primary and secondary markets and execute these bids through the Trading System

While performing the functions of the controlling body, the Central Bank shall:

- Exert control over the flotation and the circulation of the Bonds
- Obtain information on the progress of the bidding for the sale of the Bonds offered to the Trading System, determine the remaining bonds on the deposit accounts of the Dealers in the Depositary and on the movement of money in the accounts in the Trading System
- Obtain information on the state of the deposit accounts in the Sub-depositary of every Dealer
- Suspend a Dealer's transactions with the Bonds, if a violation occurs with the currently applicable legislation.

The Central Bank performs the function of the organizer of monetary settlements by the deals with the Bonds. Participants in the government Bonds market are divided into the following categories: the Issuer, Dealer and Investor. The infrastructure of the market shall consist of the Depositary System, the Settlements System, and the Trade System. The Issuer shall be the Ministry of Finance. A corporation, which is in the investment business, and is defined as a professional participant in the securities market, is called the Dealer.

A Dealer may effect Bond transactions for his own account and at his own expense, at the expense and on the orders of an Investor.

A person, who is not the Dealer, and who acquires the Bonds by the right of ownership or by another legal right, including the right of trusteeship control, and who has the right to possess the Bonds, is called the Investor.

In order to exercise this right, the Investor is required to conclude a contract with the Dealer, which shall define the procedure for effecting transactions with the Investor's deposit account and also the procedure for documenting the ownership rights to the Bonds in this account. This contract provides that the Dealer's right at effecting the transactions with the Investor's deposit account are strictly limited to transactions which are directly related to the purchase and sale of such Bonds.

In order to facilitate the transfer of title to the Bonds, as well as to register the transactions, a registration code shall be issued to every Dealer and Investor.

The Depositary System is an aggregate of organizations, authorized, by virtue of contracts with the Central Bank, to provide for recording the transfer of owner's rights to the Bonds, and also for the transfer of the Bonds to the deposit accounts during the purchase and sale transactions. The Depositary does not perform the Dealer's or the Investor's functions on the Bonds market.

The Settlement System is an aggregate of the Settlement Centers of the Securities Industry and of the Settlement Subdivisions of the Central Bank, which provides for effecting settlements of the money, involved in Bond transactions.

A Settlement Subdivision of the Central Bank is a regional branch of the Bank and the structural subdivision of the Bank, which is authorized by it to make payment settlement based upon the results of the tenders on the Bonds market.

A Trading System is an organization, authorized, on the basis of a contract with the Central Bank, to provide for the procedure for making transactions, involved in the purchase and sale of Bonds. A Trading System does not have the right to perform the Dealer's or the Investor's functions on the Bond market. A Trading System organizes the execution of transactions on the primary and secondary markets; calculates the Dealer's positions, compiles the settlement documents for consummated transactions and presents them to the

Settlement Systems and to the Depositary.

An organization, performing the functions of a Trading System, sets up a permanently functioning tribunal, or arbitrators, in conformity with the rules it establishes for the purpose of conduction examinations of disputes which may arise between the Dealer, the Trading System, the Settlement System, or the Depositary System.

The payment settlements of Investors in Bond transactions are effected exclusively through Dealers. The payment settlements of Dealers in Bond transactions are effected on a cash-less basis, only through the Settlement Centers of the Securities Industry and are effected through the Settlement Subdivisions of the Central Bank.

Bonds distribution are only made for consummated sale and purchase transactions, including pledged bonds sale transactions, through Trading systems. The offering of the Bond issues are carried out by the Central Bank at the direction of the Ministry of Finance in the form of an auction, held in the Trading System. The redemption of the Bonds shall be effected on the day of redemption in the Trading System, before the start of a tender or of an auction.

Within the infrastructure of the auction framework the Trading System records, in addition to competitive bids, the non-competitive ones as well. The competitive bid is regarded as the Buyer's offer to the Central Bank for concluding a purchase and sale contract for the Bonds on the terms, indicated in the bid. The non-competitive bids shall be regarded as the Buyer's offer to the Bank for signing a purchase and sale contract for the Bonds at terms of an average weighted price produced by the auction.

Concurrently, with the circulation of government short-term bonds, there is an issuance and distribution of the Bonds which finance federal loans. The Ministry of Finance acts as the issuer of the federal loan bonds on behalf of the Russian government. The total volume of the emission of the federal loan bonds is determined by the Ministry of Finance within the limits for national internal debt, established by federal law with respect to the federal budget for the applicable fiscal year. The emission of the federal loan bonds is carried out in the form of individual issues.

The holders of federal loan bonds may be either individuals or companies that, according to government legislation, may be either residents or non-residents, unless otherwise provided for by the conditions of the individual issue of the federal loan bonds.

A holder of a federal loan bond shall have the right to be paid the amount of the face value upon maturity, and also to receive, in accordance with the conditions of the issue, a yield in the form of interest added to the nominal value.

The redemption payments for federal loan bonds shall be made through the Central Bank and its regional offices, and also through other credit organizations in either cash or credit on account. The interest income paid on these transactions in 1995 equalled 10.6 trillion rubles. The interest rate on the federal bonds varies and is determined by the prevailing market rate of corresponding short-term bonds.

Chapter 7.3

Stock Market

In Russia's transition from a totalitarian command market to a democratic free market system, there is a need to encourage the development of personal initiative. This transition requires the transfer of at least a significant part of communal government property to private ownership. Under the pre-1993 constitution, all national resources of the country belonged to everybody - to all people. In other words everything belonged to everybody in general, but to nobody in particular. Citizens owned only particular personal effects and, only to a very insignificant extent, the tools of production. Even citizens occupied in craft industries had no right to hire employees.

In the name of all people, the country's resources, processes of material production, and services were managed in a fiduciary capacity by government employees. This management's organization chart operated from the top, consisting of the national ministries, down to supervisors in all commercial organizations such as manufacturing, plants, shops, universities, and hospitals. Every employee at the lower level strictly obeyed the directives of employees at higher levels. Business initiatives differing from specific commands had to be approved by higher management, all the way up to government officials located great distances from the point of activity. And only after their approval, was it possible to carry out an initiative. This system led to unprecedented bureaucracy, irresponsibility, and corruption. A system which eventually brought economic crisis.

Free market relations are not compatible with such a system. To create the basis of a market economy and the conditions for effective material production, it was first needed to develop a large class of owners. This was only possible by transferring state property to personal property, i.e. the "privatization process." The main goal of privatization is to increase the effectiveness of enterprise activity by transferring it from state ownership to private ownership.

The process of privatization began in 1992, and continues still, and today most enterprises and their property belong to private companies. The legal guidelines for a new private company in the form of a joint-stock company are now well established. Following are important aspects of the June 13, 1996 additions and amendments to the Federal Laws of December 26, 1995, which have established these guidelines even further:

- A joint-stock company is a commercial organization whose charter capital is divided into a defined number of shares of stock and which has organization documents setting forth the rights and obligations of the shareholders in the company, to the company.
- Shareholders are not liable for obligations of the company, but shall bear the risk of losses associated with its activity to the extent of the value of shares of stock owned by them.
- Shareholders who have not fully paid for subscribed stock are jointly liable for the obligations of the company to the extent of the unpaid portion of the value of shares of stock subscribed by them.
- A company is a legal entity existing in contemplation of law; it owns separate assets in its name which are reported in a balance sheet and it may, in its own name, acquire property and property rights, incur obligations, and be a plaintiff or defendant in legal procedures.
- A company has civil rights and possess all the attributes required to pursue any types of activity not prohibited.
- A company is considered to be created as a legal entity upon its registration according to the procedure established by federal laws.
- A company has perpetual existence unless otherwise provided for by its charter.
- A company has the right to open bank accounts in Russian territory and beyond, according to established procedures.
- A company may be open or closed, as reflected in its charter and company name.

The shareholders of an open company may dispose of the stock owned by them without the consent of their fellow share holders. Such a company has the right to hold open subscriptions to the stock it is issuing and sell such stock without limitations, subject to the requirements of Russian Law and other statutory acts. An open company also has the right to hold closed subscriptions to the stock it is issuing, except for instances when the possibility of holding closed subscriptions is limited by either the charter of the company or the requirements of statutory acts. Finally, the number of shareholders of an open company are not limited.

When stock is only distributed among a companies founders or another previously determined classifications of persons is deemed a closed company. Such a company may not hold open subscriptions to the stock it is issuing, or offer that stock for acquisition to an unlimited number of persons. The number of shareholders of a closed company does not exceed fifty.

A company may be formed by being founded and registered as a new company or by means of the reorganization of an existing legal entity through merger, acquisition, division, divestiture, or restructuring. The charter of a company shall be the foundation document of the company. All company bodies and company shareholders shall comply with the requirements of this charter. The charter of a company must contain the following information:

- the full and abbreviated names of the company
- the location of the company
- the type of company, whether open or closed
- the number of shares placed in the company, along with their par value and category (common/preferred, voting/non-voting, participating/non-participating, cumulative/non-cumulative, convertible/non-convertible, cumulative/non-cumulative)
- the rights of the shareholders in each category
- the amount of the charter capital of the company
- the composition and authority of the governing bodies of the company and the procedure for the adoption of resolutions
- the procedure for the preparation and conducting of the general meeting of shareholders, including decisions on matters to be resolved by a qualified majority or a unanimous vote of the governing bodies of the company
- information concerning branches and representative offices of the company

The company's charter may impose limits on the quantity and total par value of stock held, or the maximum number of votes cast by any one shareholder. It may also contain other provisions which are not contrary to Federal Law.

The charter capital of a company comprises the par value of the company stock acquired by its incorporators. The par value of all common stock of the company must be identical. The charter capital of a company determines the minimum amount of company property guaranteeing the interests of its creditors. A company has the right to issue common stock, and also one or several types of preferred stock. The par value of the authorized preferred stock must not exceed 25 percent of the charter capital of the company. When founding a company, all of its stock must be placed among the founders, and must be inscribed.

The quantity and par value of shares acquired by the founders, usually referred to as the incorporator's shares, must be determined by the charter of the company. An additional quantity of shares which the company is authorized to supplement the incorporator's shares, may be determined by the company charter. The option rights granted to each category of shares which it issues must be set forth in the charter of the company.

The charter capital of a company may be increased by increasing the par value of shares or by issuing additional shares of stock. The charter capital of a company may be decreased by lowering either the par value of the stock or the total quantity of shares outstanding, including the acquiring or re-purchase of some stock as treasury stock under the circumstances provided for by the Federal Law. A decrease of the charter capital of a company by acquiring and canceling some of the stock is permitted, if such action has been provided for in the company charter.

Each class of the common stock of a company grants identical rights to its holder. In the general meeting of shareholders, holders of voting classes of shares vote on all matters within its authority, and also have the right to receive declared dividends. In instances of the companies liquidation, they also have the right to receive a pro-rated share of its assets. Holders of non-voting shares of a company, however, have no right to vote at a general meeting of its shareholders.

A reserve fund in the amount provided for in the charter of the company, but not less than 15 percent of its charter capital, is created in Russian companies. A company's reserve fund is accumulated by means of obligatory annual deductions until the amount established by the company charter is achieved. These annual deductions provided for in the company charter may not be less than 5 percent of the net after-tax profits, until the amount established by the company charter is attained.

The reserve fund is earmarked to cover of operating losses, and for the redemption of company bonds and the purchase of company stock in the event of the absence of other means. The reserve fund may not be used for other purposes.

The company charter may provide for the formation of a special fund for company employees from the net after-tax profits. These assets are used exclusively for the acquisition of company stock to be sold by the shareholders for subsequent issue to its workers.

The payment for stock is carried out at market value, but not less than par value. The paying up of company stock, when it is founded, is made by its founders at par value. The company has the right to issue stock at prices lower than market value in the following instances:

- The issuance of additional common stock to existing shareholders in the exercise of their preemptive right to acquire this stock at a price which may not be lower than 90 percent of its market value.
- The issuance of additional stock with the participation of an intermediary at a price which may not be lower than its market value by more than the amount of remuneration to the intermediary as established in a percentage correlation to the price of the original issuance of the stock.

A company has the right to once a quarter, once each six months, or once a year to declare the payment of dividends on issued stock, unless otherwise provided for by the Federal Law and the charter of the company. The company is obliged to pay the dividends declared for each classification of stock. These dividends are paid in money, and, in the instances provided for by the charter of the company, by other assets. Dividends are paid from the net after-tax profits of the company's current year.

A company has the right to acquire stock issued by it, through a decision of a shareholders general meeting concerning the decrease of charter capital of the company by means of the acquisition of part of the issued stock for the purpose of reducing the total number of outstanding shares.

The company does not have the right to decrease its charter capital by means of the acquisition of part of its issued stock for the purpose of reducing its total quantity if the par value of the stock remaining in circulation becomes lower than the minimum amount of charter capital.

The company does have the right to acquire its own issued stock by a decision of its board of directors, unless provided otherwise by the Federal Law and by the charter of the company.

The company's board of directors has the right to adopt a decision concerning the acquisition by the company of its own stock, if the par value of the stock in circulation comprises less than 90 percent of the charter capital of the company.

In the normal operations of a stock market, there are two price stages. The first stage, prior to public trading, when the shares are Initially offered, and they are sold to buyers at the offering price. This Initial Public Offering is the most common method of offering shares to the general public. The second stage of operations on the stock market are daily transactions of free market buying and selling the stocks.

For the most part, only the shares of larger companies are currently being publicly traded. These companies are primarily issuing preferred shares. According to the Financial Izvestia Newspaper on January 16, 1997, the following table illustrates the existing market in such stocks:

Figure 28.
The Price of Sample Preferred Stocks from 1995 to 1996
(price in US dollars)

Oil Stocks	12/15/95	12/15/96	Annual Interest
Surgutneftegas	0.023	0.29	1161%
Lukoil	0.9	7.29	783%
Megionneftegas	0.26	2.05	688%
Uganskneftegas	1.05	6.35	505%
Noyabriskneftgas	0.68	3.95	481%
Electricity			
RAO Energasystem	0.009	0.065	622%
Communication			
Moscovskaya ITS	25	400	1500%
Rostelekom	0.12	1.80	1400%
Metal Industry			
Norilskiy Nickel	2.15	2.75	28%

Many of the larger Russian joint-stock companies currently pursue opportunities to offer shares on international markets. To facilitate this they employ the mechanism of American Depository Receipts, or ADA's, as a means of obtaining market acceptance of their shares outside Russia. ADA's indicate to potential investors that the shares exist and are recorded in the rightful owner's name. They also show that a fiduciary custodian exists for the shares, who holds Ada's representing the actual shares. Upon registration of such ADA's with the Securities Exchange Commission, the shares may then be admitted to be traded on the stock exchanges. When either underwriters, investment bankers, or dealers are able to place such shares with investors, it provides a means for the Russian companies to raise needed capital in these international markets.

The U.S. Securities Exchange Commission (SEC) has been supportive of applications of Russian companies for the registrations of ADR's

Chapter 7.4

Corporate Securities

In recent years, there have been many positive influences which have affected the existing situations in the Russian financial markets. The following are some of the more obvious of these influences:

- the results of the 1996 Presidential election
- the inclusion of Russia into the index of the International Financial Corporation
- the successful preparation and issuing of Eurobonds in Western markets
- the general admittance of Russia into the Group of *Eight* leading industrialized nations
- the acceptance of Russia into the Paris Club for Russian government debt re-financing.

Because of the Russian government's policy aimed at the strict control of the currency markets through fixed exchange rates and prevailing interest rates, government securities (GKO) have been high, only recently falling to levels of 35-45%. Lately, the Central Bank's prime lending rate and the commercial bank interest rates for commercial loans have steadily fallen. These events have resulted in lower interest rates paid by banks on deposits. Therefore, potential returns on industry investments are now more competitive as more money has become available for investments in corporate securities.

Approximately 80-90% of portfolio investments in Russian securities are made by international investors, the majority of these made by investment funds located in the United States, clearly the world's largest source of investment capital. Large British investment funds, such as Fleming and Barings, along with a growing number of other international development funds are also investing in Russian securities.

In this present early development stage, international investors providing a market for these shares, are providing a stabilizing influence upon the Russian corporate stock market. A helpful attribute of American investors is their capacity to make quick decisions and their ability to assume risk when the potential rewards are commensurate with that risk, including political risks. They realize that on a long term basis, there will be further corrections in Russian government policy and law that will ultimately convert *possibilities* into *real opportunities*. Knowing that this process will ultimately change a *speculation* into an *investment* has stimulated American participation. In the meantime Western government tax money is being made available to investors to stimulate the process until conditions are created which meet the norms of private capital expectations.

The industries in which international investors of government tax money have found the most attractive are infrastructure projects such as roads, utilities, ports, communications and transportation. Although these industries will offer very little if any short term profit, they are necessary for the profitable functioning of other industries. Meanwhile, real investors of private capital that must conserve their principal and earn a profit on their capital, have chosen those industries with short term profit potential such as oil, gas, chemistry, pharmaceutical, and natural resource development. They have particularly chosen products which are exportable and are produced in quantities greater than domestic consumption needs. This assures that the full market value of these products will be realized in the external markets, so that the value of the products' labor production will also be valued at world market prices. This will make higher Russian wages possible and improve the ability of the Russian population to pay for those things they need to consume to provide for a happy life, similar to that enjoyed by the populations in the more advanced nations. It also assures that external profits can be used to compensate international investors for the use of their capital. This provides an income to the populations of other countries through the capital they invested in Russian industry. Finally, like the Taiwan model, it provides export profits which can be invested in the production of domestic consumer goods, which will become affordable once Russian labor receives higher wages from the export on non-consumer goods and commodities. We must remember that higher wages depend upon such exports

The average daily turnover of the Russian Trading System (RTS) was between $10-$15 million USD in 1996. In October 1996, the monthly turnover volume was $541.4 million USD, but dropped to $391.7 million in November. The number of shares traded dropped once international investors acquired their shares for long term appreciation. This is normal since there was no significant change in either the earnings of the industries in which they had invested in or in their net worth, that would support or justify the major changes in market price, and the related decisions to stop losses or take profits. Accordingly, it was logical to hold on to the positions taken, allowing time for judgment on the future higher values to become evident. Accordingly, companies such as Mosenergo and Megionneftegaz saw their trading volume drop by 75%.

It was also logical that share prices should fall. Many Western investment funds bought shares they knew were overpriced in order to insure that they would not be outperformed by their competitors. The allocation of investment capital to investment funds is made on the basis of their past results. Likewise, money is transferred to different money managers based upon results.

Money managers were afraid that if they did not own Russian securities and they performed very well, their competitors would receive a transfer of capital from investors in their funds, leaving them with less money to manage and less income from such management. Accordingly, they made the decision to risk losses from paying too much, hoping that the Russian companies would perform so well that the higher prices would keep their own performance equal to that of their competitors. In the event of losses resulting from such decisions, all funds would suffer and it would not cost them customers.

This psychological motivation resulted in the participation of many investment funds, who were late buyers. Most of the investment funds were therefore forced to pay inflated prices, due to the limited supply. Once that hysteria was satisfied, an adjustment in the market took place which resulted in the declining value of shares, such as Rao Ees Rossia, which fell by 43% and Gasprom, which dropped 45% of its value.

One reason why the volume of trading has remained relatively stable, is that the capitalization of the 14 major securities constitute 50% of the Russian stock market's overall capitalization. With so few issues to choose from, it is understandable that available investment capital is concentrated on these issues. In such a limited market, availability plays a disproportionate role to value. The most probable reasons for the market's overall side-ways motion, are that:

- the market remains over-bought
- the investment funds have adjusted their portfolios to include some Russian stocks in order to overcome the potential for being outperformed by competitors
- prices are at very high multiples of earnings; many book value assets are still idle and are not as yet producing an ROI
- the potential future ROI on assets has been fully discounted by the market
- the market as a whole has started to show returns of 16% as compared to former performance of 750% annually
- the balance sheets of issuers have not as yet fully reflected their unfunded social, pension, tax and environmental liabilities.

Geometric growth is taking place throughout the Russian economy in the number of stock issuers. The larger national issuers, still partially government owned, have been over-worked and attention is being transferred to regional companies. Production of goods and services is changing and expanding from single government owned monopolies with a single production facility in a centralized location serving the national market, to multiple manufacturers with their production geographically diversified. Current signs of growth in regional companies are giving investors new opportunities to purchase shares in these new companies as private industry starts to develop in the 13 times zones and 89 autonomous regions of Russia. 1996-97 marked a turning point in Russian mentality, in the sense that confidence grew in the ideology of entrepreneurship and privately owned production, as the concept of private trade and production was learned and accepted as a workable way of functioning economically. This has contributed to the viewpoint that securities reflect real ownership in underlying tangible property rather than merely intangible paper speculation.

By autumn of 1996, shares in Sverdlovenergo were appreciating in value by 200% annually. Energy and telephone companies of this type are needed throughout the country to provide essential components of both production and consumption. People want affordable utilities, and through competition, Russia is heading in that direction. An average of these "second tier" stocks, similar to the S&P 500, appreciated 10% in value during the last week of November, 1996, with an average daily turnover of 100,000 shares. Many institutional experts in the banking and financial markets are optimistic and predict 200% growth in these stocks over the next 30 months.

The recent availability and acquisition of accurate information about individual companies and the overall market are fueling investors interest in promising stocks with realistic prospects for income growth. Initially the concern of investors was over the liquidity of these stocks, for they realized that focus was shifting toward more fundamental factors. A number of regional companies have now reached a break-even point. It remains difficult to assess the premium investors are willing to pay for the market liquidity offered by national issuers compared to these regional issues.

Based upon the growth in prices witnessed in 1996, it is becoming evident that many "second rank" regional stocks will soon reach the price levels of the national issuers. The initiative of the NAUFOR Exchange to expand the RTS electronic trading system to include second rank regional stocks is improving liquidity in the second rank markets. All the indications are that there will be continued growth in the depth of the Russian securities market and it's infrastructure.

Historically, it was in 1994 that the development of second rank stocks started. It was then that the growing interest in this level of regional securities was first evidenced. Within the past three years that trend has reached an encouraging level. In 1996, the regional power companies drew close investor attention. Kolenergo, Volgogradenergo, Permenergo, and Cheliabinskenergo stocks have experienced continuous demand. Lesser known companies such as Karelenergo, Pskovenergo, and Lipetskenergo have also received growing attention. The average price gains of these types of securities has been 35.5% annually, and there have been individual incidences of a 600% annually increase. However, the demand for new issues is still significantly lower than the number of issuers who would like to bring their issues to market. Demand remains selective. The facility to sell a stock short is offered by some Western broker-dealers to investors and this has contributed somewhat to the development markets and their liquidity.

The develop of securities markets has occurred across the board in different industrial classifications such as oil and gas processing, as well as chemicals. Those stocks in which a market is maintained and which evidence stable rate of growth in earnings, are of primary interest to investors, and Russian industry needs to concentrate on the fundamental indicators of value such as price:earnings ratios, and book value per share. The Russian market is influenced by international opinion as well as by fundamental values. Recently, when it was reported that a Western expert expressed belief that the market was undervalued, the market responded in the week that followed with a 10% increase in stock prices. By the end of November 1996, Komiinvets prices grew by 38%, Uranskneftegas grew 27%, and Purneftegas rose 21%.

Regional telecommunications have also provided attractive stock price increases. The situation in this market is somewhat different, since this market has only recently emerged, and the price of such stocks has rapidly grown by 40-50%. The average price increases for these stocks have been higher than other markets, at times increasing on average by more than 58% in a three month period. Currently, price levels have cooled down, but there seems to be room for further price increases in these "second rank" stocks. We believe the long term prospects are on the side of higher stock prices for many of these stocks once the fundamentals also increase.

The Ministry of Telecommunications and the Sviazinvest holding company are going to provide technical assistance to regional companies. They have entered into an agreement with Price Waterhouse to create a professional auditing branch specifically for the Russian telecommunications companies. Standard GAAP practices, meeting Western standards, are now being used to prepare the annual reports of these companies. The Ministry of Telecommunications has established a special securities registration department called, Registrator-Sviaz Ltd, which together with the Bank of New York provides securities registration consulting services to Russian tele-communications companies who wish to register ADR's for their issues.

A recent Russian government appraisal of the current level of capitalization in the telecommunications market is between $1.5 and $2 billion USD. After initial public offerings establish an offering price, the market value of these share could be self-boosted upwards to $9 or $10 billion USD. Despite the risks, the upward trend of these smaller stocks has continued, providing stock brokers and individual investors with share price increases.

The primary trading exchanges are located in Moscow and St. Petersburg. Regional exchanges are being formed as well, and local brokerage firms are coming into existence throughout the country. Still, the number of "second rank" stocks offered on the St. Petersburg exchange still number less than 20, and the manner of qualifying for and registering such public offerings of securities is still relatively new to most companies and their management.

It is not a secret to anyone that the biggest portion of syndication of capital to international investors is accomplished by those Russian companies who have registered their corporations "off-shore" within other jurisdictions.

Business activity in Russia is such that capital is constantly being transferred from industrial classifications, in which income and profits are declining, to more profitable industrial classifications of business. One of the most significant factors in determining profits is taxation, which can convert an activity which appears to have attractive potential for profits to a "zero" profit result. Therefore, it would be suicidal to one's own business interests to ignore, whether export or import oriented, the territories and countries that provide minimal profit tax legislation to companies incorporated under their laws. In certain instances, the company simply has to pay a flat rate either monthly or at the end of the year.

As a general rule, in Russia, in circumstances involving international trade, there are large amounts of capital deposited in the offshore bank accounts of Russian companies with their affiliates incorporated in such offshore jurisdictions. These deposits are used to either finance the growth of international sales or for other direct passive investments.

There is no need to describe all of the methods of accumulating offshore capital or the various methods for moving cash out of the country. The most common strategy has as its objective an increase in the company's after-tax profits through careful planning. The following paragraphs further examine capital movement and the principles which apply in Russia to investment management through offshore companies.

Presently, Russia has Taxation Treaties with a number of countries which preclude double taxation. Many of them were signed while the Soviet Union still existed. The most conveniently accessible and interesting of these treaties is the one with Cyprus and the opportunities which this treaty provides to both Russian investors, as well as to the international investors who invest in Russia. This was the first such international double taxation agreement and it is appealing because it does not contain the "offshore clause." This means that there is no limitation which excludes from eligibility those companies registered in both countries, but not carrying out any activity in one of the countries of registration. Although Cyprus is an offshore territory, the Treaty gives unlimited possibilities for international investors to conduct business within Russia from Cyprus even though they are not registered in Russia itself.

Let's analyze a typical arrangement of an investor who invests in Russia. First of all, an off-shore company would be registered in Cyprus to which existing offshore investment capital is transferred. The company can then, with far less bureaucracy than otherwise applicable, open bank accounts in

Russian banks. When such companies are organized for the purpose of investing, they are permitted to open special bank accounts with Russian banks. Those bank accounts of external companies are known as an "I" type. Deposits in such accounts may be invested in shares of Russian partnerships, joint-stock companies and corporations. Such companies may also open "C" type accounts which are committed to investing in Russian municipal securities under binding legal agreements. Generally, for those companies which are not Cypriot corporations, the procedure for opening an account in a Russian bank is complicated by a host of formalities. For example, one of the dozens of documents (which should be certified translated and attested) is the original of a certificate confirming registration with the Russian tax authorities. This is not a requirement for an offshore Cypriot company.

Until very recently, it has not been defined which particular agency among the numerous regional and city tax inspections in Russia, should provide the relevant document to the non-resident companies that are not registered in Russia. To resolve an issue of this type would result in significant legal fees for a non-Cypriot company. When an investment account is opened by Cypriot offshore company, interesting possibilities arise.

Presently Russian stock markets are not exactly booming. There are, however, factors which are conducive to the significant long-term appreciation in shares. For various reasons, the shares of a number of companies might be considered to be undervalued. These may include:

- poor development of public awareness of the existence of the shares
- lack of readily available information about the initial public offering
- delays in physical delivery of certificates between exchanges and their branches
- inexperience of brokers and dealers with the complexities and legal requirements of completing physical delivery of stock certificates

For these reasons there still remain many unsold shares of initial public offerings of securities, which were made at the time that subscription was limited to, and required to be by, a privatization voucher. When these under-priced situations happen to be discovered simultaneously by several investors there can be a significantly higher price movement within the ensuing two to three weeks.

The tax advantages to a Cypriot corporation are self-evident. An investor who is not a non-resident is required to pay taxes on securities profits at a present rate of 35%, as well several additional regional and local taxes. Cypriot corporations pay only 4.25% tax in Cyprus for capital gains earned in the Russian stock market.

Cypriot companies can also freely sell shares for rubles to Russian nationals. Such rubles can then be invested in shares of Russian companies. It is estimated that nearly 95% of all international investment managers and international securities broker-dealer firms who buy Russian securities are doing so through Cypriot companies. This includes for example Credit Suisse Cyprus and CS First Boston Cyprus.

Bahamian incorporation is also very popular among investors that trade in Russian securities. The key reason for this is that the Bahamas is the only significant off-shore territory that has not become a party to those international agreements which disclose confidential and private information about the identity of directors and owners of locally incorporated companies. The concepts of publicly owned companies and public disclosure of activities of companies traded publicly, as compared to the privacy of privately "closely" held corporations, or the concept of bank secrecy, are still unfamiliar to Russians. Off-shore jurisdictions are also frequented by those who wish to launder money and traffic in illegal substances and conduct arms trading.

In those instances where registration in an off-shore jurisdiction (other then Cyprus) is utilized to receive profits from investments, the activities of such companies are not covered by the Double Tax Treaty. Such companies are at a competitive disadvantage when selling shares in Russia for rubles because they are subject to the higher tax rates and they become subject to the jurisdiction of tax inspectors, some of whom are known to be corrupt.

Off-shore corporations, other then in Cyprus, therefore make a practice of selling their shares outside Russia to non-Russians. In this case, the shares are sold abroad, and then the money is being transacted from the Western currency accounts, converted into rubles, and then the process is repeated.

There are limitations on the transferability of shares in this case. The western investor would never be able to sell his shares to a resident of Russia, since for a resident national of Russia, it is still illegal to open bank accounts in banks outside of Russia and pay in foreign currency for goods, services, or securities that are available in Russia. Further the investor's profits, in the form of dividends, would be taxed by an income tax of foreign legal entities. In Russia, most taxes are withheld at the source of payment of the income, so that the earner never sees it.

The above mentioned forms and methods of tax avoidance on investment has become an everyday practice in Russia, just as "tax avoidance" rather than evasion became a normal practice some time ago in Western societies. However, the new changes in Russian business and tax planning is full of unexpected surprises and obstacles which produce growing pains, which therefore, generate revenues for legal advisors and consulting companies.

For example, during the past few years, there has been a significant jump in the price of Russian Sberbank of $20 to $190 per share. Bear in mind that the government still retains ownership of a controlling interest in the shares of Sberbank. While the increase in the price of the shares has been very large, non-residents are not legally permitted to own these shares. The same situation exists with other larger issues, such as RAO Gazprom. Special investment vehicles are still being developed specifically for dealing with such stock issues which relate to 100% international investment company owned entities. However, for Russian residents and the average tax payer, there are methods which reduce the result of these extremely high tax payments, with offsetting high profits.

The rapid evolution of the Russian banking system, as well as the integration of Russian banks into the financial systems of the world, is of course contributing to the attracting and committing of international investment capital. Today no one would be surprised to learn that a Bank in Moscow recently made a loan collateralized by property physically located in Rotterdam. Or, that when a client chooses Incombank to handle the opening of an offshore investment account for him in Cyprus, he will be able to make all transfers to Russia through that bank. Until recently such services would have seemed fantastic, if not impossible.

In Russia, these slow but constant changes sometimes proceed unnoticed. The investment climate could at any time transform into either an investment boom or bust. For those who prefer to pass now and await a further change in climate, Russia may remain an exotic country with a personal pagan approach to everything. For those who jump in now because they sense production is about to take off like a departing train, clearly the Russian market holds the promise of potential profit equal to any other world market. It will take time for Russia's possibilities to be backed by legislation and policies which will permit them to become actual economic opportunities and develop into firm results, such as are now permitted in modern developed exchanges.

Chapter 7.5

Financial Markets

The following review entitled, "St. Petersburg Financial Markets," has been prepared and was dedicated to the International Banking Congress, Saint Petersburg, 4-8 June, 1996, under the title, *"The Condition and Problems of the Development of the Securities Market in Russia."*

Financial Market Structure

The process of creating the St. Petersburg financial market was envisioned during the 1980's and 1990's to become one of the first financial markets in Russia. At present, the region's financial market is very similar in infrastructure and operation to the most important structures and characteristics of any modern financial system.

Banks have been developing channels of capital distribution throughout various regions of Russia. Concurrently, the national financial market is still in its formative stage. Due to these preparations, and the demand for financial services in a country the size of Russia, the largest in the world, recognition of the importance of regional financial markets has been growing.

Today it is possible to speak about the Saint Petersburg financial market as a reality, even though the formation process has not yet been fully completed.

Figure 29.
Financial Market Structure

Deposits	49%
Bank Loans	31%
Money Market Assets	18%
Bonds and Shares	2%

Commercial banks have become the basic financial institutions of this industry. The largest St. Petersburg banks still play the dominant role since they have emerged from the former infrastructure of specialized government owned banks. The number of these bank branches was immense, and some of them have become the largest financial institutions in the region.

In 1992, non-local banks started operating in Saint Petersburg. The city now has the second largest number of non-local bank branches of any Russian city, while having more bank deposits than any other Russian city. St. Petersburg is now the leading Russian banking city in these terms, and has two subsidiaries of international banks located in its limits which are 100% owned by three European banks.

Figure 30.
Percentage of Non-Local Banks on the Regional Market

Saint Petersburg	55%
Moscow	20%

Along with the growing number of commercial banks, a market in foreign exchange has started to form in which St. Petersburg has the second largest volume of any city in Russia. A Stock Market and Over-the-Counter market have been established along with a direct interbank market. Over the past four years, a well-developed infrastructure for trading in foreign currency cash has been created which is served by a wide network of currency exchange offices attached to the banks.

As a consequence of the special role of the Government during the transition period, the stock market has become an essential component of the money market. The Moscow banking industry played the dominant role in the development of the securities market in Government issues. However, the secondary T-bill market - MTB, called short-term bonds in Russia, has also been growing continuously. Not long ago, a trading floor offering Government securities was opened in St. Petersburg. Since last year, the Municipal Treasury Bills market, which is similar to the Government short-term bonds market, has started operating. St. Petersburg Municipal T-bills, have become the most active trading instrument among securities, and several local and non-local institutions have become holders of large amounts of these securities. Past successes in marketing these types of securities has provided the incentive to offer additional emissions of long-term municipal bonds. The possibility of offering Eurobond issues has also been under consideration.

The interbank borrowing market, which deals mainly in interbank loans had been expanding rapidly until the end of summer in 1995. The crisis of the Moscow interbank market in August of 1995, seriously affected the St. Petersburg market. After that crisis, the market was revitalized on a new basis related to a sound financial system where the market's primary function is the provision of bank liquidity. The persistent failure of industry, in general, to pay their accounts payable in a timely manner and the unavailability of account receivables in the industrial and municipal economy, prompted the emergence of public securities offerings by businesses. It would be premature to speak about the factoring market, although its infrastructure has been forming rapidly.

The establishment of these markets surpasses the development of the financial markets as a whole. On the money market, municipal authorities, banks and businesses have been searching for ways to make short-term investments and short term loans while maintaining their own liquidity. The money market consists of Government short-term securities, interbank loans, promissory notes, as well as foreign exchange (FOREX) which traditionally plays an essential role. Local FOREX trading volume exceeds the capacity of the region. Investors from outside the region conduct their trading on the St. Petersburg trading floors. Financial institutions with offices located both inside and outside of Russia are participating in trading on the St. Petersburg exchanges. St. Petersburg ranks second behind Moscow in terms of the number of non-local bank branches. The importance of some non-local and internationally-owned banks engaged in lending and borrowing transactions with regional clients has been growing constantly. Part of the short-term instrument portfolio of local financial institutions results from transactions on the domestic and international financial markets.

Bank Loan Market

Extension of commercial credit implies the existence of solvent borrowers to whom banks can lend funds. Despite the unprecedented industrial recession both in the regional economy and in the whole of the country, a solvent group of borrowers has always existed in Russia. These borrowers have been able to repay loans and to pay interest sometimes running as high three digit numbers. Such capabilities are explained by the large differences in profit margins of various industries. Despite the large number of solvent borrowers in the industrial sectors with fast turnover, on the whole there is not a real local demand for credit. While the percentage of bank loans to local businesses is small, borrowing from banks is the main source of external funds. The St. Petersburg volume of commercial bank lending for external purposes is the second largest in volume in the country.

As evidenced by the improvement in the quality and growth of the size in transactions, the banking industry has, to a large extent, begun to earn interest rates which reflect the ability of the real economy to pay for credits based upon the profit margins in their business. Between 1992 and 1995 there was a steady reduction in interest rates, approximately half in comparison with the previous year. During this same period, the stabilization of the ruble's exchange rate has further reduced the high return on loans to primary borrowers. This trend became apparent during the first half of 1994 when it became clear that real loan demand was much weaker than it seemed to be earlier.

Figure 31.
Structure of Credit Portfolio of the Saint Petersburg Banks
(million rubles)

Loans to Citizens:	150,455
Loans to Banks:	613,374
Loans to Businesses in Foreign Currency:	1,519,017
Loans to Businesses in National Currency:	2,701,573
Loans to Businesses:	4,220,590
Total Credit Portfolio:	4,984,419

Figure 32.
Major Regional Bank Loan Markets
January 1, 1996 (billion rubles)

Regional Market	Total Loans	Short-Term	Long-Term
1. Moscow and Region	32,087	30,944	1,143
2. Saint Petersburg and Region	2,863	2,513	350
3. Samara Region	2,437	2,355	82
4. Tumen Region	2,310	2,237	73
5. Sakha Republic (Yakutia)	2,183	2,036	147
6. Tatarstan Republic	2,174	1,809	365
7. Sverdlovsk Region	1,956	1,931	25
8. Bashkortostan Republic	1,939	1,841	98
9. Krasnodar Region	1,825	1,677	148
10. Nizhegorodsk Region	1,478	1,433	45

Source: "Bulletin of Banking Statistics" N1, 1996

During the years of hyper-inflation previous to 1996, the banking industry had benefitted from that inflation. Nevertheless, by the middle of 1996, loan losses had reached no less than a third of the loan portfolios, or 10% of total bank assets. At first glance, this number was critical, but nevertheless most of the banks managed to recover their loan losses through trading in FOREX where profits in excess of 100% recouped the loan losses.

In 1994, the banks started to control credit risk more strictly by demanding collateral and conducting more intensive analysis of the credit-worthiness of the borrower. The overall decline in industrial production explains why banks have reduced their commercial lending during the past 16 months. Nevertheless, the most important lending activity of banks still remains commercial lending. Since banks have close institutional links with industry, they can exercise considerable monitoring of credit risks, and their large deposit base still makes them the logical source for industry's credit needs.

Lately, banks have once again demonstrated a greater interest in financing sound businesses. Several banks are taking part in ERBD sponsored credit finance programs. By participating in such financing, the banks gain access to EBRD medium and long-term loans that the bank can then use for re-lending. Instances of long-term financing solely by means of equity capital are still rare. As a rule, where equity is involved, it is used in combination with debt financing through the acquisition by banks of a majority ownership stake. This provides time for the development of mutual trust and confidence which is a necessary prerequisite for investment in what remains a new and underdeveloped market place.

Traditionally, a large part of a bank's business comprised of loans denominated in foreign currency. During the period of hyper-inflation that was the only way to make loans at fixed interest rates. Since the summer of 1993, businesses more frequently had to face the phenomena of lag in time between the decline in the value of the ruble, expressed in the official exchange rate, and the rate of internal inflation. Under such circumstance, loans in foreign currency provided "lag shelter" for the bank and was acceptable to borrowers. Borrowers repaid a loan in foreign currency whose purchasing power temporarily lagged but was subsequently recovered when the exchange rate caught up with inflation. Lenders earned much higher net interest, which devaluation ultimately adjusted for inflation. The fixed interest rate on FOREX loans exceeded the prevailing "prime" bank rates worldwide, while all but eliminating devaluation risks. Monetary policy encouraged and led to lending in foreign currency. Since access to foreign currency loans was required by the companies involved in export and import trade, FOREX loans allowed the banks who possessed foreign currency deposit funds, put these deposits to work.

Figure 33.
Market of Lending the Primary Borrowers
(20 Major Credit Banks - Members of ACB)

	Including Loans to Businesses	Asset Share %	Including Population	Asset Share %	IBL	Asset Share %	Total credit Portfolio	Asset Share %
1.PROMSTROIBANK	810474	29	15176	1	87875	3	913525	33
2. S.P. Sberbank	638476	27	53452	2	53192	2	745120	31
3. Bank "St. Petersburg" PLC	602087	38	6036	0	81434	5	689557	44
4. Baltiysky	443328	65	2593	0	7169	1	453090	66
5. BNP-Dresdner Bank Russia	346396	54	16	0	157731	24	504143	78
6. Petrovskiy	300358	38	25216	3	111230	14	436804	56
7. Credit Lyonais Russie	262161	45	7	0	17340	3	279508	47
8. Petroagroprom-bank	238644	50	725	0	7887	2	247256	51
9. Tokobank (branch)	114293	64	7	0	6640	4	120940	68
10. Energomash-bank	95597	37	5206	2	14906	6	115709	44
11. Vitabank	87890	65	2385	2	200	0	90475	67
12. Credobank (branch)	43988	43	610	1	0	0	44598	43
13. Tavrichesky	38971	57	30	0	12650	19	51651	76
14. Export and Import Bank	34176	36	1018	1	300	0	35494	37
15. Ruscobank	19349	18	14999	14	2755	3	37103	34
16. Lenoblsber-bank	25576	4	8073	1	26126	4	59775	9
17. Viking	30175	63	1296	3	1889	4	33360	70
18. Timber Industry Bank	15001	24	6248	10	2464	4	23713	38
19. Bank for Reconstruction and Development	13180	18	387	1	8731	12	22298	31

Figure 34.
The Importance of Lending in Foreign Currency

Loans in Foreign Currency	36%
Loans in National Currency	64%

Bank Deposits Market
The main source of funds for commercial banks are deposits. These deposits are the usual method of obtaining money with which to make loans to businesses, institutions, government authorities and individuals. Funds have been accumulating in various types of bank accounts which differ only in the conditions and forms of funds withdrawn and the rates of interest they earn. On January 1, 1996, total bank deposits aggregated at 3,261 billion rubles. Traditionally, demand deposit bank balances on settlement accounts are an important source of funds. Despite the development of new trends of attracting funds over the past few years, this source of funds remains important. Competing with each other, many banks have started to pay interest on such account balances and to provide a range of new services, such as issuing payroll cards. Nevertheless, the largest banks which offer extensive services find that they can charge fees for the services they provide to their accounts, and still remain competitive.

Figure 35.
Structure of Fund Sources of the St. Petersburg Banks

Businesses Deposits	2%
Loans from Banks	12%
Equity Capital	20%
Settlement Accounts	31%
Individual Deposits	35%

Time deposits refer to the accounts which require depositor notification to the bank as a condition for early withdrawal, and such early withdrawals are subject to the payment of penalties. Since the inflation rate has been several hundred percent annually in the past, time deposits are not attractive. Banks offer depositors a higher interest rate on long-term deposits, but "long-term" is, according to Russian standards, relatively short and deposits with maturity exceeding six months remain rare. The short term of deposits narrows the duration of lending activity that Russian banks can engage in. Since 1992, inflation has twice dropped by 50% annually If this tendency continues, growth of time deposits in banks funds can soon be expected. The highest interest rates are paid for the largest deposits of the longest duration.

Figure 36.
Structure of Fund Sources of Saint Petersburg Sberbanks

Businesses Deposits	0.2%
Banks Loans	0.2%
Settlement Accounts	4.5%
Equity Capital	10.3%
Individual Deposits	84.8%

Figure 37.
Structure of Fund Sources of Saint Petersburg Banks other than Sberbanks

Businesses Deposits	3%
Individual Deposits	10%
Bank Loans	16%
Equity Capital	29%
Settlement Accounts	42%

Private individual deposits total approximately one-third of the commercial banks' deposit funds, which is about the same as for banks world-wide. Although two-thirds of this amount is deposited in the regional bank of Sberbank of Russia in St. Petersburg, a number of small and larger banks are attempting to attract deposits from individuals. As a result of their efforts, bank Petrovskiy ranks fifth according to the volume of private individual deposits, compared to other Russian cities. Banks, have begun to provide services to St. Petersburg pensioners. The percentage of individual deposits in the Saint Petersburg Industry and Construction Bank has increased greatly. It now accounts for 7% of deposits, and is second in size to Sberbank.

Figure 38.

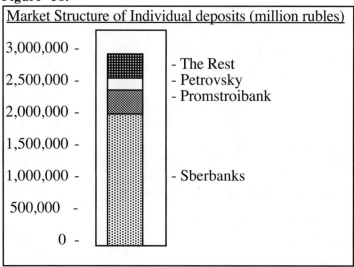

Market Structure of Individual deposits (million rubles)

- The Rest
- Petrovsky
- Promstroibank
- Sberbanks

A number of banks have started to introduce and develop credit cards, such as VISA, Mastercard, Diners Club and others. As a rule, credit cards are debit cards requiring a prepayment deposit to cover charges Despite the growing number of card holders and issuing banks, further expansion of this line of business is retarded by the significant cost of maintaining a credit card system and by the small number of retail establishments which, as yet, accept payment by credit card.

Equity Capital of Commercial Banks

St. Petersburg banks have a comparatively small financial leverage-ratio of deposits to equity capital. On average, deposits are 3.54 times capital, which is several times less than that of other OECD banks. This ratio reduces return on the banks' equity capital. A large portion of bank lending has to be provided from their equity and, as a result, less equity is available as a reserve for loan losses than in an environment where a smaller percentage of bank equity is committed to outstanding loans.

InterBank Loan Market (ILM)

The main function of interbank lending is to maintain bank liquidity, through the temporary interbank lending of idle cash assets. Interbank lending enables the transfer of funds between banks possessing a relatively well developed capacity for attracting deposits and who have low yielding portfolios, and those banks who have access to higher yielding loan portfolios. The rapid development of interbank lending is the result of wide spreads in interest rates between the regions and differences in active and passive transactions. However, interbank loan default started to occur in August, 1995, causing a reduction in interbank lending volume. As a result, leading banks to became increasingly conservative in their credit extension. Recently the presence of international banks in regional markets has grown in importance. Interbank loans were one of the earliest form of bank investment of assets. In 1992 and 1993, they predominated over other transactions between commercial banks. From the beginning of 1994 up to August of 1995, the volume of the interbank loan market grew constantly.

Moscow remains the financial center of Russia. 70% - 80% of Russian money is concentrated in Moscow. Moscow is the leading innovator in the implementation of new banking technologies and financial innovations. The development of the interbank loan business in St. Petersburg occurred along similar lines to those of Moscow, but slightly later and with some unique features of its own. In 1995, the volume of ILM totaled 598 billion rubles representing 50-70% of all short-term bank lending. St. Petersburg is estimated to conduct 1.5% to 3.6% of all Russian interbank lending or about 3% of the volume conducted in Moscow.

Figure 39.
Volume of the Interbank Loan Market
(billion rubles)

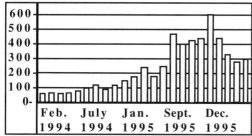

The average face amount of an interbank loan of any maturity was higher in Saint Petersburg than in Moscow. The interest rate of medium term loans significantly exceeded the re-financing rate of the Central Bank and fluctuated in tandem with it. At the time, the high interest rates for short term money were made possible by the very high profit margins in a very volatile economy which made enormous profits on short term speculation possible. In Moscow, one-day loans were common and in St. Petersburg, as a result of the slower settlement system, "short-term" money was generally lent for a term of 2-14 days.

The interest cost of such financing was lower than the re-financing rate, and on rare occasions equaled it. Variations from the average term were rare and constituted only 5-7% for a term ranging from 14-21 days, and 15% for a term shorter than that. In 1994, an increase in loan demand was seen only in the last quarters of the year and on the eve of T-bill auctions. Due to the small volume of business in T-bill investment, the significance of this type of business in Saint Petersburg was a quarter of what it was in Moscow.

In August, 1995, the crisis of interbank loan defaults in Moscow affected the Saint Petersburg market, although a slower settlement system in Saint Petersburg allowed banks there to recover their losses and that reduced the effect of the liquidity crisis. As a result, the crisis in Saint Petersburg reached its highest point 2 to 3 weeks after it hit Moscow, and shortly thereafter it was followed by a crisis of distrust. By September and October, banks were only willing to make fully collateralized loans. The most widely conducted transactions were swap transactions - an exchange of loans in different currencies. At the end of 1995, the interbank loan business became more brisk, though the difficulties that major operators faced, considerably reduced the volume of turnover in the market.

Foreign Exchange Market (FEM)

St. Petersburg FEM consists of Foreign Exchange (FE) and Over-the-Counter market (OTC). Traditionally, foreign currency makes up a considerable part of assets and revenues of local credit institutions. Increased deregulation of the country's economy, the volume of export and import transactions and the use of foreign currency as a means of payment by the majority of business brokers, were the main impetus for creating a method of exchanging other currencies. Another reason for the increase in the use of other currencies was the law requiring Russian businesses to sell their currencies back to the government.

Over-the-Counter Market (OTC)

Although the devaluation of the ruble exchange rate had greatly diminished, and the percentage of FOREX in circulation was gradually decreasing the volume in foreign currency transactions, the Saint Petersburg banks grew many fold. This is illustrated by the following figure, showing comparative data over the third quarter of the years 1993 and 1995.

Figure 40.

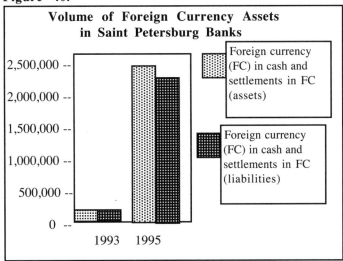

Regional Banks directly execute buying and selling transaction in foreign currency and use the Saint Petersburg Foreign Currency Exchange (FE) for these transactions. During the past few years, a network of many foreign exchange offices has been formed. The number of different currencies circulating on the market is fairly diverse. Though the prevalent currencies are US Dollars, Deutsche Marks and Finnish Marks.

Foreign Exchange Market

On January 1, 1996, 103 banks from 37 Russian cities became members of the FE.

Figure 41.
Participants of Trades

	1994	1995
Banks of European part of Russia	43%	36%
Moscow Banks	22%	28%
Saint Petersburg Banks	28%	26%
Banks of Siberia and Far East	7%	10%

Figure 42.
Results of Trades of the Main Types of Foreign Currencies
(Fixing Method of Trading)
Maximum and Minimum Volumes on Sections

	MAX volume in currency	Date	MIN volume in currency	Date
USD	29,100,000.00	04/01/95	4,280,000.00	29/04/95
DEM	15,953,000.00	24/03/95	1,407,000.00	09/02/95
FIM	9,530,000.00	16/08/95	2,340,000.00	27/12/95

Figure 43.
Maximum Differences Between the Saint Petersburg Rate
(SPFEM) and the Central Bank Rate (CBR) in 1995:

	Rate Difference	S.P.CE	CBR	Date
USD	-8.1641	4567	4973	02/03/95
DEM	-13.8232	3235	3753.91	20/06/95
FIM	2.9421	1092	1060.79	21/06/95

Figure 44.
The Following Commercial Banks Traded
Most Actively on the Exchange in 1995:

On US Dollars	On DEUTSCHE Marks	On FINNISH Marks
Promstroibank	Promstroibank	Promstroibank
Moscow International Bank	Bank "Saint Petersburg"	Bank "Saint Petersburg"
Petrovskiy	BNP Dresdner Bank	Avtovaz Bank

• In comparison with 1993, the turnover in 1994 on the SPFE on the
  US Dollar section increased 1.98 times in foreign currency and by
  4.21 times in rubles.
• In comparison with 1994, the turnover in 1995 on the SPFE on the
  US Dollar section increased 1.18 times in foreign currency and by
  2.39 times in rubles.
• In comparison with 1993, the turnover in 1994 on the SPFE on the
  Deutschmark section increased 6.41 times in foreign currency and by
  15.71 times in rubles.

- In comparison with 1994, the turnover in 1995 on the SPFE on the Deutschmark section increased 2.06 times in foreign currency and by 4.29 times in rubles.
- In comparison with 1993, the turnover in 1994 on the SPFE on the Finnmark section increased 5.36 times in foreign currency and by 15.35 times in rubles.
- In comparison with 1994, the turnover in 1995 on the SPFE on the Finnmark section increased 1.47 times in foreign currency and by 3.32 times in rubles.

Figure 45.
Results of Trades of Other Foreign Currencies (lot trading)

Currency	Number of Transactions	Volume of Trade (rubles)
AUS	2	145,700,000.00
DAK	2	133,275,000.00
FM	166	10,669,935,000.00
FRF	6	297,539,500.00
GBP	18	1,371,631,000.00
ITL	2	148,500,000.00
NOK	33	17,132,270,000.00
NLG	1	2,831,000.00
SEK	27	556,404,500.00
SFR	1	4,200,000.00
Total	**258**	**30,462,286,000.00**

In total, on January 1, 1995, lot selling of the Saint Petersburg Foreign Exchange Market (SPFEM) provided quotations on 15 types of foreign currencies. The total turnover of other foreign currencies in 1994 was estimated at 31,963,858,000 rubles. In total, on January 1, 1996, lot selling of the SPFE provided quotations on 15 types of foreign currencies. The total turnover of other foreign currencies in 1995 was estimated at 30,462,286,000 rubles.

Interbank Foreign Exchange Market (IFEM)

In 1994, the IFEM was considerably influenced by the mandatory requirement imposed upon Russian businesses to sell 50% of foreign currency revenues back to the Russian government at the fixed exchange rate, through the foreign exchanges. The existence of only a limited number of bank-dealers who could participate in trading on the FE, allowed them to dictate terms on commission and settlement dates to their agents. Brokerage services were not as yet well-developed and consisted only in introducing out of town firms to the FE. Later on, expansion of the system for communicating the foreign currency positions of banks, made it possible for them to engage in speculative transactions on the interbank markets. Banks in the North-West region of Russia started to appear on the FE market more frequently. The lack of a system for communicating quotations enabled dealers to make exchange rate decisions on transactions quite independently of any knowledge of broadly prevailing exchange rates. The abolishment of the mandatory requirement to sell the proceeds from foreign currency sales through the FEM in the summer of 1995, allowed the IFEM to become more active in this market.

The amount of direct interbank transactions increased in the summer of 1995, but at the same time, banks started to employ limits upon agents in the form of quotas. In August, the first default of banks with a wide branch network occurred on the interbank market. As a result, banks cut quotas on a whole range of transactions, including foreign currency transactions. They stopped making "counter" payments and started to make delayed payments. Subsequently, the percentage of foreign exchange transactions increased again. Quotas were no longer imposed upon brokers. These quotas were was not reduced due to the growing importance of the role of the broker as third party intermediary, and someone who validated performance in the transaction. In the Autumn of 1995, the introduction of high yielding Government securities brought about the elimination of the trading accounts of foreign currency departments of banks. Foreign currency transactions were thereafter made mainly on behalf of the clients of the bank, and that no longer enabled dealers to act independently and earn a large spread from taking positions in foreign currency.

After the beginning of 1996, quotas were again actively re-introduced. The turnover of the Saint Petersburg Financial House trading floor totaled $25-35 million dollars a month. Using a big spread between exchange rate quotes of the IFEM and OTC markets, swap transactions and by obtaining low interest rate ruble loans, traders earned profits up to 80 to 90% on these transactions.

Arbitrage transactions between the Moscow and Saint Petersburg Exchanges, despite a considerable difference in rate, were not enjoying popularity because of the slow settlement of ruble payments. Return on such transactions did not exceed 20-30% in April 1996. Saint Petersburg has the highest exchange rate in the country. First, because the number of buyers exceeded the number sellers thereby creating a shortage of supply for FOREX. Second, there is yet no fast electronic system of payment, either inside or outside Saint Petersburg. So, short-term currency speculations are not profitable, based on arbitrage with rates in Moscow, and this encourages non-local banks to maintain ruble balances on correspondent accounts in Moscow.

Derivatives Market (DM)

The derivatives instruments market (DM) provides a wide range of products linked to the key factors affecting financial and commercial performance. In 1995, the futures and options market became one of the most dynamic markets in terms of both instrument expansion and growth in market participants. Derivatives trading is conducted on two trading-floors: Commodity Stock Exchange St. Petersburg (CSE) and St. Petersburg Futures Exchange (SPFE), where 95 participants were registered and allowed to trade.

One of the first financial instruments of the futures market were cash-settled dollar contracts, but in June, 1995, futures settled through the clearing system started to appear. They enjoyed popularity because it was possible to speculate on the unpredictability of the exchange rate or to hedge risks arising out of the buying of foreign currency. This was utilized before the "corridor" for dollar exchange rates was introduced on the Moscow Interbank Foreign Exchange. But, during 1995, new types of instruments, interest futures, futures contracts on state securities, T-bills and GMDB were introduced. The volume of these transactions has dropped lately due to their high political risks.

Aside from the sharp fluctuations of T-bills, yields in April of 1996 made the market itself very risky. On the same exchange, in 1996, there was an attempt to offer futures contracts on interest rates - MIBOR (Moscow Interbank Offered Rate - similar to LIBOR). But, after the banking crisis in August, 1995, the demand for this type of futures declined significantly. After the crisis, trading of futures contracts on the Interbank market was stopped. In August of 1995, Western type options and futures contracts were introduced on the CFE Saint Petersburg.

Participants of the Market

Among the 95 participating traders in the futures market who serve more than 235 clients through CFE SP, investment companies dominate all others, constituting about 70% of the traders, while brokerage companies comprises about 20% and banks 10%. To arrange settlements, a Clearing House was established, to which banks such as Promstroybank (Industry and Construction), St. Petersburg, Mosbusinessbank, Inkombank, International Moscow Bank, Petrovskiy, and members of other major financial institutions became members. In 1996, the market was in a stage of decline due to the perception of increased political risks stemming from the presidential election.

As a result, several large speculation-oriented instruments have disappeared from the market. The most perceptible was the cessation of interest bearing futures based on government securities. It had produced an increasing percentage of hedgers, most of which were bought by banks.

Since January 1, 1996, all settlements have been carried out through special companies, which form a Clearing House. Settlement of variational margin and mutual settlements are made at the end of every trading day.

Interbank Market of Futures Contracts

In 1995, the risk of default on futures became minimum, so despite the ever decreasing profit margins, the volume of trading in futures had reached $40 million by April. After the Central Bank imposed measures to stabilizing the ruble, in May, despite the effect this change has had upon the situation, participants in the market did not change their strategy. Turnover of Saint Petersburg Financial House by summer, had reached $50 million. In the middle of the summer, contracts continued to grow at 5% a month in anticipation of the exchange rate increase, at a time when the real stock exchange rate had dropped.

Market participants started to change their strategy only after the introduction of the "currency corridor". Forward contracts in the conditions of falling foreign currency rates ceased to be only speculative instruments and were more frequently used for the hedging of risks. Since September of 1995, mainly large companies have been operating on the futures market while the number of banks has dropped. Mainly, highly profitable transactions of the futures market became arbitrage transactions between the stock, both futures and the over-the-counter, forward floors. Due to the reduced number of participants after the August crisis in 1995, the volume of trading in the Saint Petersburg market decreased to $25 million.

The priorities of the financial market changed in the beginning of 1996. The foreign currency policy had been forecast and the use of speculative forward transactions appeared to be potentially less profitable. In order to maintain the previous level of earnings, by March participants were forced to increase the number of their transactions. At the same time, forward contracts began to be used for providing arbitrage low-risk transactions between neighboring sectors of the money market. The turnover of the Saint Petersburg Financial House in the Spring of 1996, increased to $70 million a month.

Government and Municipal Securities Market

The State securities market of St. Petersburg consists of Federal issues and Municipal issues. The most popular Federal securities are discount Treasury Bills, both T-bills and coupon bonds with longer maturity known in Russia as Federal Debt Bonds (FDB). A special role among securities belongs to Internal Foreign Currency Dept Bonds (ICDB), which emerged as a result of restructuring of Vnesheconombank's debt. In 1994, the first tranches of Municipal Bills (MB) known in Russia as Municipal short-term bonds were issued. They were similar to T-bills, but issued on the regional level. At the present time there is a growing market of these securities.

Government Treasury Bills (GTB) and Federal Debt Bonds (FDB)
In Russia, the most developed sector of the financial market is the Government T-Bills sector, which today represents a highly liquid financial instrument. The first issue of T-bills took place in 1993. At present, market capitalization at par value exceeds 100 billion rubles. The growing volume of offerings is used for repayment of previous issues. Other then at times of price fluctuations, the T-bills market has been characterized by transparency in available information. They serve a purpose in bank liquidity management.

The Moscow market is connected with the St. Petersburg market through two local banks, which act as its dealers along with Saint Petersburg branches of Moscow banks. On December 19, 1995, the FCE trading floor, which is a remote from the Moscow Interbank Foreign Exchange, started to operate. It provides the banks and financial institutions the opportunity to operate on the Moscow GTB/FDB market.

Figure 46.
Saint Petersburg Banks Portfolio of GTB (January 1, 1996)

Bank	GTB Portfolio	Share's in Portfolio	Bank Asset Share
1. S.P. Sberbank	733673	52%	20%
2. Promstroibank	286691	20%	7%
3. Lenoblsberbank	222932	16%	28%
4. Credit Lyonais Bank	60909	4%	9%
5. Bank "Saint Petersburg"	21886	2%	0%
6. Petroagroprombank	21532	2%	4%
7. Petrovskiy	17199	2%	1%
8. Rossia	16538	1%	24%
9. Ruscobank	9821	1%	9%
10. Social and Commercial Bank	5666	1%	7%

A regional floor for trading Federal securities is situated on Saint Petersburg Foreign Currency Exchange (FCE). It was the second regional exchange for trading of T-bills after the FCE in Novosibirsk.

Figure 47.
Bank Shares in Government T-Bills Investment

S.P Sberbank	52%
Promstroibank	20%
Lenoblsberbank	16%
Credit Lyonais Russia	4%
Others	8%

Internal Foreign Currency Debt Bonds of the Ministry of Finance

The most liquid financial instruments denominated in foreign currency are Internal Foreign Currency Dept bonds (ICDB). On the date of issue, Foreign Currency Internal Loans constituted the largest issue of State securities in Russia. On January 1, 1991, it took up 29% of the overall trading in Russian securities.

Figure 48.
Structure of the Internal Foreign Currency Debt After the Redemption of the First and Second Tranches.

3rd Tranche	21%
4th Tranche	43%
5th Tranche	36%

After the previous redemption there were bonds of the third tranche, which totaled at $1.307 billion dollars at par value, and the fourth tranche totaled at $2.167 billion dollars. Very shortly bonds of the sixth and the seventh tranches will be issued. Establishing this foreign currency corridor has made the IFCD bonds disadvantageous for national conservative investors, since investments in government securities and the purchase of futures have provided several times the rate of profits. Nevertheless, demand was stimulated by foreign investors. Opportunities to make speculative long term investment are provided by Foreign Currency bonds. Medium term opportunities are provided by high liquidity yield to maturity bonds and the yield on coupon payments. Short-term opportunities are to be found in the yield on coupon payments and in currency speculation. The Reduction of standard spreads from 50 to 25 points per lot, also enhances the opportunity for investing. The Regional market for IFCD Bonds traditionally is considered to be sluggish and fairly conservative.

For example, in St. Petersburg, IFCD Bonds are quoted only by 2 or 3 banks and the financial company Glavstroyinvest. Sluggishness is explained by the presence of conservative investors in the market who use IFCD bonds for acquisition of soft loan terms or for contribution to the authorized fund, by weekly settlement of transactions and, finally, for investment of excess currency resources.

Municipal Securities

The St. Petersburg financial markets are characterized by the active circulation of municipal securities. First, among them are discount short-term municipal bills which were issued by St. Petersburg's instrumentalities of government. The total amount of the first issue realized 2.1 billion rubles. Trading in MB's is conducted at the auction. The Yield is the difference between the buying price and the selling price. Redemption of MTB's is conducted at the nominal par value of 100,000 rubles. Primarily MTB's were supported by tax on real estate from the St. Petersburg Real Estate Fund. After the changes in the MTB issue, enhancing of volume of issue amount up to 5 billion rubles from the initial 2.1 billion rubles, the issue was supported by the value added tax, flowing into the city's budget. Auctions and secondary trades of MTB take place on the St. Petersburg Foreign Exchange (SPFE), Commodity and Stock Exchange St. Petersburg (CSE) and St. Petersburg Stock Exchange (SE). Registration of bonds trading is provided for by the St. Petersburg Settlement and Depository Center. As far as the procedure for Federal issues is concerned, FTB's are tax exempt. When the floating of MTB began on March 23, 1995, the main trading floor for the first offering and the second trading was the St. Petersburg Foreign Exchange. The total offering reached more than 2 billion rubles, which was 63% of the MTB market.

Figure 49.
Structure of MTB Dealers

Saint Petersburg Banks	42%
Investment Companies	26%
Moscow Banks	21%
Regional Banks	11%

In 1995, there were 16 auctions conducted where 12 issues of three month maturity, 3 issues of six month maturity and 1 issue of 12 month maturity have been successfully floated. 11 issues were redeemed at maturity date in full at their par value. Analysis of the auction results indicate that the offering of MTB was made at a price corresponding to the yield of issues with similar terms of payment. Conversely, market yield of MTB/T-bills has fluctuated widely.

In 1995, there were 100 trade sessions. At first, they took place twice a week, and then from mid-September of 1995, 4 times a week. From February 1, 1996, secondary MTB trades were taking place 5 times a week, with the exclusion of the days of MTB auctions.

Figure 50.
Dynamics of MTB Turnover on the
Saint Petersburg Foreign Exchange
(million rubles)

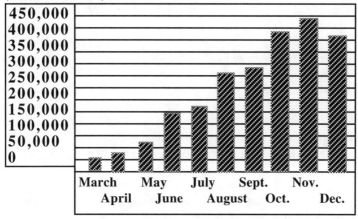

Figure 51.
A Comparative Yield of MTB and GTB Issues Annual Return %

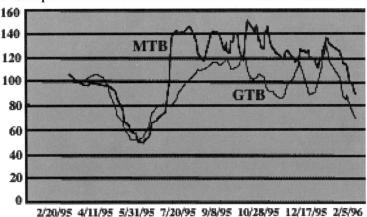

For investors, the most important requirement for MTB is their liquidity. This index on the MTB is high enough. The average turnover during one trade makes 2-5% of the current market turnover.

Commercial Papers Market

In 1995, the Government issued bills aimed at making settlements with subcontracting organizations carrying out work within the framework of local budget programs. Their main feature is primarily a limited circulation within one region. Municipal bills with a guarantee from large Russian banks are the only exception. St. Petersburg has one of the few markets where bills of other local governments are circulated. In that case, we speak not only about bills of the north-west region, but also about bills issued by Saratov, Kemerovo, Yamalo-Nenets and other administrations. Bills issued by the Mayors Office account for the largest volume on the secondary market. Basically bank bills are the only instrument of this kind investors are interested in.

Figure 52.
Structure of Money Supply

Rubles in Cash and Bank Deposits	33%
Non-Payments	33%
Dollars and DM in Cash	17%
Promissory Notes and Other Quasi	17%

212

Due to the greater appeal of bank bills to international investors, and their unlimited potential market with reference to trading, and their area of circulation, the number of those trading in this security are much greater than with others. The market of bank bills is relatively liquid and contributes to the development of secondary bills market as a whole.

Organization of the Secondary Market
This is represented by two trading floors where bills of Tver universal Bank and Incombank are traded, as well as by direct transactions between participants. Securities by issuers from the Baltic to the Amur regions are included in the trading volume of these markets. Monthly trading volume of the North-West regional bills trading floor of Tveruniversal Bank, the largest in the region, reached 100 billion rubles in corporate bill transactions. Trading in bank bills accounts for more than 20 billion rubles monthly. However, a large portion of trading volume in the bills of local issuers take place in private placements. This is explained by the limited number of participants and established networking connections.

Investors are generally interested only in the trading conducted on the trading floors. In this instance, participants of the brokerage firms mentioned above account for a greater part of the market. Therefore, bills by the largest Saint Petersburg issuers, such as Vodokanal, Lenen ergo, Leningrad nuclear plant, Lentransgas, KEG (municipal bills) usually are available on the trading floor in limited quantities. Under these conditions, the role of the trading floor is reduced to performing a statistical function which consists in establishing, by way of quotations, indicators of potential supply and demand. The industry issuers are represented by transport (railways), the energy complex, ferrous and non ferrous metallurgy, machine building, oil, chemistry and others.

Stock Market
The Saint Petersburg capital market began to take form concurrently with the money market. However, real transformation of a corporate securities market into an integral part of the financial system became possible only after privatization, when the majority of St. Petersburg's large enterprises became publicly owned corporations. Although, from the viewpoint of the size of the capitalization and turnover, the stock market still occupies a modest place, but its institutional structure has been established. There are two exchanges in St. Petersburg where securities are traded, the Commodity and Stock Exchanges. However, the over-the-counter stock market plays the most important role. Investment companies now form the basis of trading. A number of the largest ones are closely connected to the leading banks.

Turnover and Structure of the Stock Market

The total turnover of the over-the-counter stock market in Saint Petersburg constituted 107 billion rubles in 1994. During the entire year that trading was conducted by investment institutions, an indirect indication of its current transition to a new stage of development was given. In 1995, the turnover of the over-the-counter stock market exceeded 500 billion rubles. This figure is much higher than that for exchange trading volume. However, there was also a trend toward a decrease in corporate issues traded, if the share of federal and municipal securities in the trading volume of the largest brokerage firms in the city is excluded from the 1994 figures. During the past year the share of federal short-term bonds constituted about 10% of the turnover and the share of municipal short-term bonds of the Saint Petersburg government made up over 8%.

The most attractive shares on the Saint Petersburg stock market in 1995 were those of transport, communication and large publicly traded companies. If in the first half of 1994, shares of Saint Petersburg issuers constituted the largest part of the industry, then beginning in the autumn, securities from other cities began to play a greater part. These were primarily shares of oil companies, which are blue chips by Russian standards. In 1995, the number of Saint Petersburg issuers increased considerably as their securities were traded. Shares of Saint Petersburg companies also ranked highest in terms of liquidity. With respect to bank shares, investors are increasingly becoming interested in the large banks. The recent incidents of bank failures has somewhat worsened the investment climate in this sector. However, the attractiveness of bank shares from the investor's viewpoint, still remains very strong.

Figure 53.
Structure of the Stock Market

Shares	63%
GTB	10%
MTB	8%
Bonds	3%
IFCDB	1%
Bills	1%
Others	14%

214

Figure 54.
Turnover According to the Types of Issuers in 1995

Type	Turnover (bln. rubles)	Turnover %
Privatized Enterprises	32,214	55.13%
Banks	3,449	5.9%
Investment Industrial Companies	3,247	5.56%
Investment Funds	1,470	0.25%
Others	19,382	33.16%

One of the unexpected developments of 1995 was the rising prices for shares of the so-called second echelon, which frequently includes not only separate enterprises, but all industries. Stock quotations of enterprises of ferrous metals and forestry moved a bit faster than others in 1996. It is worth noting that, in terms of investment volume, forestry occupies one of the first places. In the Spring there was a rather long period of active purchases, after which the industry experienced a period of decline and operating losses. There was, nevertheless, a shortage of shares on the market. Investors, particularly international investors, were very interested in forestry investments.

Figure 55.

Issuer	Number of Traders	Average Ratio of Purchase/Sale Prices	Turnover Volume (ruble)	Turnover Volume %
North-West Shipping Co.	362	0.88	25751	7.37
Telephone Network	274	0.87	23401	6.69
Sea Trade Port	147	0.93	19466	5.57
Lenenergo	335	1.05	16570	4.47
Industry and Construction Bank	192	0.87	13158	3.376
Baltic Shipping Co.	294	0.81	10954	3.13
Kirovsky Works	359	0.84	8667	2,48
LOMO	296	0.89	7573	2.17
MMT (St. Pb)	179	0.82	5450	1.56
Elektrosila	268	0.78	3825	1.09

In the near future, shares in the chemical, ferrous metals, energy, and forestry industries are likely to perform well. The possibility for growth in the market for companies in the food processing and communications industries, which recently have received large investments, undoubtedly exists.

Buying and selling ratios have changed on the stock market with emphasis on issues of privatized companies. Sharply increased activity in this sector was caused by the interest on the part of large institutional investors, mainly international. German, American, and Swedish investors were active in St. Petersburg. In the first place, they were interested in machine-building, ship-building, energy and forestry. Dutch and English investors took an interest in the food and confectionery industries. There were not many investments in traded securities and practically all operations were carried out as private placements. It is very difficulty for an industrial company to obtain capital through the stock market. The largest volume of funds received by an industrial company through an initial public offering of its shares amounted to the equivalent of 2.8 million dollars. Beginning in mid-1995, large Russian banks began to successfully compete with international investors. Russian banks have the right to own shares of industrial companies. Large banks account for the major portion of all bank industry ownership of such shares. It is difficult to determine their actual market value because they represent not only investment assets, but one of the formulating elements of finance and the industrial groups developing around the leading banks.

Figure 56.
Structure of Bank Portfolio of Shares of Businesses

Promstroibank	50%
Bank "Saint Petersburg"	21%
Baltiysky	17%
Others	12%

Participants of the Securities Markets

Key institutions in the over-the-counter securities market are brokerage firms. By the end of last year, dozens of firms had been carrying on business in Saint Petersburg's over-the-counter securities market. However, 70% of the turnover was accounted for by four of the largest investment companies.

216

Figure 57.
Share on the Securities Market

Lenstroimaterials	33%
Romecs-invest	14%
Glavstroyinvest	14%
Baltic Finance Agency	10%
Others	29%

Financial stabilization, considerable expansion of the federal securities market and certain other macro-economic processes greatly influenced the over-the-counter stock market in 1995. One of the most important events in St. Petersburg was the signing of a preliminary agreement on the activity of professional participants in the stock market, signed by the seven leading brokerage firms. The main purpose of the agreement was to represent the interests of those who signed it and solving controversies by way of negotiation and compromise. In 1995, according to the resolution of the local government commission on securities, the requirements for the registration of broker-dealers was introduced. All participants in stock market trading are recommended to apply to the securities commission for accreditation.

Stock Index FIP - 30

Towards the end of 1994, with the participation of the Baltic finance agency, Research Institute of Mathematics and the Management Processes of the Saint Petersburg University and Saint Petersburg stock exchange. The stock index of Saint Petersburg, called the FIP-30, was based upon the number of enterprises included in the index. In mid-1995, after analysis that took half a year, the index was approved by the Committee of professional participants of the stock market, as the official index, reflecting the most important trends of the over-the-counter stock market. Initially, the list of enterprises included in the calculation of the index consists of:

• **Machine and Instrument Building**
   "Kirovsky Plant", ZMZ, LOMO, "Diamond", "Izhora Plants", "Electrosila", "Nevsky Plant", "Svetlana"
• **Chemical Industry**
   "Medpolimer","Farmacon", "Plastpolimer", "Foil-Rolling Mill"
• **Light and Food Industry**
   "Skorokhod","Butter and Fat Combine", "Lenribrom", "Bolshoi Gostini Dvor", "Aroma", "Baltica", "Neva", "Beriozka"

- **Fuel Energy Complex**
    "Lenenergo","Kirishinefteorgsyntes".
- **Transport and Communication**
    "BMP","Sea Trade Port", "North-West Shipping Company", "Saint P. MMT"
- **Finance**
    "Industry and Construction Bank","Vitabank", Bank "Saint Petersburg", "Timber Industry Bank"

In the middle of last year, the index was passed to the Committee of professional participants of the securities market and from that moment, the calculation and the accompanying of the index have been carried out by the Expert Council of the Committee, which consists of representatives of the largest investment institutions of the city: Baltic Finance Agency, Glavstroyinvest, Deviz, Cartel, Course, Lenstroymateriali, ORIMI - broker, Rendezvous, the Saint Petersburg Stock Exchange and others. Total index FIP-30 for thirty of the largest Saint Petersburg public limited companies and six branch indexes are calculated every week.

UNIT 8

Clearing as a Method of Saving Money

Introduction

Behind the mechanical processes of clearing physical matter with offsetting money values, lies the identical spiritual principle of clearing the non-physical values underlying all human interaction. Each of us continuously produces value. Spiritual clearing is created when the expectation of the production of such value prompts reliance upon its delivery. Spiritual clearing eliminates loss of creative potential. Such relationships become possible and grow as a community develops standards of honor, honesty, integrity, dependability, trust, ethics, morality and love. These are the fertilizers of commerce (material creation).

One of Pushkin's "Decemberist" friends once said "When I look at my poor Mother Russia, I sometimes think that God created it in order to show other people how not to Live". To the contrary, the knowledge of how to live has always existed in Russia and has never quite been forgotten. It is now experiencing a period of intense revival. "Clearing" is one of its expressions and manifestations.

Chapter 8.1

Overview

Theoretical background and development of clearing in Russia.

While doing business, every company operating on a commercial basis continuously creates cash flow, which results in accounts receivable. The company can then become a creditor or a debtor. Accounts receivable and payable circulate money. Money circulation creates a multiplier effect in the economy. The longer working capital is tied up in circulation, the less efficient it will be.

Clearing shortens the time that working capital is unavailable to a business. It is a mechanism which enables business to meet money obligations (accounts payable) with claims to money (accounts receivable) without or with minimal use of cash. In this manner accounts payable and accounts receivable offset each other, which reduces overdue outstanding accounts payable. In academic terms, clearing is defined as a method of cashless money transmission which facilitates payments.

Without a doubt, promptness of payments is a valuable benefit of clearing but the equally important benefit is that less money (both cash and cashless) is needed. Therefore, less working capital is required to finance production.

The theoretical background for implementing and maintaining clearing is that *money*, while circulating in the economy, performs Four Functions:

- measure of value
- means of payment
- means of circulation
- means of accumulation

As money circulates it serves as the equivalent of goods, and exists physically as coins, banknotes, bank account transactions and as computer entries if money balances and transfers are maintained in computers.

Money exists in the above forms to carry out the functions of payment, circulation or accumulation. In measurement of value no physical form for money is needed because it is an ideal function. Money is also used for counting. Ideal counting of money is required for pricing, evaluation of national wealth, accounting, assessment of financial obligations and claims.

The ideal form of money is enough to assess the price of a commodity or the size of a financial obligation, while to purchase a product or meet a financial claim one would need real, physical money, either in cash or as a bank account. To draw a cheque or money request real money is not needed, while to settle these documents one would then need real money.

The use of money as the measure of value only is the theoretical basis to carry out clearing. Clearing becomes possible when outstanding payments accumulate in one place and there is an opportunity to offset counter claims without the use of real money. If we weight the money requests of party A to B, B to C, A to G, G to A, etc., they will offset each other to a certain extent as positive and negative values. No real money need be involved. In this case money would be a measure of value for the price of shipped goods on the one hand, and the price of received goods on the other hand. Therefore, except for the ideal form of measurement of value, money is not really involved.

There are two types of classifications of Clearing Operations:
- frequency
- status of participants

First, clearing may happen on a casual basis when accounts payable and receivable accrue, or are continuous with no regard to the extent money claims and obligations are in arrears. Second, involved parties might be either corporate, private individuals, or a combination of both from the same industry or region.

Clearing is possible if counterparts have business or other relations with the involvement of money, such as:
- bilateral
- multilateral
- sporadic

In bilateral business relations, value moves from one counterpart to the other and vice versa. In such relations mutual money obligations and claims meet each other.

In practice we find bilateral business relations less often than multilateral when there is a one way movement of value through a number of economically independent parties. As a result of such one way movement of value, cash flows also proceed on one direction. Clearing becomes possible if business relations are followed by a multilateral chain of money transactions. Every member of clearing shall be the unit of this chain. It is a prerequisite that these units are linked by money claims on the one hand and money claims on the other hand.

Most effective is a multiparty clearing when involved parties have claims or obligations to other participants. In the settlement of debts by clearing, the participants perform a large number of documented transactions, which are presented to the clearing center for settlement and recorded on the current accounts (see Figure 58). In the international community, such accounts are referred to as a transit account-position.

Figure 58.
Clearing and Involvement of Real Money (thousands rubles)

Clearing Participate	Transaction Center	on the Clearing current account	Settled in clearing	Involvement Real	of Money
	obligations	claims		To pay debts	To receive debts
1	100	400	100		300
2	400	600	400		200
3	600	500	500	100	
4	850	1000	850		150
5	200	80	80	120	
6	300	200	200	100	
7	250	300	250	650	50
8	1000	350	350		
9	80	150	80		70
10	150	350	150		200
Total	3930	3930	2960	970	970

In this table, obligations are shown on the debit of clearing the participant's current account, which then means he has an accounts receivable. Claims are shown on the credit of clearing participant's current account, which means they have accounts payable. Effectiveness of clearing is shown by the offset ratio, which represents amount of debts registered for clearing to the amount of the off-set debts (in our above example 75%).

Therefore, in doing clearing, money does not serve as a means of circulation. Instead, it is involved as a measure of value shown for the price of goods and services, registered in documents and received for offset. The reduced funds taken to service the sphere of circulation, lowers the overall demand for capital in circulation from corporations and saves the banks' credit resources.

Clearing centers based on banks originated in England back in the 18th century. In Russia, clearing grew from the Settlement Chambers of the State Bank branches in 1898. By the time of World War I, there were 45 Clearing Chambers encompassing 430 banking and other institutions in Russia. In the times of War Communism, when the credit system was destroyed, clearing settlements were also abolished.

With the rise of the New Economic Policy, restoration of the credit system and clearing centers began. In July 1922, the Clearing Center was established by the Board of the State Bank of the USSR Department of Mutual Settlements. By the end of the year, 775 institutions were serviced in this department. As of October 1, 1925, the State Bank had 12 such departments in major cities to offset payments between state and cooperative enterprises. About two-thirds of registered claims, primarily checks, were off-set.

In July 1931, the Board of the State Bank USSR approved the standard Rules for Departments of Mutual Settlements for branches of the State Bank. According to these Rules, the settlement participants could be local or federal cooperatives, public or trade-union organizations, government entities and enterprises with current or budget accounts in a given city, as well as nonresident corporations, only if they had special settlement accounts with the Central Bank.

The participants held daily meetings on which they exchanged documents ascertaining their mutual obligations and money claims. They also worked out daily balances of outstanding obligations and unsatisfied claims, which were paid by money transfers. In order to warrant timeliness and continuation of settlements, reserve funds of legal tenders were established at each branch at the expense of the participants. The order of setting up reserve funds was determined by a general meeting of the participants. Banking institutions made credit funds available to build up reserve funds.

A disadvantage of settlements through casual selection of participants, was that they could incorporate business entities which had no business relations with the other participants. This technique of settlements was bulky and required daily meetings of all participants, while those who hosted the given meeting had no obligations or claims in the meeting. Absence of representative on two successive meetings caused automatic exclusion from the system.

In the beginning of the 1930's, the official government Department of Mutual Settlements (DMS), was replaced by the Offices of Mutual Settlements (OMS). As opposed to the DMS, participants of the OMS clearing were enterprises united by industry or region, and in essence the OMS were structural divisions of banks. Originally OMS was called "Local Offices of Mutual Settlements" (LOMS). By 1940, there were 62 such clearing centers, and by 1954 their number increased to 243.

Alongside with the Local Offices of Mutual Settlements in 1940, eight Centralized Offices of Mutual Settlements (COMS) were organized by the Board of the State Bank. Each of these made regular offsets between enterprises throughout the rest of the country. In a number of cases, operating offices were situated far away from both the payer and the payee. Documents supporting money requests and obligations were sent by post, which caused further delays in settlements.

With the increase in business relations, interbranch specialization and cooperation expanded and highlighted the short-comings of LOMS and COMS. Without the speed of today's technology and telecommunications, final settlements by results of offset were often confusing. Having performed a positive role in the reduction of legal tenders in arrears and in acceleration of settlements, clearing carried out by LOMS and COMS eventually became an obstacle in economic turnover. In 1955, these institutions were replaced by a clearing system of decentralized offsets, called Dezachet, which covered the entire

Soviet Union.

The main attribute of clearing in decentralized offset, was the use of money as a measure of value shown in fixed prices, with documents ascertaining mutual obligations and money claims. Obligations are offset as negative and positive values. Money as a means of payment, was used for payment of outstanding obligations or claims. The source of money for each organization was its own resources or bank credits.

In the Soviet Union, the clearing system required each participant to open a Dezachet Current Account in addition to their existing settlement account. At maturity, the money was transferred from the Dezachet Current Account to the payee. Money was transferred to the same account of the economic organization when its money claims for goods were satisfied. Once a week the totals of operations were calculated, or settled.

Outstanding money claims of the participant were paid from borrowed funds. Because of an extremely low level of offset, the Dezachet system turned into a form of unlimited bank crediting.

Since 1974, Special Credit Accounts were implemented in the State Bank credit-clearing arena. These are accounts with a limited overdraft. The Dezachet system became useless, because corporations gained access to operational bank credit, and the system of clearing was liquidated. Since then, the State Bank of the Soviet Union ceased to pay attention to the development of clearing, which caused additional need for real money and fueled inflation.

In 1992, the government of Russia in consideration of urgent measures to recover the situation with settlements, offered the heads of local administration, ministries and departments, together with the heads of senior Departments of the Central Bank and commercial banks, to make regional, industrial and intercompany offsets of mutual indebtedness. However, these offsets turned out to be inefficient and as Dezachet before, funneled large sums of credit resources into non-payment .

Chapter 8.2

Interbank Clearing

Interbank Clearing operated successfully in many Russian cities with more than three branches of state and specialized banks, before the two-level banking system was created. For the purposes of clearing Settlement, Chambers were established at the local USSR State Bank divisions. Each participating bank opened an account. Results of daily clearing (debit and credit balances) were recorded on the subcorrespondent account of the specialized bank's branch, irrespective of availability of money on this account. This was possible because local branches were not private corporations and full range correspondent relations existed at the level of Boards of the State Bank and of specialized banks. At this level bank correspondent accounts were active.

The branches of specialized banks received limit notices to issue money without the transfer of appropriate sums. As a result, subcorrespondent accounts on their balances were a liability. Payment of debit account in the settlement department only increased the passive balance, while on the account of the State Bank, branch settlement of debit balance in essence was an issue of a loan to complete the offsets.

A major prerequisite of Russia's transition to a market economy was the commercialization of the state special banks and the foundation of new commercial banks. Their operations are limited to the owning of capital and equal money resources. They independently picked up credit applicants, determined the order of making deposits, and the interest rates on assets and liability operations. This becomes possible only if the commercial bank independently disposes of the correspondent account. These circumstances have caused the liquidation of interbank clearing because settlement departments as clearing centers paid credit balances and covered debit balances on offset through system of subcorrespondent accounts or by letter of advice through the system of Interbranch Settlements (IBS). In the meantime, subcorrespondent accounts and IBS are not used in the relations between the Central Bank and independent commercial banks.

Cash Centers (CC) were created in order to effect settlements between commercial banks and local Central Bank branches. Settlements through CC have the same major imperfections that were mentioned before. Many Russian banks carry out settlements between each other by direct remittance of money through mutual correspondent accounts. This enables better settlement procedures but does not reduce the amount of real money involved, because it immobilizes significant amounts of money at the level of the correspondent accounts. The size of these funds is comparable to the current capital, including CC balances.

In 1992 the Central Bank, together with a group of commercial banks, conducted research on the opportunities of setting up interbank clearing under the revised circumstances of a market economy. As a result temporary bylaws on clearing agencies were introduced. These bylaws said that a clearing agency could be founded in any form of private ownership allowed by legislation and that it could carry out business on a commercial basis.

The activity of a clearing agency is prescribed by its charter and is carried out on the basis of a license issued by the Central Bank. Commercial banks, the Central Bank and other corporations and individuals, except for state authorities at all levels, their executive bodies, political organizations and specialized public funds, can be founders of a clearing agency. The main tasks of clearing agency are as follows:

- the acceleration and optimization of settlements between banks and other credit institutions, both Russian and international
- the rise of settlement reliability and authenticity
- the implementation and maintenance of the new forms of the clearing settlements, whether checks, bills, credit cards, etc.
- the most rational use of temporarily free bank resources
- the introduction of modern international technologies, standards and protocols, creating a gradual entry into the global banking system
- the implementation of a modern informational bank structure
- the receipt and transfer of data through communication channels with script secured hardware and software (electronic signature), methods of data coding certified by authorized body
- the reliable multilevel data protection against unauthorized access, use, distortion and falsification at stages of processing and storage
- the control of informational reliability at all stages

In the meantime, there are two models for the setting up of a clearing agency. By the first model, clearing is made after all clearing agency members have made a deposit. By the second, no advance deposit is needed.

One of the main problems of the interbank clearing system is the elimination of debit balances. This means that the final settlement is made by the results of clearing. There are three possible variants of this:

1. The founders set up a reserve fund in the clearing center, which is used for settlement of debit balances, if any member is not capable to pay.

A Reserve fund is maintained on a correspondent account of the clearing center at the local Central Bank branch. Remittances from debtor banks are transferred onto the same account. In this case members may open sub-correspondent accounts in the clearing center where clearing is effected by the transfer of real money between these accounts. This variant requires banks to keep money in the clearing center.

2. By results of offset the clearing center submits a debit balance for payment to the members' correspondent account in the appropriate Central Bank branch.

Payment is effected irrespective of availability of money in the member bank account for a debit balance may accrue on the account. In essence, it is a credit issued by the completion of account offsets. The credit will be short-term, for the commercial bank can't continue operations if there is a debit balance on correspondent account. In such cases, the commercial bank may apply for a special short-term loan from the local Central Bank branch for the benefit of clearing center to cover debt.

3. If after all credit and debit offsets the member is not in the position to settle debit balance, recalculation of multilateral claims is made to revalue payments and obligations. After recalculation each participant may pay a larger sum or it may receive a smaller sum. Even those participants which did not conduct any operations with defaulters may need to increase their liquidity in the event that the participants which might lack liquidity because of a delay in debit balance settlements with the other participants. Thus, insolvency of one participant of the clearing process spreads between the rest.

The second variant is pure classical clearing. It is also the simplest and suits the interests of all participants of clearing and the body which carries out offsetting. Besides, due to modern means of communication, clearing may be regional and interregional if necessary.

Techniques of clearing by the second variant requires a certain sequence of operations. First of all, each participant opens a transit account which serves for records only. These records are entered on the basis of documents delivered through the computer system. Thus, an electronic identification of the holder of this account is needed. Simultaneously, the clearing agency opens a correspondent account in the local Central Bank branch and the founders then make their contributions accordingly.

In the first half of each operating day, the clearing center receives payment orders (checks) through electronic communication and a computer debits the payer's account and credits the payee's. In the second half of the day the computer calculates all debit (credit) balances of the members' accounts. At day's end, the clearing agency produces the balance sheet through its results in clearing and transmits it to the local Central Bank branch which writes off debit balances from the accounts of member banks in favor of the clearing agency's correspondent account. From this account money is remitted to the correspondent accounts of the member banks which then create a positive offset (credit balance). On the basis of the correspondent account statement the clearing center makes respective entries in the members' current account.

Let's study a conditional example with five banks in the clearing center.

Operation 1. *Bank 1 transmits electronic payment orders to:*

Bank 2	500
Bank 4	300
Bank 5	400
Total	1200

Operation 2. *Bank 2 transmits electronic payment orders to:*

Bank 1	300
Bank 3	550
Bank 4	250
Total	1100

Operation 3. *Bank 3 transmits electronic payment orders to:*

Bank 1	400
Bank 2	100
Bank 4	70
Bank 5	130
Total	700

Operation 4. *Bank 4 sends checks for accounts receivable from:*

from Bank 1	80
from Bank 2	30
from Bank 3	50
from Bank 5	40
Total	200

Operation 5. *Bank 5 transmits electronic payment orders to:*

Bank 1	180
Bank 2	270
Bank 3	250
Total	700

Operation 6. *Bank 4 transmits electronic payment orders to:*

Bank 1	90
Bank 2	100
Bank 3	60
Bank 5	240
Total	500

Operation 7, 7a. The clearing center calculates the final balances of the current accounts and the results of offset.

Operation 8. A balance sheet is produced and delivered to the Central Bank branch for execution.

Figure 59.
Balance Sheet (Clearing Results of Operating Day ___Month____ 199 __ (thousand rubles)

Name of Bank #Correspondent Account	Clearing	Center	Information	
	Current	Account Entries	Offset	Amount
	Debit	Credit	Debit	Credit
1	1280	970	310	-
2	1130	980	150	-
3	750	860		110
4	500	820		320
5	740	770		30
Total	**4400**	**4400**	**460**	**460**

Operation 9 (1, 2, 3, 4, 5). On the basis of similar sheets, money from correspondent accounts is transmitted to the correspondent account of the clearing center. On the basis of this sheet money from the account of the clearing center is transmitted to the creditor banks. Records on the clearing center correspondent account provide information to reflect the results of clearing on the appropriate member current accounts. The above mentioned example may be reflected on the T (current) accounts in the clearing center and in the Central Bank.

Clearing with Advance Deposits on the Clearing Center Correspondent Account have a number of disputable issues, such as:

Figure 60.

Current Account in Clearing Center

BANK 1	BANK 1	BANK 2	BANK 2	BANK 3	BANK 3
D-T	CR-T	D-T	CR-T	D-T	CR-T
1) 1200	2) 300	2)1100	1)500	3)700	2)500
4) 80	3) 400	4) 30	3) 100	4) 50	5) 250
	5) 180		5) 270		6) 60
	6) 90		6) 110		
7) 1280	7) 970	7) 1130	7) 980	7) 750	7) 860
7a) 310	9.1) 310	7a) 150	9.2) 150	9.3) 110	7a) 110

BANK 4	BANK 4	BANK 5	BANK 5	CLEARING	CENTER
D-T	CR-T	D-T	CR-T	D-T	CR-T
	1) 300	4) 40	1) 400	9.1) 310	9.3) 110
	2) 250		3) 130	9.2) 150	9.4) 320
6) 500	3) 70	5) 700	6) 240		9.5) 30
	4) 200				
7) 500	7) 820	7) 740	7) 770		
9.4) 320	7a) 310	9.5) 30	7a) 30		

Figure 61.

Accounts in the Central Bank Local Branch

BANK 1	BANK 1	BANK 2	BANK 2	BANK 3	BANK 3
D-T	CR-T	D-T	CR-T	D-T	CR-T
9.1) 310	Balance	9.2) 150	Balance	Balance	9.3)110

BANK 4	BANK 4	BANK 5	BANK 5	CLEARING	CENTER
D-T	CR-T	D-T	CR-T	D-T	CR-T
	Balance		Balance	9.3) 110	9.1) 310
	9.4) 320		9.5) 30	9.4) 30	9.2) 150
				5) 30	

The clearing agency is established as a bank with functions of common commercial banking operations, with deposit accounts of member banks. This requires continuous immobilization of funds on these member bank accounts. Money requests of the participant are taken to fulfill the claim if there is enough money for this obligation on the deposit account of the contractor. Short-term debit balance is not allowed, which reduces to zero the advantages of clearing payments and in essence replaces them with real money payments.

The main idea of any multilateral clearing, including bank clearing, presumes that only the debit balance that appears on the current account after offset should periodically be repaid by real money, which is transferred at the disposal of the clearing agency and is used by it to repay credit balances of other participants.

APPENDIX 1

The Constitution of the Russian Federation

Introduction

The adoption of the constitution of the Russian Federation comes at a time of both enormous internal change in Russia as well as Global reawakening and refocusing upon our original objectives. It is by no coincidence that Russia chose this time to express its communion with this global process. To understand the significance of this document, one must understand the global context within which it occurs.

At present, all nations seem to experience a profound sense of dissatisfaction and restlessness with the way things are. We are looking for more fulfillment. This restlessness is what's behind the *me-first* attitude that has characterized recent decades. Learning how to find such fulfillment occurs when we become conscious of the apparent *coincidences* in our lives, and discover they are not coincidences after all. We are discovering that coincidences mean something. This awareness is the first clue to fulfillment. Quite simply, the truth.

We are in the process of structuring a new world view reflecting this new awareness. This idea seems more valid once we see the historical background of our new awareness. History is more the evolution of thought than of technology. What people are feeling and thinking is more important than what is happening. At the end of the sixteenth century, the world became preoccupied with creating a secular and economic security to replace the spiritual security we had previously, but lost. History shows that for the following 400 years, we have been preoccupied with an attempt to define the universe by means of the scientific method. We had decided to master this planet.

Getting those answers has taken longer than expected, so we became preoccupied with settling into the world and making ourselves comfortable. We concentrated on using the earth's resources to better our lives. We pushed aside the original question that the scientific method was supposed to answer. Why are we Alive. Working to establish physical comfort grew to feel complete, and of itself, a reason to live.

Present dissatisfaction and restlessness results from the fact that many nations have accomplished what we collectively had set out to do. A 400 year old obsession has been completed. The preoccupation is breaking down, and we are waking up to something else. To consider our original question. What's

232

behind life on this planet? Why are we really here? Many nations have created the means of material security and discovered that they are not enough, many more are on the verge of prosperity. The critical mass now exists to help the remaining nations achieve material security, and now we are ready to find out why we have done it.

It is entirely comprehensible that Russia, with its educated population and wealth of natural resources, and rich spiritual traditions, should constitute an indispensable component to this process, and be an essential pioneer in this awakening. We can believe nothing less to explain these utterances emanating from a nation which has endured such turmoil in its recent past.

APPENDIX 1

The Constitution of the Russian Federation

We, the multinational people of the Russian Federation, united by a common fate on our land, establishing human rights and freedoms, civic peace and accord, preserving the historically established state unity, proceeding from the universally recognized principles of equality and self-determination of peoples, revering the memory of ancestors who have conveyed to us the love for the Fatherland, belief in the good and justice, reviving the sovereign statehood of Russia and asserting the firmness of its democratic basis, striving to ensure the well-being and prosperity of Russia, proceeding from the responsibility for our Fatherland before the present and future generations, recognizing ourselves as part of the world community, adopt the CONSTITUTION OF THE RUSSIAN FEDERATION.

I. THE FUNDAMENTALS OF THE CONSTITUTIONAL SYSTEM

Article 1

The Russian Federation - Russia is a democratic federal law-bound State with a republican form of government. The names "Russian Federation" and "Russia" shall be equal.

Article 2

Man, his rights and freedoms are the supreme value. The recognition, observance and protection of the rights and freedoms of man and citizen shall be the obligation of the State.

Article 3

1. The bearer of sovereignty and the only source of power in the Russian Federation shall be its multinational people.

2. The people shall exercise their power directly, and also through the bodies of state power and local self-government.

3. The supreme direct expression of the power of the people shall be referenda and free elections.

4. No one may usurp power in the Russian Federation. Seizure of power or usurping state authority shall be prosecuted by federal law.

Article 4

1. The sovereignty of the Russian Federation shall cover the whole of its territory.

2. The Constitution of the Russian Federation and federal laws shall have

supremacy in the whole territory of the Russian Federation.

3. The Russian Federation shall ensure the integrity and inviolability of its territory.

Article 5

1. The Russian Federation consists of Republics, territories, regions, cities of federal importance, an autonomous region and autonomous areas - equal subjects of the Russian Federation.

2. The Republic (State) shall have its own constitution and legislation. The territory, region, city of federal importance, autonomous region and autonomous area shall have its charter and legislation.

3. The federal structure of the Russian Federation is based on its state integrity, the unity of the system of state authority, the division of subjects of authority and powers between the bodies of state power of the Russian Federation and bodies of state power of the subjects of the Russian Federation, the equality and self-determination of peoples in the Russian Federation.

4. In relations with federal bodies of state authority all the subjects of the Russian Federation shall be equal among themselves.

Article 6

1. The citizenship of the Russian Federation shall be acquired and terminated according to federal law; it shall be one and equal, irrespective of the grounds of acquisition.

2. Every citizen of the Russian Federation shall enjoy in its territory all the rights and freedoms and bear equal duties provided for by the Constitution of the Russian Federation.

3. A citizen of the Russian Federation may be deprived of his or her citizenship or of the right to change it.

    Concerning the Citizenship of the Russian Federation, see the Law of the RSFSR No. 1948-1 of November 28, 1991.

Article 7

1. The Russian Federation is a social State whose policy is aimed at creating conditions for a worthy life and a free development of man.

2. In the Russian Federation the labor and health of people shall be protected, a guaranteed minimum wages and salaries shall be established, state support ensured to the family, maternity, paternity and childhood, to disabled persons and the elderly, the system of social services developed, state pensions, allowances and other social security guarantees shall be established.

Article 8

1. In the Russian Federation guarantees shall be provided for the integrity of economic space, a free flow of goods, services and financial resources, support for competition, and *the freedom of economic activity*.

2. In the Russian Federation recognition and equal protection shall be given to the private, state, municipal and other forms of ownership.

Article 9

1. Land and other natural resources shall be utilized and protected in the Russian Federation as the basis of life and activity of the people living in corresponding territories.

2. Land and other natural resources may be in private, state, municipal and other forms of ownership.

Article 10

The state power in the Russian Federation shall be exercised on the basis of its division into legislative, executive and judicial power. The bodies of legislative, executive and judicial power shall be independent.

Article 11

1. The state power in the Russian Federation shall be exercised by the President of the Russian Federation, the Federal Assembly (the Council of the Federation and the State Duma), the Government of the Russian Federation, and the courts of the Russian Federation.

2. The state power in the subjects of the Russian Federation shall be exercised by the bodies of state authority created by them.

3. The division of subjects of authority and power among the bodies of state power of the Russian Federation and the bodies of state power of the subjects of the Russian Federation shall be fixed by the given Constitution, the Federal and other treaties on the delimitation of the subjects of authority and powers.

Article 12

In the Russian Federation local self-government shall be recognized and guaranteed. Local self-government shall be independent within the limits of its authority. The bodies of local self-government shall not be part of the system of bodies of state authority.

Article 13

1. In the Russian Federation ideological diversity shall be recognized.

2. No ideology may be established as state or obligatory one.

3. In the Russian Federation political diversity and a multi-party system shall be recognized.

4. Public associations shall be equal before the law.

5. The creation and activities of public associations whose aims and actions are aimed at a forced change of the fundamental principles of the constitutional system and at violating the integrity of the Russian Federation, at undermining its security, at setting up armed units, and at instigating social, racial, national and religious strife shall be prohibited.

Concerning activities of public associations see Federal Law No. 82-FZ of May 19, 1995 on Public Associations.

Article 14

1. The Russian Federation is a secular state. No religion may be established as a state or obligatory one.

2. Religious associations shall be separated from the State and shall be equal before the law.

Article 15

1. The Constitution of the Russian Federation shall have the supreme juridical force, direct action and shall be used on the whole territory of the Russian Federation. Laws and other legal acts adopted in the Russian Federation shall not contradict the Constitution of the Russian Federation.

2. The bodies of state authority, the bodies of local self-government, officials, private citizens and their associations shall be obliged to observe the Constitution of the Russian Federation and laws.

3. Laws shall be officially published. Unpublished laws shall not be used. Any normative legal acts concerning human rights, freedoms and duties of man and citizen may not by used, if they are not officially published for general knowledge.

4. The universally-recognized norms of international law and international treaties and agreements of the Russian Federation shall be a component part of its legal system. If an international treaty or agreement of the Russian Federation fixes other rules than those envisaged by law, the rules of the international agreement shall be applied.

Article 16

1. The provisions of the present chapter of the Constitution comprise the fundamental principles of the constitutional system of the Russian Federation, and may not be changed otherwise than according to the rules established by the present Constitution.

2. No other provision of the present Constitution may contradict the fundamental principles of the constitutional system of the Russian Federation.

II. RIGHTS AND FREEDOMS OF MAN AND CITIZEN
Article 17

1. In the Russian Federation recognition and guarantees shall be provided for the rights and freedoms of man and citizen according to the universally recognized principles and norms of international law and according to the present Constitution.

2. Fundamental human rights and freedoms are inalienable and shall be enjoyed by everyone since the day of birth.

3. The exercise of the rights and freedoms of man and citizen shall not violate the rights and freedoms of other people.

Article 18

The rights and freedoms of man and citizen shall be directly operative. They determine the essence, meaning and implementation of laws, the activities of the legislative and executive authorities, local self-government and shall be ensured by the administration of justice.

Article 19

1. All people shall be equal before the law and court.

2. The State shall guarantee the equality of rights and freedoms of man and citizen, regardless of sex, race, nationality, language, origin, property and official status, place of residence, religion, convictions, membership of public associations, and also of other circumstances. All forms of limitations of human rights on social, racial, national, linguistic or religious grounds shall be banned.

3. Man and woman shall enjoy equal rights and freedoms and have equal possibilities to exercise them.

Article 20

1. Everyone shall have the right to life.

2. Capital punishment until its complete elimination may be envisaged by a federal law as an exclusive penalty for especially grave crimes against life, and the accused shall be granted the right to have his case examined by jury trial.

Article 21

1. Human dignity shall be protected by the State. Nothing may serve as a basis for its derogation.

2. No one shall be subject to torture, violence or other severe or humiliating treatments or punishment. No one may be subject to medical, scientific and other experiments without voluntary consent.

Article 22

1. Everyone shall have the right to freedom and personal immunity.

2. Arrest, detention and remaining in custody shall be allowed only by court decision. Without the court's decision, a person may be detained for a term no more than 48 hours.

Article 23

1. Everyone shall have the right to the inviolability of private life, personal and family secrets, the protection of honor and good name.

2. Everyone shall have the right to privacy of correspondence, of telephone conversations, postal, telegraph and other messages. Limitations of this right shall be allowed only by court decision.

Article 24

1. The collection, keeping, use and dissemination of information about the private life of a person shall not be allowed without his or her consent.

2. The bodies of state authority and local self-government, their officials

shall ensure for everyone the possibility of acquainting with the documents and materials directly affecting his or her rights and freedoms, unless otherwise provided for by law.

Article 25

The home shall be inviolable. No one shall have the right to get into a house against the will of those living there, except for the cases established by a federal law or by court decision.

Article 26

1. Everyone shall have the right to determine and indicate his nationality. No one may be forced to determine and indicate his or her nationality.

2. Everyone shall have the right to use his or her native language, to a free choice of the language of communication, upbringing, education and creative work.

Article 27

1. Everyone who legally stays in the territory of the Russian Federation shall have the right to free travel, choice of place of stay or residence.

2. Everyone may freely leave the Russian Federation. Citizens of the Russian Federation shall have the right to freely return to the Russian Federation.

> On the Procedure of Exit from the Russian Federation and Entry into the Russian Federation see Federal Law No. 114-FZ of August 15, 1996.

Article 28

Everyone shall be guaranteed the freedom of conscience, the freedom of religion, including the right to profess individually or together with any other religion or to profess no religion at all, to freely choose, possess and disseminate religious and other views and act according to them.

Article 29

1. Everyone shall be guaranteed the freedom of ideas and speech.

2. The propaganda or agitation instigating social, racial, national or religious hatred and strife shall not be allowed. The propaganda of social, racial, national, religious or linguistic supremacy shall be banned.

3. No one may by forced to express his views and convictions or to reject them

4. Everyone shall have the right to freely look for, receive, transmit, produce and distribute information by any legal way. The list of data comprising state secrets shall be determined by a federal law.

5. The freedom of mass communication shall be guaranteed. Censorship shall be banned.

Article 30

1. Everyone shall have the right to association, including the right to create trade unions for the protection of his or her interests. The freedom of

activity of public association shall be guaranteed.

2. No one may be compelled to join any association and remain in it.

Concerning the trade unions, their rights and guarantees for their activity see Federal Law No. 10-FZ of January 12, 1996.

Article 31

Citizens of the Russian Federation shall have the right assemble peacefully, without weapons, hold rallies, meetings and demonstrations, marches and pickets.

Article 32

1. Citizens of the Russian Federation shall have the right to participate in managing state affairs both directly and through their representatives.

2. Citizens of the Russian Federation shall have the right to elect and be elected to state bodies of power and local self-government bodies, and also to participate in referenda.

3. Deprived of the right to elect and be elected shall be citizens recognized by the court as legally unfit, as well as citizens kept in places of confinement by a court sentence.

4. Citizens of the Russian Federation shall enjoy equal access to state services.

5. Citizens of the expenditures shall have the right to participate in administering justice.

Article 33

Citizens of the Russian Federation shall have the right to address personally, as well as to submit individual and collective appeals to state organs and local self-government bodies.

Article 34

1. Everyone shall have the right to a free use of his abilities and property for *entrepreneurial* and economic activities not prohibited by law.

2. The economic activity aimed at monopolization and unfair competition shall not be allowed.

Article 35

1. The right of private property shall be protected by law.

2. Everyone shall have the right to have property, possess, use and dispose of it both personally and jointly with other people.

3. No one may be deprived of property otherwise than by a court decision. Forced confiscation of property for state needs may be carried out only on the proviso of preliminary and complete compensation.

4. The right of inheritance shall be guaranteed.

Article 36

1. Citizens and their associations shall have the right to possess land as private property.

2. Possession, utilization and disposal of land and other natural resources

shall be exercised by the owners freely, if it is not detrimental to the environment and does not violate the rights and lawful interests of other people.

3. The terms and rules for the use of land shall be fixed by a federal law.

Article 37

1. Labor is free. Everyone shall have the right to freely use his labor capabilities, to choose the type of activity and profession.

2. Forced labor shall be banned.

3. Everyone shall have the right to labor conditions meeting the safety and hygienic requirements, for labor remuneration without any discrimination whatsoever and not lower than minimum wages and salaries established by the federal law, as well as the right to protection against unemployment.

4. Recognition shall be given to the right to individual and collective labor disputes with the use of methods of their adjustment fixed by the federal law, including the right to strike.

5. Everyone shall have the right to rest and license. Those working by labor contracts shall be guaranteed the fixed duration of the working time, days off and holidays, and the annual paid leave established by the federal law.

Article 38

1. Maternity and childhood, and the family shall be protected by the State.

2. Care for children, their upbringing shall be equally the right and obligation of parents.

3. Able-bodied children over 18 years of age shall take care of disabled parents.

Article 39

1. Everyone shall be guaranteed social security at the expense of the State in old age, in case of an illness, disabilities, loss of bread-winner, for upbringing of children and in other cases established by law.

2. State pensions and social allowances shall be established by law.

3. Promotion shall be given to voluntary social insurance and the creation of additional forms of social security and charity.

Article 40

1. Everyone shall have the right to a home. No one may be arbitrarily deprived of his or her home.

2. The bodies of state authority and local self-government shall encourage housing construction and create conditions for exercising the right to a home.

3. Low-income people and other persons mentioned in law and in need of a home shall receive it gratis or for reasonable payment from the state, municipal and other housing stocks according to the norms fixed by law.

Article 41

1. Everyone shall have the right to health protection and medical aid.

Medical aid in state and municipal health establishments shall be rendered to individuals gratis, at the expense of the corresponding budget, insurance contributions, and other proceeds.

2. In the Russian Federation federal programs of protecting and strengthening the health of the population shall be financed by the State; measures shall be adopted to develop state, municipal and private health services; activities shall be promoted which facilitate the strengthening of health, the development of physical culture and sport, ecological and sanitary-epidemiological well-being.

3. The concealment by officials of the facts and circumstances posing a threat to the life and health of people shall entail responsibility according to the federal law.

Article 42

Everyone shall have the right to favorable environment, reliable information about its state and for a restitution of damage inflicted on his health and property by ecological transgressions.

Article 43

1. Everyone shall have the right to education.

2. Guarantees shall be provided for general access to and free pre-school, secondary and high vocational education in state or municipal educational establishments and at enterprises.

3. Everyone shall have the right to receive on a competitive basis a free higher education in a state or municipal educational establishment and at an enterprise.

4. The basic general education shall be free of charge. Parents or persons in law parents shall enable their children to receive a basic general education.

5. The Russian Federation shall establish federal state educational standards and support various forms of education and self-education.

See Law of the Russian Federation on Education in the wording of January 13, 1996.

Article 44

1. Everyone shall be guaranteed the freedom of literacy, artistic, scientific, technical and other types of creative activity, and teaching. Intellectual property shall be protected by law.

2. Everyone shall have the right to participate in cultural life and use cultural establishments and to an access to cultural values.

3. Everyone shall be obliged to care for the preservation of cultural and historical heritage and protect monuments of history and culture.

Article 45

1. State protection of the rights and freedoms of man and citizen shall be guaranteed in the Russian Federation.

2. Everyone shall be free to protect his rights and freedoms by all means not

prohibited by law.

Article 46

1. Everyone shall be guaranteed judicial protection of his rights and freedoms.

2. Decisions and actions (or inaction) of bodies of state authority and local self-government, public associations and officials may be appealed against in court.

3. Everyone shall have the right to appeal, according to international treaties of the Russian Federation, to international bodies for the protection of human rights and freedoms, if all the existing internal state means of legal protection have been exhausted.

Article 47

1. No one may be deprived of the right to the consideration of his or her case in that court and by that judge in whose cognizance the case is according to law.

2. The accused of committing a crime shall have the right to the examination of his case by a court of jury in cases envisaged by the federal law.

Article 48

1. Everyone shall be guaranteed the right to qualified legal assistance. In cases detained, taken into custody, accused of committing a crime shall have the right to receive assistance of a lawyer (council for the defense) from the moment of detention, confinement in custody or facing charges accordingly.

Article 49

1.Everyone accused of committing a crime shall be considered innocent until his guilt is proved according to the rules fixed by the federal law and confirmed by the sentence of a court which has come into legal force.

2. The accused shall not be obliged to prove his innocence.

3. Unremovable doubts about the guilt of a person shall be interpreted in favor of the accused.

Article 50

1. No one may be convicted twice for one and the same crime.

2. In administering justice it shall not be allowed to use evidence received by violating the federal law.

3. Everyone convicted for a crime shall have the right to appeal against the judgement of a superior court according to the rules envisaged by the federal law, as well as to ask for pardon or a mitigation of punishment.

Article 51

1. No one shall be obliged to give incriminating evidence, husband or wife and close relatives the range of whom is determined by the federal law.

2. The federal law may envisage other cases of absolution from the obligation to testify.

Article 52

The rights of victims of crimes and of abuse of office shall be protected by law. The State shall provide access to justice for them and a compensation for sustained damage.

Article 53

Everyone shall have the right for a state compensation for damages caused by unlawful actions (inaction) of bodies of state authority and their officials.

Article 54

1. A law introducing or aggravating responsibility shall not have retrospective effect.

2. No one may bear responsibility for the action which was not regarded as a crime when it was committed (grandfathered). If after violating law the responsibility for that is eliminated or mitigated, a new law shall be applied.

Article 55

1. The listing in the Constitution of the Russian Federation of the fundamental rights and freedoms shall not be interpreted as a rejection or derogation of other universally recognized human rights and freedoms.

2. In the Russian Federation no laws shall be adopted canceling or derogating human rights and freedoms.

3. The rights and freedoms of man and citizen may be limited by the federal law only to such an extent to which it is necessary for the protection of the fundamental principles of the constitutional system, morality, health, the rights and lawful interest of other people, for ensuring defence of the country and security of the State.

Article 56

1. In conditions of a state of emergency in order to ensure the safety of citizens and the protection of the constitutional system and in accordance with the federal constitutional law certain limitations may be placed on human rights and freedoms with the establishment of their framework and time period.

2. A state of emergency may be introduced in the whole territory of the Russian Federation and in its certain parts in case there are circumstances and according to the rules fixed by the federal constitutional law.

3. The rights and freedoms envisaged in Articles 20, 21, 23 (the first part), 24, 28, 34 (the first part), 40 (the first part), 46-54 of the Constitution of the Russian Federation, shall not be liable to limitations.

Article 57

Everyone shall be obliged to pay the legally established taxes and dues. Laws introducing new taxes or deteriorating the position of taxpayers may not have retroactive effect.

Article 58

Everyone shall be obliged to preserve nature and the environment, carefully treat the natural wealth.

Article 59

1. Defence of the Fatherland shall be a duty and obligation of citizens of the Russian Federation.

2. A citizen shall carry out military service according to the federal law.

3. A citizen of the Russian Federation shall have the right to replace military service by alternative civilian service in case his convictions or religious belief contradict military service and also in other cases envisaged by the federal law.

Article 60

A citizen of the Russian Federation may exercise his or her rights and duties in full from the age of 18.

Article 61

1. A citizen of the Russian Federation may not be deported from Russia or extradited to another State.

2. The Russian Federation shall guarantee to its citizens protection and patronage abroad.

Article 62

1. A citizen of the Russian Federation may have the citizenship of a foreign State (dual citizenship) according to the federal law or an international agreement of the Russian Federation.

2. The possession of a foreign citizenship by a citizen of the Russian Federation shall not derogate his rights and freedoms and shall not free him from the obligations stipulated by the Russian citizenship, unless otherwise provided for by federal law or an international agreement of the Russian Federation.

3. Foreign nationals and stateless persons shall enjoy in the Russian Federation the rights and bear the obligations of citizens of the Russian Federation, except for cases envisaged by the federal law or the international agreement of the Russian Federation.

Article 63

1. The Russian Federation shall grant political asylum to foreign nationals and stateless persons according to the universally recognized norms of international law.

2. In the Russian Federation it shall not be allowed to extradite to other States those people who are persecuted for political convictions, as well as for actions (or inaction) not recognized as a crime in the Russian Federation. The extradition of people accused of a crime, and also the hand-over of convicts for serving sentences in other States shall be carried out on the basis of the federal law or the international agreement of the Russian Federation.

Article 64

The provisions of the present chapter comprise the basis of the legal status of the individual in the Russian Federation and may not be changed otherwise then according to the rules introduced by the present Constitution.

III. THE FEDERAL STRUCTURE
Article 65

1. The Russian Federation includes the following subjects of the Russian Federation:

> Concerning new designations of the Ingush Republic and the Republic of North Ossetia see Decree of the President of the Russian Federation No. 20 of January 9, 1996.

Decree of the President of the Russian Federation No. 173 of February 10, 1996 included the new designation of the entity of the Russian Federation - the Republic of Kalmykia - in paragraph 1 of Article 65 of the Constitution instead of the designation the Republic of Kalmykia - Khalm Tangch the Republic of Adygeya, the Republic of Altai, the Republic of Bashkortostan, the Republic of Buryatia, the Republic of Daghestan, the Ingush Republic, the Kabardino-Balkarian Republic, the Republic of Kalmykia - Halmg Tangch, the Karachayevo-Circassian Republic, the Republic of Karelia, the Komi Republic, the Republic of Marii El, the Republic of Mordovia, the Republic of Sakha (Yakutia), the Republic of North Ossetia, the Republic of Tatarstan (Tatarstan), the Republic of Tuva, the Udmurtian Republic, the Republic of Khakassia, the *Chechen* Republic, the Chuvsash Republic - Chavash respubliki; the Altai Territory, the Krasnodar Territory, the Krasnoyarsk Territory, the Primorie Territory, the Stavropol Territory, and the Khabarovsk Territory; the Amur Region, the Archangel Region, the Astrakhan Region, the Belgorod Region, the Bryansk Region, the Vladimir Region, the Volgograd Region, the Vologda Region, the Voronezh Region, the Ivanovo Region, the Irkutsk Region, the Kaliningrad Region, the Kaluga Region, the Kamchatka Region, the Kemerovo Region, the Kirov Region, the Kostroma Region, the Kurgan Region, the Kursk Region, the Leningrad Region, the Lipetsk Region, the Magadan Region, the Moscow Region, the Murmansk Region, the Nizhni Novgorod Region, the Novgorod Region, the Novosibirsk Region, the Omsk Region, the Orenburg Region, the Orel Region, the Penza Region, the Perm Region, the Pskov Region, the Rostov Region, the Ryazan Region, the Samara Region, the Saratov Region, the Sakhalin Region, the Sverdlovsk Region, the Smolensk Region, the Tambov Region, the Tver Region, the Tomsk Region, the Tula Region, the Tyumen Region, the Ulyanovsk Region, the Chelyabinsk Region, the Chita Region, and the Yaroslavl Region; Moscow, St. Petersburg - cities of federal importance, the Jewish

Autonomous Region, the Aginsk Buryat Autonomous Area, the Komi-Permyak Autonomous Area, the Koryak Autonomous Area, the Nenets Autonomous Area, the Taimyr (Dolgano-Nenets) Autonomous Area, the Ust-Ordyn Buryat Autonomous Area, the Khanty-Mansi Autonomous Area, the Chukotka Autonomous Area, the Evenki Autonomous Area, and the Yamalo-Nents Autonomous Area.

2. The admission of the Russian Federation and the creation in it of a new subject shall be carried out according to the rules established by the federal constitutional law.

Article 66

1. The status of a Republic shall be determined by the Constitution of the Russian Federation and the Constitution of the Republic.

2. The status of a territory, region, city of federal importance, autonomous region and autonomous area shall be determined by the Constitution of the Russian Federation and the Charter of the territory, region, city of federal importance, autonomous region or autonomous area, adopted by the legislative (representative) body of the corresponding subject of the Russian Federation.

3. Upon the proposal of the legislative and executive bodies of the autonomous region or autonomous area a federal law on autonomous region or autonomous area may by adopted.

4. The relations between the autonomous area within a territory or region may be regulated by the federal law or a treaty between the bodies of state authority of the autonomous area and, accordingly, the bodies of state authority of the territory or region.

5. The status of a subject of the Russian Federation may be changed upon mutual agreement of the Russian Federation and the subject of the Russian Federation and according to the federal constitutional law.

Article 67

1. The territory of the Russian Federation shall include the territories of its subjects, inland waters and territorial sea, and the air space over them.

2. The Russian Federation shall possess sovereign rights and exercise the jurisdiction on the continental shelf and in the exclusive economic zone of the Russian Federation according to the rules fixed by the federal law and the norms of international law.

> See Federal Law No. 187-FZ of November 30, 1995 on the Continental Shelf of the Russian Federation

3. The borders between the subjects of the Russian Federation may be changed upon their mutual consent.

Article 68

1. The Russian language shall be a state language on the whole territory of the Russian Federation.

2. The Republics shall have the right to establish their own state languages. In the bodies of state authority and local self-government, state institutions of the Republics they shall be used together with the state language of the Russian Federation.

3. The Russian Federation shall guarantee to all of its peoples the right to preserve their native language and to create conditions for its study and development.

Article 69

The Russian Federation shall guarantee the rights of the indigenous small peoples according to the universally recognized principles and norms of international law and international treaties and agreements of the Russian Federation.

Article 70

1. The state flag, coat of arms and anthem of the Russian Federation, their description and rules of official use shall be established by the federal constitutional law.

The capital of the Russian Federation is the city of Moscow. The status of the capital shall be determined by the federal law.

Article 71

The jurisdiction of the Russian Federation includes:

a) adoption and amending of the Constitution of the Russian Federation and federal laws, control over their observance;

b) federal structure and the territory of the Russian Federation;

c) regulation and protection of the rights and freedoms of man and citizen; citizenship in the Russian Federation, regulation and protection of the rights of national minorities;

d) establishment of the system of federal bodies of legislative, executive and judicial authority, the rules of their organization and activities, formation of federal bodies of state authority;

e) federal state property and its management;

f) establishment of the principles of federal policy and federal programs in the sphere of state, economic, ecological, social, cultural and national development of the Russian Federation;

See the Fundamentals of the Legislation of the Russian Federation on Culture approved by Law of the Russian Federation No. 3612-1 of October 9, 1992

g) establishment of legal groups for a single market; financial, currency, credit, and customs regulation, money issue, the principles of pricing policy; federal economic services, including federal banks;

h) federal budget, federal taxes and dues, federal funds of regional development;

i) federal power systems, nuclear power-engineering, fission materials, federal transport, railways, information and communication, outer space activities;

j) foreign policy and international relations of the Russian Federation, international treaties and agreements of the Russian Federation, issues of war and peace;

k) foreign economic relations of the Russian Federation;

l) defence and security; military production; determination of rules of selling and purchasing weapons, ammunition, military equipment and other military property; production of poisonous substances, narcotic substances and rules of their use;

m) determination of the status and protection of the state border, territorial sea, air space, exclusive economic zone and continental shelf of the expenditures;

n) judicial system, procurator's office, criminal, criminal procedure and criminal-executive legislation, amnesty and pardoning, civil, civil procedure and arbitration procedure legislation, legal regulation of intellectual property;

o) federal law of conflict of laws;

p) meteorological service, standards, metric system, horometry accounting, geodesy and cartography, names of geographical units, official statistics and accounting;

q) state awards and honorary titles of the Russian Federation;

r) federal state service.

Article 72

1. The joint jurisdiction of the Russian Federation and the subjects of the Russian Federation includes:

a) providing for the correspondence of the constitutions and laws of the Republics, the charters and other normative legal acts of the territories, regions, cities of federal importance, autonomous regions or autonomous areas to the Constitution of the Russian Federation and the federal laws;

b) protection of the rights and freedoms of man and citizen; protection of the rights of national minorities; ensuring the rule of law, law and order, public security, border zone regime;

c) issues of possession, use and disposal of land, subsoil, water and other natural resources;

d) delimitation of state property;

e) nature utilization, protection of the environment and ensuring ecological safety; specially protected natural territories, protection of historical and cultural monuments;

f) general issues of upbringing, education, science, culture, physical culture and sports;

g) coordination of issues of health care; protection of the family, maternity, paternity and childhood; social protection, including social security;

h) carrying out measures against catastrophes, natural calamities, epidemics, elimination of their aftermath;

i) establishment of common principles of taxation and dues in the Russian Federation;

j) administrative, administrative procedure, labor, family, housing, land, water, and forest legislation; legislation on subsoil and environmental protection;

k) personnel of the judicial and law enforcement agencies; the Bar, notaryship;

l) protection of traditional living habitat and of traditional way of life of small ethnic communities;

m) establishment of common principles of organization of the system of bodies of state authority and local self-government;

n) coordination of international and foreign economic relations of the subjects of the Russian Federation, fulfillment of international treaties and agreements of the Russian Federation.

2. Provisions of this Article shall be equally valid for the Republics, territories, regions, cities of federal importance, autonomous regions or autonomous areas.

Article 73

Outside the limits of authority of the Russian Federation and the powers of the Russian Federation on issues under joint jurisdiction of the Russian Federation and the subjects of the Russian Federation, the subjects of the Russian Federation, the subjects of the Russian Federation shall possess full state power.

Article 74

1. In the territory of the Russian Federation it shall not be allowed to establish customs borders, dues or any other barriers for a free flow of goods, services and financial resources.

2. Limitations on the transfer of goods and services may be introduced according to the federal law, if it is necessary to ensure security, protect the life and health of people, protect nature and cultural values.

Article 75

1. The monetary unit in the Russian Federation shall be the ruble. Money issue shall be carried out exclusively by the Central Bank of the Russian Federation. Introduction and issue of other currencies in Russia shall not be allowed.

2. The protection and ensuring the stability of the ruble shall be the major task of the Central Bank of the Russian Federation, which it shall fulfil independently of the other bodies of state authority.

3. The system of taxes paid to the federal budget and the general principles

of taxation and dues in the Russian Federation shall be fixed by the federal law.

4. State loans shall be issued according to the rules fixed by the federal law and shall be floated on a voluntary basis.

Article 76

1. On the issues under the jurisdiction of the Russian Federation federal constitutional laws and federal laws shall be adopted and have direct action in the whole territory of the Russian Federation.

2. On the issues under the joint jurisdiction of the Russian Federation and subjects of the Russian Federation federal laws shall issued and laws and other normative acts of the subjects of the Russian Federation shall be adopted according to them.

3. Federal laws may not contradict the federal constitutional laws.

4. Outside the limits of authority of the Russian Federation, of the joint jurisdiction of the Russian Federation and the subjects of the Russian Federation, the Republics, territories, regions, cities of federal importance, autonomous regions or autonomous areas shall exercise their own legal regulation, including the adoption of laws and other normative acts.

5. The laws and other legislative acts of the subjects of the Russian Federation may not contradict the federal laws adopted according to the first and second parts of this Article. In case of a contradiction between a federal law and an act issued in the Russian Federation the federal law shall be applied.

6. In case of a contradiction between a federal law and a normative act of a subject of the Russian Federation adopted according to the fourth part of this Article, the normative legal act of the subject of the Russian Federation shall be applied.

Article 77

1. The system of bodies of state authority of the Republics, territories, regions, cities of federal importance, autonomous regions or autonomous areas shall be established by the subjects of the Russian Federation independently and according to the principles of the constitutional system of the Russian Federation and the general principles of the organization of representative and executive bodies of state authority fixed by federal law.

2. Within the limits of jurisdiction of the Russian Federation and the powers of the Russian Federation on the issue under the joint jurisdiction of the Russian Federation and the subjects of the Russian Federation, the federal bodies of executive authority and the bodies of executive authority of the subjects of the Russian Federation shall make up a single system of executive power of the Russian Federation.

Article 78

1. The federal bodies of executive power in order to exercise their powers

may create their own territorial organs and appoint corresponding officials.

2. The federal bodies of executive power by agreement with the bodies of executive power of the subjects of the Russian Federation may transfer to them the fulfillment of a part of their powers, if it does not contradict the Constitution of the Russian Federation and the federal laws.

3. The bodies of executive power of the subjects of the Russian Federation by agreement with the federal bodies of executive authority may transfer to them the fulfillment of a part of their powers.

4. The President of the Russian Federation and the Government of the Russian Federation shall ensure, according to the Constitution of the Russian Federation, the implementation of the powers of the federal state authority in the whole territory of the Russian Federation.

Article 79

The Russian Federation may participate in interstate associations and transfer to them part of its powers according to international treaties and agreements, if this does not involve the limitation of the rights and freedoms of man and citizen and does not contradict the principles of the constitutional system of the Russian Federation.

IV. THE PRESIDENT OF THE RUSSIAN FEDERATION

Article 80

1. The President of the Russian Federation shall be the head of the State.

2. The President of the Russian Federation shall be guarantor of the Constitution of the Russian Federation, of the rights and freedoms of man and citizen. According to the rules fixed by the Constitution of the Russian Federation, he shall adopt measures to protect the sovereignty of the Russian Federation, its independence and state integrity, ensure coordinated functioning and interaction of all the bodies of state power.

3. According to the Constitution of the Russian Federation and the federal laws, the President of the Russian Federation shall determine the guidelines of the internal and foreign policies of the State.

4. As the head of the State, the President of the Russian Federation represents the Russian Federation within the country and in international relations.

Article 81

1. The President of the Russian Federation shall be elected for four years by citizens of the Russian Federation on the basis of universal, equal, direct suffrage by secret ballot.

2. Any citizen of the Russian Federation not younger than 35 years of age and with a permanent residence record in the Russian Federation of not less than 10 years may be elected President of the Russian Federation.

3. One and the same person may not be elected President of the Russian

Federation for more than two terms running.

4. The rules of electing the President of the Russian Federation shall be determined by the federal law.

Article 82

1. When taking office the President of the Russian Federation shall take the following oath of loyalty to the people:

> "I swear in exercising the powers of the President of the Russian Federation to respect and safeguard the rights and freedoms of man and citizen, to observe and protect the Constitution of the Russian Federation, to protect the sovereignty and independence, security and integrity of the State, to faithfully serve the people."

2. The oath shall be taken in a solemn atmosphere in the presence of members of the Council of the Federation, deputies of the State Duma and judges of the Constitution Court of the Russian Federation.

Article 83

The President of the Russian Federation shall:

a) appoint by agreement with the State Duma the Chairman of the Government of the Russian Federation;

b) have the right to chair meetings of the Government of the Russian Federation;

c) adopt decision on the registration of the Government of the Russian Federation;

d) present to the State Duma a candidate for the appointment to the post of the Chairman of the Central Bank of the Russian Federation, raise before the State Duma the issue of dismissing the Chairman of the Central Bank of the Russian Federation;

e) on the proposal by the Chairman of the Government of the Russian Federation appoint and dismiss deputy chairman of the Government of the Russian Federation and federal ministers;

f) present to the Council of the Federation candidates for appointment as judges of the Constitution Court of the Russian Federation, the Supreme Court of the Russian Federation, the Higher Court of Arbitration of the Russian Federation, as well as a candidate for the post of the Procurator-General of the Russian Federation; appoint judges of other federal courts;

g) form and head the Security Council of the Russian Federation, the status of which is determined by the federal law;

h) approve the military doctrine of the Russian Federation;

i) form the Administration of the President of the Russian Federation;

j) appoint and dismiss plenipotentiary representatives of the President of the Russian Federation;

k) appoint and dismiss the supreme command of the Armed Forces of the Russian Federation;

l) after consultations with corresponding committees and commissions of the chambers of the Federal Assembly appoint and recall diplomatic representatives of the Russian Federation in foreign States and international organizations.

Article 84

The President of the Russian Federation shall:

a) announce elections to the State Duma according to the Constitution of the Russian Federation and the federal law;

b) dissolve the State Duma in cases and according to the rules fixed by the Constitution of the Russian Federation;

c) announce a referendum according to the rules fixed by the federal constitutional law;

d) submit bills to the State Duma;

e) sign and make public the federal laws;

f) address the Federal Assembly with annual messages on the situation in the country, on the guidelines of the internal and foreign policy of the State.

Article 85

1. The President of the Russian Federation may use conciliatory procedures to solve disputes between the bodies of state authority of the Russian Federation and bodies of state authority of the subjects of the Russian Federation, as well as between bodies of state authority of the subjects of the Russian Federation. In case no agreed decision is reached, he shall have the right to submit the dispute for the consideration of a corresponding court.

2. The President of the Russian Federation shall have the right to suspend acts of the Bodies of executive power of the subjects of the Russian Federation in case these acts contradict the Constitution of the Russian Federation and the federal laws, international commitments of the Russian Federation or violate the rights and freedoms of man and citizen until the issue is solved by a corresponding court.

Article 86

The President of the Russian Federation shall:

a) govern the foreign policy of the Russian Federation;

b) hold negotiations and sign international treaties and agreements of the Russian Federation;

c) sign ratification instruments;

d) receive credentials and letters of recall of diplomatic representatives accredited to him.

Article 87

1. The President of the Russian Federation shall be the Supreme Commander-in-Chief of the Armed Forces of the Russian Federation.

2. In case of an aggression against the Russian Federation or of a direct

254

threat of aggression the President of the Russian Federation shall introduce in the territory of the Russian Federation or in its certain parts a martial law and immediately inform the Council of the Federation and the State Duma about this.

3. The regime of the martial law shall be defined by the federal constitutional law.

Article 88

The President of the Russian Federation, in circumstances and according to the rules envisaged by the federal constitutional law, shall introduce a state of emergency in the territory of the Russian Federation or in its certain parts and immediately inform the Council of the Federation and the State Duma about this.

Article 89

The President of the Russian Federation shall:

a) solve the issues of citizenship of the Russian Federation and of granting political asylum;

b) decorate with state awards of the Russian Federation, award honorary titles of the Russian Federation, higher military and higher special ranks;

c) decide on pardoning.

Article 90

1. The President of the Russian Federation shall issue decrees and orders.

2. The decrees and orders of the President of the Russian Federation shall be obligatory for fulfillment in the whole territory of the Russian Federation.

3. Decrees and orders of the President of the Russian Federation shall not run counter to the Constitution of the Russian Federation and the federal laws.

Article 91

The President of the Russian Federation shall possess immunity.

Article 92

1. The President of the Russian Federation shall take up his powers from the moment of taking the oath of loyalty and cease to fulfill them with the expiration of the term of office and from the moment a newly-elected president is sworn in.

2. The President of the Russian Federation shall cease to exercise his powers short of the term in case of his resignation, stable inability because of health reasons to exercise the powers vested in him or in case of impeachment. In this case, the election of the President of the Russian Federation shall take place not later than three months from the termination of the powers short of the term.

3. In all cases when the President of the Russian Federation is incapable of fulfilling his duties, they shall temporarily be fulfilled by the Chairman of the Government of the Russian Federation. The Acting President of the

Russian Federation shall have no right to dissolve the State Duma, appoint a referendum, and also provisions of the Constitution of the Russian Federation.

Article 93

1. The President of the Russian Federation may be impeached by the Council of the Federation only on the basis of the charges of high treason or another grave crime, advanced by the State Duma and confirmed by the conclusion of the Supreme Court of the Russian Federation on the presence of the elements of crime in the actions of the President of the Russian Federation and by the conclusion of the Constitutional Court of the Russian Federation confirming that the rules of advancing the charges were observed.

2. The decision of the State Duma on advancing charges and the decision of the Council of the Federation on impeaching the President shall be adopted by two thirds of the votes of the total number of members of each chamber and on the initiative of not less than one third of the deputies of the State Duma and with the conclusion of a special commission set up by the State Duma.

3. The decision of the Council of the Federation on impeaching the President of the Russian Federation shall be adopted not later than three months after the State Duma advanced the charges against the President. If a decision of the Council of the Federation is not adopted during this time, the charges against the President shall be regarded as rejected.

V. THE FEDERAL ASSEMBLY

Article 94

The Federal Assembly - the parliament of the Russian Federation - shall be the representative and legislative body of the Russian Federation.

Article 95

1. The Federal Assembly consists of two chambers - the Council of the Federation and the State Duma.

2. The Council of the Federation includes two representatives from each subject of the Russian Federation: one from the legislative and one from the executive body of state authority.

3. The State Duma consists of 450 deputies.

Article 96

1. The State Duma shall be elected for a term of four years.

2. The rules of forming the Council of the Federation and the rules of electing deputies to the State Duma shall be introduced in federal laws.

Article 97

1. A citizen of the Russian Federation over 21 years of age and with the right to participate in elections may be elected deputy of the State Duma.

2. One and the same person may not be simultaneously a member of the

Council of the Federation and a deputy of the State Duma. A deputy of the State Duma may not be a deputy of other representative bodies of state authority and local self-government.

3. Deputies of the State Duma shall work on a permanent professional basis. Deputies of the State Duma may not be employed in the state service, engage in other paid activities, except for teaching, scientific and other creative work.

Article 98

1. Members of the Council of the Federation and deputies of the State Duma shall possess immunity during the whole term of their mandate. They may not be detained, arrested, searched, except for cases of detention at the site of crime. They may not be personally inspected, except for the cases envisaged by the federal law in order to ensure the safety of other people.

2. The issue of depriving immunity shall be solved upon the proposal of the Procurator General of the Russian Federation to the corresponding chamber of the Federal Assembly.

Article 99

1. The Federal Assembly shall work on a permanent basis.

2. The State Duma shall be convened at its first sitting on the 13th day after the elections. The President of the Russian Federation may convene a sitting of the State Duma earlier then the mentioned time.

3. The first sitting of the State Duma shall be opened by the oldest deputy.

4. From the time the State Duma of a new convocation begins to work the mandate of the State Duma of the previous convocation shall expire.

Article 100

1. The Council of the Federation and the State Duma shall hold separate sittings.

2. Sittings of the Council of the Federation and of the State Duma shall open. In cases envisaged by procedural rules the chambers shall have the right to hold closed-door sittings.

3. The chambers may hold joint sittings for the consideration of the messages of the President of the Russian Federation, the messages of the Constitutional Court of the Russian Federation, and speeches of leaders of foreign states.

Article 101

1. The Council of the Federation shall elect from among its deputies the Chairman of the Council of the Federation and his deputies. The State Duma shall elect from among its deputies the Chairman of the State Duma and his deputies.

2. The Chairman of the Council of the Federation and his deputies, the Chairman of the State Duma and his deputies chair sittings and shall be in charge of the internal routine work of the respective chamber.

3. The Council of the Federation and the State Duma shall set up committees and commissions, hold parliamentary hearings on issues in their authority.

4. Each of the chambers shall adopt its procedural rules and solve issues of procedure for its work.

5. For controlling the implementation of the federal budget the Council of the Federation and the State Duma shall create the Accounting Chamber, the composition and the rules of work of which are fixed by the federal law.

Article 102

1. The jurisdiction of the Council of the Federation includes:

a) approval of changes in borders between subjects of the Russian Federation;

b) approval of the decree of the President of the Russian Federation on the introduction of a martial law;

c) approval of the decree of the President of the Russian Federation on the introduction of a state of emergency;

d) deciding on the possibility of using the Armed Forces of the Russian Federation outside the territory of the Russian Federation;

e) appointment of elections of the President of the Russian Federation;

f) impeachment of the President of the Russian Federation;

g) appointment of judges of the Constitutional Court of the Russian Federation, of the Supreme Court of the Russian Federation, of the Higher Arbitration Court of the Russian Federation;

h) appointment and dismissal of the Procurator-General of the Russian Federation;

i) appointment and dismissal of Deputy Chairman and half of the auditors of the all Accounting Chamber.

2. The Council of the Federation shall adopt resolutions on the issues referred to its authority by the Constitution of the Russian Federation.

3. Resolution of the Council of the Federation shall be adopted by a majority of the total number of the members of the Council of the Federation, if other rules for adopting decisions are not envisaged by the Constitution of the Russian Federation.

Article 103

1. The jurisdiction of the State Duma includes:

a) approving the appointment of the Chairman of the Government of the Russian Federation by the President of the Russian Federation;

b) solution of the issue of confidence in the Government of the Russian Federation;

c) appointment and dismissal of the Chairman of the Central Bank of the Russian Federation;

d) appointment and dismissal of the Chairman and half of the auditors of the

258

Accounting Chamber;

e) appointment and dismissal of the Commissioner for human rights, who acts according to the federal constitutional law;

f) proclamation of amnesty;

g) advancing of charges against the President of the Russian Federation for his impeachment.

2. The State Duma shall adopt resolutions on the issues referred to its authority by the Constitution of the Russian Federation.

> Concerning interpretation of the third part of Article 103 of the Constitution, see Decision of the Constitutional Court of the Russian Federation No. 2-P of April 12, 1995.

3. Resolutions of the State Duma shall be adopted by a majority of the total number of the deputies of the State Duma, if other rules for adopting decisions are not stipulated by the Constitution of the Russian Federation.

Article 104

1. The power to initiate legislation shall belong to the President of the Russian Federation, the Council of the Federation, the members of the Council of the Federation, the deputies of the State Duma, the Government of the Russian Federation, and the legislative (representative) bodies of the subjects of the Russian Federation. The power to initiate legislation shall also belong to the Constitution Court of the Russian Federation, the Supreme Court of the Russian Federation, the Higher Arbitration Court of the Russian Federation on the issues in their authority.

2. Bills shall be submitted to the State Duma.

3. Bills on the introduction or cancellation of taxes, on exemption from their payment, on the issue of state loans, on changes in the financial obligations of the State, and other bills envisaging expenses covered from the federal budget may be submitted only upon the conclusion of the Government of the Russian Federation.

> Concerning the interpretation of Articles 105 and 106 of the Constitution, see Decision of the Constitutional Court of the Russian Federation No. 1-P of March 23, 1995.

Article 105

1. Federal laws shall be adopted by the State Duma.

> Concerning interpretation of the second part of Article 105 of the Constitution, see Decision of the Constitutional Court of the Russian Federation No. 2-P of April 12, 1995.

2. Federal laws shall be adopted by a majority of votes of the total number of the deputies of the State Duma, unless otherwise envisaged by the Constitution of the Russian Federation.

3. The federal laws adopted by the State Duma shall be submitted in five days for the consideration of the Council of the Federation.

4. A federal law shall be considered to be approved by the Council of the Federation, if over a half of the total number of the members of the chamber have voted for it, or it the Council of the Federation does not consider it in fourteen days. In case the Council of the Federation rejects a law, the chambers may create a conciliatory commission for overcoming the contradictions that arose, after which the federal law shall be recognized by the State Duma.

> Concerning interpretation of the fifth part of Article 105 of the Constitution, see Decision of the Constitutional Court of the Russian Federation No. 2-P of April 12, 1995.

5. In case the State Duma disagrees with the decision of the Council of the Federation, a federal law shall be considered adopted, if during the second vote not less than two thirds of the total number of the deputies of the State Duma supported it.

> Concerning interpretation of Articles 105 and 106 of the Constitution, see Decision of the Constitutional Court of the Russian Federation No. 1-P of March 23, 1995.

Article 106

Liable to obligatory consideration by the Council of the Federation shall be the federal laws adopted by the State Duma on the following issues:

a) federal budget;

b) federal taxes and dues;

c) financial, currency, credit, customs regulation, and money issue;

d) ratification and denunciation of international treaties and agreements of the Russian Federation;

e) the status and protection of the state border of the Russian Federation;

f) *peace* and war.

Article 107

1. The adopted federal law shall be submitted in five days to the President of the Russian Federation for signing and making it public.

2. The President of the Russian Federation shall sign the federal law and make it public in fourteen days.

> Concerning interpretation of the third part of Article 107 of the Constitution, see Decision of the Constitutional Court of the Russian Federation No. 2-P of April 12, 1995.

3. If in fourteen days since the moment of receiving the federal law the President rejects it, the State Duma and the Council of the Federation shall reconsider the given law according to the rules fixed by the Constitution of the Russian Federation. If during the second vote, the law is approved in the earlier adopted wording by not less than two thirds of the total number of the members of the Council of the Federation and of the deputies of the Duma, it shall be signed by the President in seven days and made public.

Article 108

1. Federal constitutional laws shall be adopted on the issues envisaged by the Constitution of the Russian Federation.

Concerning interpretation of the second part of Article 108 of the Constitution, see Decision of the Constitutional Court of the Russian Federation No. 2-P of April 12, 1995.

2. A federal constitutional law shall be considered to be adopted, if it is approved by not less than three fourths of the total number of the members of the Council of the Federation and not less than two thirds of the total number of the deputies of the State Duma. The adopted federal constitutional law shall be signed by the President of the Russian Federation in fourteen days and made public.

Article 109

1. The State Duma may be dissolved by the President of the Russian Federation in cases envisaged in Articles 111 and 117 of the Constitution of the Russian Federation.

2. In case the State Duma is dissolved, the President of the Russian Federation shall appoint the date of election so that a newly-elected State Duma could meet not later than four months from the moment of dissolution.

3. The State Duma may not be dissolved on the grounds envisaged in Article 117 of the Constitution of the Russian Federation during a year after it was elected.

4. The State Duma may not be dissolved from the moment it advances charges against the President of the Russian Federation until the Council of the Federation adopts a decision on the issue.

5. The State Duma may not be dissolved while a state of emergency or a martial law operate in the whole territory of the Russian Federation, as well as during six months before the term of office of the President expires.

VI. THE GOVERNMENT OF THE RUSSIAN FEDERATION

Article 110

1. The executive power in Russia shall be exercised by the Government of the Russian Federation.

2. The Government of the Russian Federation consists of the Chairman of the Government of the Russian Federation, Deputy Chairman of the Government of the Russian Federation and federal ministries.

Article 111

1. The Chairman of the Government of the Russian Federation shall be appointed by the President of the Russian Federation with the consent of the State Duma.

2. The proposal on the candidate to the post of the Chairman of the

Government of the Russian Federation shall be submitted not later than two weeks after a newly-elected President of the Russian Federation takes office or after the resignation of the Government of the Russian Federation or one week after the State Duma rejects the candidate.

3. The State Duma shall consider the candidate nominated by the President of the Russian Federation for the post of the Chairman of the Government of the Russian Federation during the week after the submission of the nomination.

4. In case the State Duma rejects three times the candidates for the post of the Chairman of the Government of the Russian Federation, dissolve the State Duma and appoint new elections.

Article 112

1. Not later than a week after the appointment shall submit to the President of the Russian Federation proposals on the structure of the federal bodies of executive power. The Structure of the Federal Bodies of Executive Power was approved by Decree of the President of the Russian Federation No. 1177 of August 14, 1996.

2. The Chairman of the Government of the Russian Federation shall propose to the President of the Russian Federation candidates for the posts of Deputy chairmen of the Government of the Russian Federation and federal ministries.

Article 113

According to the Constitution of the Russian Federation, the federal laws and decrees of the President of the Russian Federation the Chairman of the Government of the Russian Federation shall determine the guidelines of the activities of the Government of the Russian Federation and organize its work.

Article 114

1. The Government of the Russian Federation shall:

a) work out and submit to the State Duma the federal budget and ensure its implementation, submit to the State Duma a report on the implementation of the federal budget;

b) ensure the implementation in the Russian Federation of a single financial, credit and monetary policy;

c) ensure the implementation in the Russian Federation of a single state policy in the sphere of culture, science, education, health protection, social security and ecology;

d) manages the federal property;

e) carry out measures to secure the defence of the country, the state security, and the implementation of the foreign policy of the Russian Federation;

f) implement measures to ensure the rule of law, human rights and freedoms, protection of property and public order, and *crime control*;

g) exercise other powers vested in it by the Constitution of the Russian Federation, the federal laws and decrees of the President of the Russian Federation.

2. The rules of activities of the Government of the Russian Federation shall be determined by the federal constitutional law.

Article 115

1. On the basis and for the sake of implementation of the Constitution of the Russian Federation, the federal laws, normative decrees of the President of the Russian Federation, the Government of the Russian Federation shall issue decisions and orders and ensures their implementation.

2. The decisions and orders of the Government of the Russian Federation shall be obligatory for fulfillment in the Russian Federation.

3. The decisions and orders of the Government of the Russian Federation, if they are inconsistent with the Constitution of the Russian Federation, federal laws and decrees of the President of the Russian Federation, may by canceled by the President of the Russian Federation.

Article 116

The Government of the Russian Federation shall resign before a newly-elected President of the Russian Federation.

Article 117

1. The Government of the Russian Federation may offer to resign and the President of the Russian Federation either shall accept or reject the resignation.

2. The President of the Russian Federation may make a decision on the resignation of the Government of the Russian Federation.

> Concerning interpretation of the third part of Article 117 of the Constitution, see Decision of the Constitutional Court of the Russian Federation No. 2-P of April 12, 1995.

3. The State Duma may express no-confidence to the Government of the Russian Federation. A no-confidence resolution shall be adopted by a majority of votes of the total number of the deputies of the State Duma. After the State Duma expresses no-confidence to the Government of the Russian Federation, the President of the Russian Federation shall be free to announce the resignation of the Government or to reject the decision of the State Duma. In case the State Duma again expresses no-confidence to the Government of the Russian Federation during three months, the President of the Russian Federation shall announce the resignation of the Government or dissolve the State Duma.

4. The Chairman of the Government of the Russian Federation may raise before the State Duma the issues of no-confidence to the Government of the Russian Federation. If the State Duma votes no-confidence, the President shall adopt in seven days a decision on the resignation of the Government of

the Russian Federation or dissolve the State Duma and announce new elections.

5. In case of a resignation of the Government of the Russian Federation, it shall continue to work on the instruction of the President of the Russian Federation until a new Government of the Russian Federation is formed.

VII. JUDICIAL POWER
Article 118
1. Justice in the Russian Federation shall be administered by the courts alone.

2. The judicial power shall be exercised by means of constitutional, civil, administrative and criminal proceedings.

3. The judicial system of the Russian Federation shall be instituted by the Constitution of the Russian Federation and the federal constitutional law. The creation of extraordinary courts shall not be allowed.

Article 119
Judges may be citizens of the Russian Federation over 25 years of age with a higher education in law and a law service record of not less than five years. The federal law may introduce additional requirements for judges of the courts of the Russian Federation.

Article 120
1. Judges shall be independent and submit only to the Constitution and the federal law.

2. If after considering a case, the court of law decides that an act of a state or other body contradicts the law, it shall pass an appropriate decision according to the law.

Article 121
1. Judges shall be irremovable.

2. The powers of a judge can be ceased or suspended only on the grounds and according to the rules fixed by the federal law.

Article 122
1. Judges shall possess immunity.

2. A judge may not face criminal responsibility otherwise than according to the rules fixed by the federal law.

Article 123
1. Examination of cases in all courts shall be open. Examinations in camera shall be allowed only in cases envisaged by the federal law.

2. Trial by default in criminal courts shall not be allowed except in cases fixed by the federal law.

3. Judicial proceedings shall be held on the basis of controversy and equality of the parties.

4. In cases fixed by the federal law justice shall be administered by a jury.

Article 124

The courts shall be financed only from the federal budget and the possibility of the complete and independent administration of justice shall be ensured in keeping with the requirements of federal law.

Article 125

1. The Constitution Court of the Russian Federation consists of 19 judges.

2. The Constitution Court of the Russian Federation upon requests of the President of the Russian Federation, the Council of the Federation, the State Duma, one fifth of the members of the Council of the Federation or of the deputies of the State Duma, the Government of the Russian Federation, the Supreme Court of the Russian Federation and the Higher Arbitration Court of the Russian Federation, the bodies of legislative and executive power of the subjects of the Russian Federation shall consider cases on the correspondence to the Constitution of the Russian Federation of:

a) the federal laws, normative acts of the President of the Russian Federation, the Council of the Federation, the State Duma, the Government of the Russia;

b) the constitutions of republics, charters, and also the laws and other normative acts of the subjects of the Russian Federation adopted on the issues under the jurisdiction of the bodies of state authority of the Russian Federation or under the joint jurisdiction of the bodies of state authority of the Russian Federation and the bodies of state authority of the subjects of the Russian Federation;

c) the treaties concluded between the bodies of state authority of the Russian Federation and the bodies of state authority of the subjects of the Russian Federation, the treaties concluded between the bodies of state authority of the subjects of the Russian Federation;

d) international treaties and agreements of the Russian Federation which have not come into force.

3. The Constitutional Court of the Russian Federation shall resolve disputes on jurisdiction matters:

a) between the federal bodies of state authority;

b) between the bodies of state authority of the Russian Federation and the bodies of state authority of the subjects of the Russian Federation;

c) between the higher bodies of state authority of the subjects of the Russian Federation.

4. The Constitutional Court of the Russian Federation, upon complaints about violations of constitutional rights and freedoms of citizens and upon court requests shall check, according to the rules fixed by the federal law, the constitutionality of a law applied or subjects to be applied in a concrete case.

5. The Constitution Court of the Russian Federation, upon the requests of

the President of the Russian Federation, the Council of the Federation, the State Duma, the Government of the Russian Federation, the bodies of the legislative power of the subjects of the Russian Federation, shall give its interpretation of the Constitution of the Russian Federation.

6. Acts or their certain provisions recognized as unconstitutional shall become invalid; international treaties and agreements not corresponding to the Constitution of the Russian Federation shall not be liable for enforcement and application.

7. The Constitution Court of the Russian Federation, upon the request of the Council of the Federation, shall provide a conclusion on the observance of the fixed procedure for advancing charges of treason or of another grave crime against the President of the Russian Federation.

Article 126

The Supreme Court of the Russian Federation shall be the supreme judicial body for civil, criminal, administrative and other cases under the jurisdiction of common courts, shall carry out judicial supervision over their activities according to federal law-envisaged procedural forms and provide explanations on the issues of court proceedings.

Article 127

The Higher Arbitration Court of the Russian Federation shall be the supreme judicial body for settling economic disputes and other cases examined by courts of arbitration, shall carry out judicial supervision over their activities according to federal law-envisaged procedural forms and provide explanations on the issues of court proceedings.

Concerning the Arbitration Courts in the Russian Federation, see Federal Constitutional Law No. 1-FKZ of April 28, 1995.

Article 128

1. The judges of the Constitution Court of the Russian Federation, the Supreme Court of the Russian Federation, the Higher Arbitration Court of the Russian Federation shall be appointed by the Council of the Federation upon the proposals by the President of the Russian Federation.

2. Judges of other federal courts shall be appointed by the President of the Russian Federation according to the rules fixed by the federal law.

3. The powers, the rules for forming and functioning of the Constitution Court of the Russian Federation, of the Supreme Court of the Russian Federation and the Higher Arbitration Court of the Russian Federation shall be fixed by the federal constitutional law.

Article 129

1. The Procurator's Office of the Russian Federation shall form a single centralized structure in which procurators are subordinate to superior procurators and the Procurator-General of the Russian Federation.

2. The Procurator-General of the Russian Federation shall be appointed and

dismissed by the Council of the Federation upon the proposal of the President of the Russian Federation.

3. The procurators of the subjects of the Russian Federation shall be appointed by the Procurator-General of the Russian Federation by agreement with the subjects.

4. Other procurators shall be appointed by the Procurator-General of the Russian Federation.

5. The powers, organization and the rules of the functioning of the Procurator's Office of the Russian Federation shall be determined by the federal law.

VIII. LOCAL SELF-GOVERNMENT

Concerning the general principles of the organization of local self-government in the Russian Federation, see Federal Law No. 154-FZ of August 28, 1995.

Article 130

1. Local self-government in the Russian Federation shall ensure the independent solution by the population of the issues of local importance, of possession, use and disposal of municipal property.

2. Local self-government shall be exercised by citizens through a referendum, election, other forms of direct expression of the will of the people, through elected and other bodies of local self-government.

Article 131

1. Local self-government shall be administered in urban and rural settlements and in other areas with the consideration of the historical and other local traditions. The structure of local self-government bodies shall be determined by the population independently.

2. Changes in borders of the areas in which local self-government is administered shall be made with the consideration of the opinion of the population of the corresponding areas.

Article 132

1. The local self-government bodies shall independently manage municipal property, form, adopt and implement the local budgets, introduce local taxes and dues, ensure the protection of public order, and also solve other issues of local importance.

2. The local self-government bodies may be vested by law with certain state powers and receive the necessary material and financial resources for their implementation. The implementation of the delegated powers shall be controlled by the State.

Article 133

Local self-government in the Russian Federation shall be guaranteed by the right for judicial protection, for a compensation for additional expenses emerging   as a result of decisions adopted by state authority bodies, by a ban on the limitations on the rights of local self-government fixed by the Constitution of the Russian Federation and the federal laws.

IX.   CONSTITUTIONAL AMENDMENTS AND REVIEW OF THE CONSTITUTION

Article 134

Proposals on amendments and review of the provisions of the Constitution of the Russian Federation may be submitted by the President of the Russian Federation, the Council of the Federation, the State Duma, the Government of the Russian Federation, the legislative (representative) bodies of the subjects of the Russian Federation, and also by groups numbering not less than one fifth of the number of the members of the Council of the Federation or of the deputies of the State Duma.

Article 135

1. Provisions of Chapters 1, 2, and 9 of the Constitution of the Russian Federation may not be revised by the Federal Assembly.

Concerning interpretation of the second part of Article 135 of the Constitution, see Decision of the Constitution Court of the Russian Federation No. 2-P of April 12, 1995.

2. If a proposal on the review of the provisions of Chapter 1, 2, and 9 of the Constitution of the Russian Federation is supported by the three fifths of the total number of the members of the Council of the Federation and the deputies of the State Duma, then according to federal constitutional law a Constitutional Assembly shall be convened.

3. The Constitutional Assembly shall either confirm the invariability of the Constitution of the Russian Federation or draft a new Constitution of the Russian Federation, which shall be adopted by the Constitutional Assembly by two thirds of the total number of its members or submitted to a referendum. In case of a referendum the Constitution of the Russian Federation shall be considered adopted, if over half of the voters who came to the polls supported it and under the condition that over half of the electorate participated in the referendum.

Article 136

Concerning interpretation of Article 136 of the Constitution of the Russian Federation, see Decision of the Constitution Court of the Russian Federation No. 12-P of October 31, 1995.

Amendments to the provisions of Chapters 3-8 of the Constitution of the Russian Federation shall be adopted according to the rules fixed for adoption of federal constitutional laws and come into force after they are approved by the bodies of legislative power of not less than two thirds of the subjects of the Russian Federation.

Article 137

1. Amendments in Article 65 of the Constitution of the Russian Federation determining the structure of the Russian Federation shall be introduced on the basis of the federal constitutional law on the admission to the Russian Federation and the creation of new subjects of the Russian Federation within it, on changes in the constitutional-legal status of a subject of the Russian Federation.

Concerning interpretation of the second part of Article 137 of this Constitution, see Decision of the Constitution Court of the Russian Federation No. 15-P of November 28, 1995.

SECOND SECTION
CONCLUDING AND TRANSITIONAL PROVISIONS

1. The Constitution of the Russian Federation shall come into force from the moment of its official publication according to the results of a nationwide referendum.

The day of the nationwide referendum of December 12, 1993 shall be considered to be the day of adopting the Constitution of the Russian Federation.

Simultaneously, the Constitution (Fundamental Law) of the Russian Federation, adopted on April 12, 1978 with all amendments and changes, shall become invalid.

In case of non-compliance with the Constitution of the Russian Federation of the provisions of the Federal treaty - the Treaty on the Division of Subjects of Jurisdiction and Powers Between the Federal Bodies of State Power of the Russian Federation and the Bodies of Authority of the Sovereign Republics within the Russian Federation, the Treaty on the Division of Subjects of Jurisdiction and Powers Between the Federal Bodies of State Power of the Russian Federation and the Bodies of Authority of the Territories, Regions, Cities of Moscow and St. Petersburg of the Russian Federation, the Treaty on the Division of Subjects of Jurisdiction and Powers Between the Federal Bodies of State Power of the Russian Federation and the Bodies of Authority of the Autonomous Region, and Autonomous Areas within the Russian Federation, and also other treaties concluded between the federal bodies of state authority of the Russian Federation and bodies of state authority of the subjects of the Russian Federation, treaties between the bodies of state authority of the subjects of the Russian Federation, the provisions of the Constitution of the Russian Federation shall be applicable

2. The laws and other legal acts acting in the territory of the Russian Federation before the given Constitution comes into force shall be applied in that part which does not contradict the Constitution of Russia.

3. The President of the Russian Federation, elected according to the Constitution (Fundamental Law) of the Russian Federation - Russia, since the given Constitution comes into force, since carry out the powers fixed in it until the term of office for which he was elected expires.

4. The Council of Ministers (Government) of the Russian Federation from the moment when the given Constitution comes into force shall acquire the rights, obligations and responsibilities of the Government of the Russian Federation fixed by the Constitution of the Russian Federation and since then shall be called the Government of the Russian Federation.

5. The courts of the Russian Federation shall administer justice according to their powers fixed by the given Constitution.

After the Constitution comes into force, the judges of all the courts of the Russian Federation shall retain their powers until the term they were elected for expires. Vacant positions shall be filled in according to the rules fixed by the given Constitution.

6. Until the adoption and coming into force of the federal law establishing the rules for considering cases by a court of jury, the existing rules of court examination of corresponding cases shall be preserved.

Until the criminal procedure legislation of the Russian Federation is brought into conformity with the provisions of the present Constitution, the previous rules for arrest, detention and keeping in custody of people suspected of committing crime shall be preserved.

7. The Council of the Federation of the first convocation and the State Duma of the first convocation shall be elected for a period of two years.

8. The Council of the Federation shall meet in its first sitting on the 13th day after its election. The first sitting of the Council of the Federation shall be opened by the President of the Russian Federation.

9. A deputy of the State Duma of the first convocation may be simultaneously a member of the Government of the Russian Federation. The provisions of the present Constitution on the immunity of deputies in that part which concerns the actions (inaction) connected with fulfillment of office duties shall not extend to the deputies of the State Duma, members of the Government of the Russian Federation.

The deputies of the Council of the Federation of the first convocation shall exercise their powers on a non-permanent basis.

APPENDIX 2

Russia's Historical Economic Development

Introduction

As we enter the 21st Century, Russia and the nations of the West have become wiser. Both countries still have much to teach each other, and much to learn from one another. Jointly they have demonstrated that it is people who support the government and not governments that support the people. From each other they have learned that private hands-on ownership produces better custodians and efficiency than communal absentee ownership. They have learned that extremes in the form of social unfairness and injustice in their societies produces chaos. The time has now come to benefit from each other's experience.

If the cold war was indeed a contest between the U.S. and the U.S.S.R, with their competing systems, and the objective of achieving well-being in a socially moral and just society, the jury is still out. While the U.S. was able to create greater material wealth, paradoxically its population is less fulfilled due to the erosion of traditional moral values within its culture. It is ironic that now it is again possible for the U.S. and Russia to share experiences, the U.S. has misplaced the one thing of most value that it once had to offer; moral, ethical and spiritual principles of conduct.

Until recently, most Americans had overlooked or misunderstood cultural changes which were occurring within its nation. Americans noticed these changes, but did not understand that far from isolated curiosities, these were harbingers of a new culture that would shortly burst upon them and sweep their land into a new United States that Americans would hardly be able to recognize. Americans now endure in the new culture of modern liberalism, with rap songs calling for the killing of policeman, sexual mutilation, high homicide figures, collapse of the criminal justice systems, high illegitimate birth rates, the growth of aids, corruption, the popularization of violence in entertainment, a disoriented and less than well-educated youth, distrust of government, and growing loss of freedom as many increasingly seek to legislate equality of outcomes in their efforts to create an egalitarian society. With each new evidence of deterioration, Americans lament for a moment and then become accustomed to it. Many Americans now realize that ethics, moral principles and spiritual foundations are more important to a just society and well-being than material goods.

Russia, which has already tried egalitarianism, could be reminding the U.S. And its leaders that it doesn't work. The U.S., which has achieved economic success, could be reminding Russia that economic progress without traditional moral values does not produce a just society, or human well-being.

Culture, as used here, refers to all human behavior and institutions, including popular entertainment, art, religion, education, scholarship, economic activity, science, technology, laws, and morality. Of that list, only science, technology and the economy may be said to be healthy in the U.S. today. And it is problematical how long that will last. It seems highly unlikely that a vigorous U.S. economy can be sustained in an enfeebled hedonistic culture, particularly when personal achievement is increasingly rejected in the U.S. as the criteria for the distribution of rewards. Ironically, Russia's difficult and painful experience with this phenomena is no longer fully understood or accepted in the U.S.. Perhaps the time to get real has arrived?

Who has the most money, is less significant than the fact that the cultural and spiritual trajectories of both countries continues downward. This is not to deny that much in both cultures remains healthy, that many families are intact and continue to raise children with strong moral values. Both Russian and American culture is complex and resilient. But it is also not to be denied that there are aspects of almost every branch of both cultures that are now worse.

Large chunks of the moral and ethical life of the United States and Russia, major features of their culture, have disappeared altogether and more are in the process of extinction. These have been replaced by new and frightening ways of viewing morality, that are very unwelcome. As behavior worsens, the community adjusts its standards, so that conduct once thought reprehensible is no longer deemed so. It is the collapse of these moral forces that has brought the U.S. to offer Russia the advice that corruption is to be expected in creating a democracy. It is not.

Now, together the people of the U.S. and Russia have an opportunity to join once again, as they did in the generation of the 1940's. This time it would be a war on the poverty, injustice, immorality, corruption and unethical practices, which destroy democracies. A nation's moral life is of course the foundation of its culture.

The democratic principle is in rhetorical ascendancy everywhere, and yet it is worth asking whether in actuality, as a matter of practice rather then declamation, it is not in retreat. Our greatest joint hope lies in a moral and spiritual regeneration which could be produced by either a religious revival or the revival of public discourse about morality. It may yet develop that the nation who designs a system that serves the true well-being of the individual people, will be the one that provides leadership in restoring morality, ethics, and spirituality to the economy of the human equation.

This appendix, about Russia's historical economic development, provides clues to the compatibility of aspirations of the Russian and the U.S. populations, who jointly share a hunger to transcend their inadequate past whether it be economic, moral or spiritual.

APPENDIX 2

Russia's Historical Economic Development

1917 October Revolution to World War II

For more than three centuries, from 1613 to 1917, the Romanov Dynasty built upon the previous Moscovite Empire by extending its rule from the Arctic Ocean to the Black Sea, from the Baltic Sea to the Pacific Ocean. The Romanov's ruled as an absolute monarchy, without any democracy.

The Decembrist officers' revolt of 1825, marks the first stirring of democratic passions. After Alexander II freed the surfs in 1861, a revolutionary movement led by the gentry gathered strength, leading to the tsar's assassination in 1881. Russia's defeat in the Russo-Japanese War shook confidence in the monarchy, which relinquished some authority after a series of strikes and protests in 1905.

The first democratic parliament, or Duma (which in English translates into *think*), met in 1906. Supported by parties on the right and left, the 1917 February Revolution toppled the monarchy. Then Lenin returned from exile to lead the leftist Bolsheviks in their struggle for control of the revolution and they seized power in a coup on October 25, 1917.

The March 1918 Breast Treaty with Germany, released the Bolsheviks from an unwanted role in World War I. In the process, they lost control over the Ukraine, the Baltics, and other czarist lands. They then moved their capital from Petrograd (Petersburg) to Moscow, and renamed themselves Communists.

Lenin dissolved the popularly elected Constituent Assembly on January 6, 1918, killing in one stroke the democratic movement begun in 1906. Nicholas II and his family were murdered in July 1918, as a three year civil war begins between the Red and White Armies - the latter a loose coalition of anti-communist factions. Lenin uses charisma and inflammatory propaganda to rally support for the Bolsheviks and the highly centralized war economy, known as War Communism.

With a failing economy, Lenin started the New Economic Policy (NEP) - an admitted *Retreat from Socialism*. It began in 1921, and continued beyond his death in 1924. Lenin's aspiring successors, Joseph Stalin and Leon Trotsky, debated the future of communism. Stalin, with his policy of *socialism in one country*, triumphs over his rival, which ignited their global revolution.

In 1927, Trotsky was expelled from the party and later he was exiled and murdered. With his Five-Year Plan of 1928, Stalin takes iron-fisted control of the economy.

During 1928 to 1938, Stalin began a total transformation of Soviet society, by regimenting every aspect of public life. Heavy industry is emphasized, along with massive public works projects. But the peasants, Russia's largest class, remained the major obstacle to *the dictatorship of the proletariat*. To transform them from traditional farmers into rural workers, collective and state farms were instituted. The peasants, however, resisted fiercely.

Reigns of terror began in 1929, as Stalin invaded the countryside to crush the resistance. *Better-off* farmers whom he vilifies as *kulaks*, or *rich peasants*, were targeted. Confiscated crops lead to famine, and millions starved. In show trials from 1936 to 1938, Stalin purged the Communist Party of half its members - some 1.2 million people. Millions more were slain or exiled.

In 1933, fascism came to power in Germany. In 1937, the people of Europe realized that the expansionary aggressive policies of German fascism would inevitably lead to the beginning of World War II. France and Great Britain offered the Soviet Union a pact of mutual help in case of German aggression in any of the European countries. These negotiations were successful and culminated, in August of 1939, in the passing of an agreement on mutual help among the three governments. There was nothing left to do but sign the treaty. However, Stalin decided to interrupt further negotiations and concluded a Non-Aggression Pact with Hitler. Hitler had only one goal with this pact, to exclude the U.S.S.R. (a potential enemy in the future war) from the struggle.

In November of 1939, the U.S.S.R. made a successful attack against Finland. The victory cost an enormous number of Russian casualties and the war with Finland demonstrated the Soviet army's extremely low level of readiness for modern war conditions. After Hitler and his associates quickly assessed the results of the Soviet-Finish War and the internal situation in the U.S.S.R., they decided to prepare for the *blitzkrieg*, that is, a lightning strike on the Soviet Union. This preparation was taking place at the same time as Germany was heavily engaged in combat with England. On June 22, 1941, Germany started the war against the Soviet Union. The Soviet Union was unprepared and vulnerable to the German attack.

Hitler estimated that the defeat of the Soviet Union was possible in one to two months. His optimism was based on the lack of leaders in the Soviet high command and the army's officers corps, plus extreme dissatisfaction of the population with the nation's internal political leadership. In reality, at the beginning of the war, the leadership of the Soviet Army was also decimated. It had suffered enormous fatal casualties during the Soviet-Finish War of 1939, and at the beginning of World War II with Germany.

The repressions which started in the Soviet Union at the end of the 1920's, reached monstrous sizes by the end of the 1930's. In May of 1937, there were 350 thousand people in concentration camps, and in 1941, there were 2.3 million people. Among those who were shot, were three of the five Marshals of the Soviet Union, almost all commanders of the military district, and many other prominent military leaders. During 1938 alone, all commanders of the corps, division, brigades, plus half of the regiment commanders, the military science theorists, and the instructors of the highest schools were imprisoned and most were shot. Stalin ordered all the Soviet military personnel sent to the Spanish Civil War in 1939 shot dead, because he did not want the revolutionary ideas returning home. There were then few people in the Armed Forces of the country able to offer and implement modern military techniques.

Soviet secret service agents, England and other countries warned the U.S.S.R. about Germany's preparation for an attack. However, in accordance with Stalin's personal instructions, the actions to prepare the military readiness of the army were not taken. Stalin was afraid to have the Soviet Union take steps which could undermine confidence in the Soviet-German Non-Aggression Pact.

In three weeks, Germany caused severe defeat to the Red Army and advanced up to 600 kilometers into the country. By the end of 1941, the German armies moved forward up to 1200 kilometers into the country, taking captive about one million people and annexing the most economically developed territories with almost a third of the country's population (75 million people). The Soviet armies sustained losses not seen in any previous war. The Soviet army was decimated with the loss of 7 million people, 22 thousand tanks, and 25 thousand planes.

Even though Stalin's regime of personal power had caused the terrible distress throughout, the peoples of the Soviet Union rose up to defend their Motherland. Ultimately, even in the face of unforeseen difficulties, they were victorious over Germany and its satellites. The victory cost over 27 million Soviet lives.

After the end of the war, the same totalitarian regime continued to exist in the Soviet Union and the propaganda of Stalin's cult reached an even larger scale. The country had to restore the economy destroyed by the war. Dictatorship methods to mobilize resources allowed for the restoration of the destroyed regions' economies, and these areas were able to achieve the pre-war levels of production within four years. Simultaneously, because of the regime's continued severe suppression of freedom of speech and thought, the people started to show dissatisfaction more openly. After the restoration of the economy, the conditions and level of life for the people remained at poverty level. Inspired by the victory and the successes in the liberation of the European countries from the fascist tyranny, the Soviet people started to express their opinions about the necessity for fundamental reform of the Soviet system with orientation toward Western democracy.

The tense economic situation and clear signs of political instability posed a dilemma for the country's leaders (of course their only concern was their own personal power and benefits). They needed either radical political and economic reforms, or terror to drive the people back to their former course of absolute obedience to authorities. Stalin and his associates chose the second way and the suppression campaign was intensified. The increasing social instability contributed to a vicious tax press on peasants and unrest in concentration camps. Between 1945 and 1953 (the year of Stalin's death!), an additional million people were added to the 1.5 million people who were already in concentration camps at the end of the war. Stalin and his associates, relying upon repression and the propagandist machinery, tried to isolate the country from the influence of Western democracy. They aggressively pursued the policy of the *Iron Curtain* between the Soviet Union and the other countries of the world community.

From Stalin's death in 1953 until 1985, the country's leadership tried to put into effect economic reforms to create more liberal conditions of production development and some democratization of the society. This period was characterized by significant discrepancy between the decrees made and the political actions actually taken. All reforms were deadlocked in a severe centralized system of economic control, a one party system, and the desire to follow the principles of socialism. All reforms were based on the necessity to keep and strengthen the unshakable base of socialism-state-bureaucratic property. Foreign policy was based on the necessity to provide military superiority over Western countries and to render huge economic assistance for countries which oriented their politics towards the Soviet Union.

Expenses for the militarization of the economy was growing disproportionately to the country's ability to support it. In all areas of the economy, with the exception of the military sector, the Soviet Union was falling more and more behind the developed capitalist countries. In cities and other populated areas, the shortages of provisions and goods were growing, and there appeared indications of starvation in many regions. Corruption and misappropriation penetrated all levels of power throughout the Soviet Union. At the same time, it should be noted that the Soviet Union exported raw, non-recoverable resources, especially oil and gas, at dumping, *below world market value*, prices. The inflow of funds provided some opportunity to support relatively satisfactory supplies for large industrial centers by importing basic consumer goods.

At the beginning of the 1980's, the Soviet Union came close to a crisis throughout its entire social and economic system. Poverty level living for tens of millions of people, the absence of opportunity to meet everyday requirements, and the lack of material interest in the results of their labor, brought on physical and moral degeneracy of the people.

In April of 1985, Mikhail Gorbachev took the helm of internal and foreign policies in the Soviet Union. His name is associated with two new terms, which are now included in world lexicon: *perestroika* (restructuring) and *glasnost* (openness).

Perestroika (which touched mainly the political life in the country) directly effected the democratization of the Soviet society, but the economic basis of the state was kept unshakable until 1991. The authorities preserved all means of production as state property, centralized planning, and centralized resource distribution. The state continued to pay subsidies to unprofitable enterprises and did not allow their liquidation or bankruptcy. Peasants did not receive the right to own land and agriculture management was still centralized. The authorities continued to give the peasants instructions about when, where, and how much to produce. That produce was taken from the peasants at fixed prices below that needed to reimburse their production expenses. Gorbachev's perestroika and glasnost did not change the economy, and it only continued its decline to the point of collapse. At the same time, it should be noted, that perestroika and glasnost facilitated the people's transition from blindly obeying the communist party to a new direction of self-awareness. This new realization, however, created bitterness and disillusionment towards their ideals and convictions and made it impossible to continue under the old system.

In 1990, for the first time, there was a democratic election of the Congress of Peoples Deputies, which deprived the Communist Party of its controlling role in economies and politics. An opposition group, headed by Boris Yeltsin, formed inside the party itself and called for radical reform to improve the economy. During the same period, a multi-party political system began to form in Russia. Before perestroika, any political activity not controlled by the communist was suppressed by the authorities. Any opposition was limited to illegal meetings of small groups. Since the beginning of perestroika, various groups started to form small political parties to express their interests. Origination and development of the multi-party system is a necessary development in the move toward democracy, as is freedom of speech.

The government was forced to allow the activity of independent trade unions and strikes. The authorities passed a decree to create cooperatives and the first small private businesses began to operate independent of the state. In the beginning of 1992, the government took a difficult but essential step toward a free market by canceling control over prices. Producers immediately took advantage of the freedom and raised the prices of their goods ten times over previous prices.

Gorbachev's foreign policies were very popular outside the Soviet Union, but many people inside perceived his policies negatively. The army and a large part of the population did not support the unification of Eastern and Western Germany. Neither did they support the removal of Soviet troops from Eastern European countries, and the politics of non-interference into the internal affairs of these countries. Perestroika and glasnost brought unexpected consequences to Gorbachev.

At the beginning of 1990, Gorbachev's authority began to erode noticeably. Boris Yeltsin entered the political arena. Within a year he converted from the high official of the central communist party machinery, into the leader of the democratic movement. He was inundated by the multiple forces affecting the country's destiny and which required immediate radical steps to improve the conditions of people's lives. Meanwhile, the economic and social upheaval started with strikes and escalated to armed conflicts, which were sparked by ethnic dissention. The republics of the Soviet Union demanded complete economic independence and limits to federal authority.

In August of 1991, the hardline leaders of the former Soviet Union attempted to retake the country using anti-democratic methods. In their coup, they introduced a state of emergency. However, the residents of Moscow, Leningrad (St. Petersburg) and other large cities firmly stood against it. The majority of the population refused to recognize the state of emergency and the communist government was forced to resign. All power in the republics was transferred to the local presidents and parliaments, as they declared themselves to be independent countries and applied for recognition by the world community.

The Soviet Union, one of the great powers of the world, ceased to exist. Russia became the successor to the Soviet Union. The following information provides some aspects about the potential of Russia's economy. Using this potential with active mutually profitable assistance of foreign countries, will allow Russia to take its place among the developed countries of the world in the future.

The following points support this statement of Russia's market potential:

- Russia has the largest mining industry in the world. In 1992 it was the largest producer of different types of mineral and energy resources, including aluminum, copper, coal, diamonds, gold, iron-ore, lead, manganese ore, natural gas, oil, tin, and zinc. United Nations experts have estimated it at about 28.5 trillion USD. Russia intends to provide a reliable supply of mineral resources to the world market into the next century. One of the main principles of the creation of this reliable supply, is the liquidation of the state monopoly in geology and assistance in the development of easily accessible resources by providing licenses to national and international investors.
- Six of the world's forty-five largest metallurgical plants are located in Russia. Currently their capacity is under-utilized by 50%.
- Russia is first in the world with timber reserves of 75 billion cubic meters, including 55 billion cubic meters of the conifer type. To compare, let's note that timber production in the former U.S.S.R. came to 400 million cubic meters a year and in France timber production was 200 million cubic meters.

- The wages of highly qualified workers in electrical engineering, machine building, and other branches of industry in Russia and other states of the Newly Independent States are much lower than in Western European countries and the U.S.A.. For example, an equipment adjuster's hourly wage is about 1-2 dollars, while wages for similar workers in the U.S. and Western Europe are 6-8 times higher.
- There are huge geographic areas equipped with productive equipment for producing military goods. This production capacity is for the most part idle, because of Russia's conversion to the production of consumer goods. The conversion of this military industrial complex opens the door for consumer goods production. These consumer goods will be needed to meet the new growing demands of Russian consumers.
- Infrastructure in Russia and other N.I.S. countries is developed in a quantitative respect. But it is old-fashioned in qualitative respect. Thus, there exists opportunity for profitable investments.
- A middle class with disposable income is developing in Russia. This new middle class is beginning to demand goods and services. The demand for high quality consumer goods and a service industry provides an attractive market for Western companies wishing to expand.

The collapse of the Soviet Union was followed by the breaking off of the multi-year production connections between separate regions and enterprises. The cessation of these connections deepened the economic crisis even more. Rates of production continued to decrease and inflation increased. Russia inherited the debts of the former Soviet Union and was left with a stagnant economy. The time for serious steps to economical reform was long over due and was the only choice for the country.

The governments of the newly independent countries began efforts to take their economies out of crisis, each in their own way. All of these governments were committed to replacing their totalitarian economic system with a free market. This long and tedious change requires careful decisions which are heavily affected by material and moral factors, and the traditions and customs of the people. A free market requires the following minimum conditions:

- The existence of private property and land for the majority as a means of production.
- Competition between producers and the possibility of bankruptcy.
- An advanced banking and insurance system.
- A stable monetary system.

- An organized financial market.
- An opportunity for social security for the poorest strata of the population.
- A liberalization of external economic trade relations and guarantees for international investments.

None of these conditions reliably existed in the countries of the NIS in 1991.

The government of Russia was headed by the young economist Gaidar, and other scientists who did not have very much experience in the management of an economy. The government decided to attempt economic reform at an intensive rate and to convert to a free market by using *shock therapy* methods. The government instantly canceled centralized planning, centralized price control, and centralized material and technical supply, which were formed during the previous several decades. The result of these hasty decisions included breaking up connections in production, cooperation and sales. Enterprises producing consumer goods sharply decreased the amount of production and greatly raised prices. Output from the industrial enterprises producing the means of production and from the military enterprises slowed down significantly.

Government budget revenues decreased, prices increased, and the need for financial support of industry and agriculture caused an increase in budget expenses and deficits. The budget deficit was covered by printing money which was not supported by goods. This caused the subsequent increase of prices. The inflation rate, which came close to hyper level, shocked the people. The government decided to try to get out of the crisis by regulation of the currency and through financial policies or monetary policies.

At the end of 1993, there were national elections for the highest positions of government. The majority of the population confirmed their support for reforms to transfer the country to a capitalist economy, but they expressed disagreement with the methods used to achieve this reform. The government headed by Gaidar was forced to resign. Gaidar's government had envisioned that the only way to transfer to a free market was to immediately stop the direct state interference in the economy. In spite of the election results, Gaidar's government did play a positive role in the country's transformation. The process of overcoming the totalitarian state economy and creating multiple forms and types of business, was accelerated. The formation of market economy infrastructures and appropriate mechanisms started to work, along with the mechanisms of supply and demand. Additionally, there appeared the first indications of competition, which could be seen in the increased quality of goods available and the improved conditions of the stores. The mentality of managerial personnel started to improve as they began adapting to market economy conditions. A new generation of leaders, educated, energetic and free from the shackles of the old dogmas and customs, came into management positions on varying levels of business. At the initiative of the government, tens of thousands of state enterprises including all shops, restaurants and service companies, were transferred to private ownership. These newly privatized enterprises extended production capacity and variety of consumer goods and services. A strata of entrepreneurs began to form.

At the beginning of 1994, the new government was headed by an experienced businessman and the former minister of the oil and gas industry, Victor Chernomyrdin. His government agreed with the necessary steps out of the economic crisis, but the rate and methods where changed. Chernomyrdin's government had to choose between two approaches: first, by slowing the reduction of the budget deficit, and second, by a sharp reduction of the support of subsidies for the enterprises, which were headed for bankruptcy without government assistance. A consequence of the second approach meant the bankruptcies of many enterprises, the growth of unemployment, the sharpening of political confrontation, and an opportunity for social unrest. The government is looking for and finding compromise decisions to ease the transition. It was decided to mobilize additional budget revenues by also taking into consideration the financial assistance of international finance organizations. The government increased wages for pensions, employees of budget organizations, and expenditures for health care. The government continued to pay salaries to employees of the military industrial complex enterprises during the period of production reduction caused by the conversion of the military-industrial enterprises to consumer goods production.

The new government declared that it would carry out socially oriented politics much slower, but with an unconditional transition to a free market economy. The government restored state regulations to their more natural, generally accepted scales. The government intended also to support more active production of manufactured goods and to stimulate investment activity. The goal is to establish industry at a modern free enterprise level, and to encourage competitiveness of domestic goods in Russia and international markets. There continues to be a great need for improved tax and budget policies, which will improve overall stability of the economy. The government is working to overcome corruption and to develop reliable business legislation. Without such legislation, it is not possible to successfully function as a market economy and increase foreign capital investment.

In 1996 and the beginning of 1997, the Russian parliament passed laws to improve the foundation of the market economy. With Yeltsin's reelection in June of 1996, political stability helped keep Russia on the right path toward a free market. Russia became a member of the IMF (International Monetary Fund), World Bank, and other financial international organizations.

Why do many leaders mislead, by not accepting the reality that a return of power to the local level, minimal government interference in the economy, incentive based reduced taxing (a fair flat-tax for all), protection of individual citizens rights, protection of ones boarders, and open freedom will make prosperity? A balance of truth and justice must exist, humanely. Self-reliance has proven prosperous to the individual as well as to the whole.

Such democratic ideals as freedom, equality, superiority of law, honor, child and disabled care, have taken deep root into the consciousness of a majority of the Russian people. The road toward capitalism and freedom cannot be turned back.

APPENDIX 3

Saint Petersburg State
University of Economics and Finance

The Saint Petersburg State University of Economics and Finance is open for eduction, research and cooperation. All those who strive for these humanitarian aims are welcome. The University is located in the heart of the city and housed in a magnificent building, one of the glorious old monuments built by Giacomo Quarengi for the State Assignation Bank of the Russian Empire. The history of the University spans more than sixty years, for the then called Leningrad Economic Institute opened its doors in 1930. What was once a small educational institute, grew into one of the Soviet Union's leading centers of education and research. Today, the name has been changed to the Saint Petersburg State University of Economics and Finance by decree of the Russian Government.

The University prepares students for work in a wide, growing field of economic specialties. Graduates can be found working in practically all economic departments and institutions in St. Petersburg, and in many other cities throughout Russia, as well as the former Soviet Union and internationally. The University's educational and research complex has a very well developed network. Many of the successful alumni, well-known scholars and economists are engaged in the elaboration and modernization of the University's plans. The University maintains 10 faculties for day courses, night courses, and uniquely qualified faculties for foreign exchange students. There are 32 Chairs, providing higher education and specialized courses for their students.

The Faculty of General Economics
>Chairs:
>- Philosophy
>- Politology
>- General Economic Theory
>- Advanced Mathematics
>- Economic Informatics and Automated Control Systems
>- Physical Education

The Faculty of Economic Theory and Politics
>Chairs:
>- Prediction of Economic and Social Systems
>- Economic Theory and World Economics

- Territorial Organization of Society and Social Ecology
- Economic History

The Faculty of Economics and Management

Chairs:
- Production Management
- The Economics of Industrial Production and Innovation
- Economic Cybernetics and Methods of Econ-Mathematics
- Economic Projecting
- The Economy and Planning of Enterprises

The Faculty of Human Resource Management

Chairs:
- The Economy of Labor and Human Resources
- Sociology and Scientific Methods of Labor Organization Law

The Faculty of Finance, Credit and International Economic Relations

Chairs:
- International Economic Relations
- Finance
- Currency Circulation
- Banking

The Faculty of Statistics, Accounting and Economic Analysis

Chairs:
- Accounting and Auditing
- Economic Analysis of the Production Effectiveness
- Statistics

The Faculty of Commerce

Chairs:
- Commercial Logistic and Wholesale Trade
- Technological and Commodity Systems
- *Marketing*
- Price Formation

Other Academic Chairs:
- Foreign Languages
- Russian
- Military

Educational Work

Education is most successful when its high quality is ensured by creating favorable conditions to help all of the students discover their abilities. The educational plan of the University comprises mandatory courses (up to 70 percent of the total course of study), and elective subjects to be chosen at the discretion of the students and faculty.

284

During the first two years, all students pursue a common plan of study. The following two years the student may choose the faculty and chair for their desired education. Those students with the highest grades are given preferential treatment when choosing chairs. After four years of study, the students may be presented diplomas and awarded a Bachelors Degree in such disciplines as economics, statistics, management and commerce.

The fifth year the students devote to the attainment of economist's qualifications. This study includes intensive professional specialization completed with submission of the student's thesis papers. Graduates demonstrating an inclination to research may continue their education (according to an individual plan) and work towards a Master's Degree.

Research Work

The Saint Petersburg State University of Economics and Finance is one of the leading economic research centers in Russia. Research is carried out in the following areas:

- macro-economics
- theories of economic growth and prosperity
- finance, banking and insurance
- management
- marketing
- auditing and consulting
- accounting and statistics
- economic diagnostics
- management of human resources
- mathematical models as applied to economics
- economic informatics and the computerization of economics

Scholars from the University often provide consultation for the government and parliament of Russia, governing bodies of St. Petersburg, as well as close cooperation with business organizations. The University publishes scholarly works, text books, and monographs. The University also offers post-graduate study, as well as 14 Councils for awarding Doctoral degrees. For maintaining and organizing the applied researches, the University uses its own Research center, laboratories, completes creative groups for certain works needed in searching and thorough thinking.

International Relations

The Saint Petersburg State University of Economics and Finance has a broad network of international connections. They are cooperating in such spheres as the course of study, research, advancing qualifications, consulting and marketing. Since 1948, they have been educating foreign students. In the past 45 years, approximately 3,000 foreign citizens from 70 countries have attained higher education in economics, defended dissertations, and advanced their qualifications within the walls of the University.

In recent years, the University of Economics and Finance has developed active contacts with universities and colleges in developed countries such as France, Germany, Sweden, Holland, England, the USA, South Korea, China, and Vietnam. The University has been numbered among universities - participants of Sasakava - Fund (Japan). Frequent guests of the University are delegations of scholars, entrepreneurs, youth groups, and members of the media. The first Honorary Doctorate of St. Petersburg State University of Economics and Finance was awarded to the eminent economist, Vasily Leontiev.

Sports and Recreation

Students of the State University of Economics and Finance enjoy sports and often compete in them with distinctions. Most popular are swimming, light athletics, Greco-Roman wrestling, crew, basketball, volleyball and chess. The Student Club is to a large extent responsible for organizing extracurricular activities on campus. Students may develop their talents in the choir, as well as in the dance, theater and variety troupes.

APPENDIX 4

Securities Investment Firm ZAO Konto

ZAO Konto was established in 1995 in St. Petersburg. The Founders of the Company are ZAO Milord and private individuals. The company has obtained a license for activity on the securities market, as an investment consultant and financial broker. The license, No. 194, dated April 30, 1994, was issued by the Committee of Economy and Finance of the St. Petersburg Mayor's office.

The company has considerable experience in dealing with corporate securities of large joint-stock companies in the oil and gas industry, such as Surgutneftgas, RAO EES Rossija, Gasprom, Komineft, and Bashkirenergo. The company also has experience in organization of forming the larger offerings of securities against purchase orders in various regions.

The Company has many representative offices and affiliates, including Moscow, Surgut, and Ufa. They are experienced in working with the leading Russian regional operators in the stock market, such as the Investment Company, Troika Dialog, ZAO Kondor-Invest, ZAO Eastern Investment Company, MC-BBL Finance Ltd, Bridmar Investments Ltd., and others. They perform work for both legal entities and individuals, dealing in both large and small quantities of securities. The company is a member of the Non-Commercial Partnership Stock Exchange of St. Petersburg, and a shareholder and full-right member of ZAO St. Petersburg Stock Exchange.

The Company is applying communication technology, modern software applications, and streamlining their offices to continually improve the efficiency of services offered. Although the Company has a small number of employees, fewer than 30 people, they manage to fulfill a comparatively large volume of transactions due to the high qualification of the personnel in the company. All employees have higher education, including ten specialist with the primary category certificate, giving the right to operate on the securities market. Therefore, within the first quarter of 1997, the total volume of transactions with securities amounted to more than 25 billion rubles.

In its work, the company is acting according to the regulations and recommendations of the *National Association of the Participants of the Stock Market* (its Russian acronym is NAUFOR), and the *Federal Committee on the Securities Market* (FKTB).

Developing the company's range of services in the securities market, they are planning to provide their clients with *trust management* of investment portfolio's. Currently, they have already worked out several variants of portfolio investment, such as:

Statutory (conservative)

The money assets of the Client are fully invested into statutory securities. These investments provide a maximum guarantee of return.

Corporate (risky)

The money assets of the client are fully invested into the most liquid shares and bonds of Russian joint-stock companies (corporate securities). Such investments are more risky than those described above, but can result in higher returns and larger profits.

Mixed (moderate)

The money assets of the client are invested into both statutory and corporate securities, which provides suitable profitability with moderate risk. The Company has developed several different ways of forming an investment portfolio.

Collective Form (Fund)

Money assets and securities of the Client are consolidated with the money assets and securities of other Clients of the company, but accounting of the Client's property is always maintained on its individual investment-broker account (IBS). The collective form enables the Client to save money on the overhead expenses, which are proportionally divided among all participants of the collective portfolio and give the possibility of achieving larger profit due to the transactions with larger amounts of shares involved.

Individual Form

The control over the money assets of the Client is carried out on an individual basis, and money assets and securities of the Client are not consolidated with any other clients. This form is used by the Company in cases when the Client is willing to invest money assets into those securities which are not the objective investment of the collective portfolio of the Company. The percentage of securities is determined by the agreement between the Client and the Company, and when the Client chooses the collective way to form the portfolio, the standard percentage for the collective portfolio is used.

Services Rendered on the Stock Market in Russia

The Company renders its services to control money assets and securities of the Client that is willing to invest in the financial market for the purpose of making profits. An individual investment-broker account (IBS) is opened for each client. The IBS is a complex system of control, accounting, and estimation of the property value controlled by the Company. According to the agreement between the Company and the Client, all transactions with shares and monetary funds are carried out. Depending on the terms of the agreement, the Company renders to the Client a variety of additional services which includes the preparation of reports, consultations, assistance in accounting and taxation in respect to the operations with securities.

A Client working with the Company has the possibility to:

- constantly control and receive regular information about an IBS status (i.e. Bank statements, financial reports, and manager's comments)
- perform sale-purchase activities
- receive the Company's advice, recommendations, and survey's of the stock and financial market

Client's Participation in Managing of Own Stocks

Depending on the level of readiness of the Client, their experience on the stock market, "Konto" Company offers different forms of participation of the Client in managing their own property:

Trust

The Company itself, without consultations with the Client, determines the strategy on the stock market and makes all transactions. When the contract expires, the client receives a report with the description of all transactions.

Active

The Client is managing his account himself, periodically giving the Company orders for the transactions on the stock market. In this case, the Company fulfill's the Client's orders, performs accounting services, and holds the paper asset's and property. This type of participation is recommended primarily to qualified investors.

Automatic

The Company will perform all transactions with the Client's property according to the strategy determined beforehand. Unlike the active form of investment, the order is given by the Client only once at the moment the contract is signed.

Informational-Analytic Support of the Client

The Client regularly receives a review of the market based upon data from the information system Ros Business Consulting, justification of the Stock Exchange St. Petersburg, MMVB (Moscow International Currency Exchange), RTS-1 and RTS-2. The review is performed by the specialist of the Company in respect to the types of securities provided by the agreement with the Client. The review's given to the Clients in an agreed way include statistical data on the market, the results of tenders and auctions, reports, and charts.

In situations where a trust form is used, the Company gives to the Client free consultations and advice about the transactions. For active or automatic accounts, the Client can receive consultations for a special discounted price. Additionally, the Company can give the Client political and economical surveys, the possibility of access to the databases and systems of the exchanges.

Reports of the Company to the Client

The Company provides to the Client within the specified time agreed to in the contract the following:

- regular statements showing the status of the Client's assets
- reports reflecting the fulfilled operations of the IBS of the Client for the reporting period
- reports on the fulfillment of the order when the Company is working under the Client's order

The Company will also consider all suggestions on rendering additional services to the Client.

List of Russian Banks as of January 1997 (rubles)

As published in the newspaper *Finansova Izvestia*, No. 10 (361), February 13, 1997:

#	BANK	NUMBER OF BRANCHES	TOTAL ASSETS	AMOUNT OF REGISTERED CAPITAL	TOTAL DEPOSITS	AMOUNT of RESOURCES	AMOUNT OF RUBLE LOANS	FOREIGN CURRENCY LOANS	TOTAL PROFIT	STATE SECURITIES
1	Sberbank Russia	33824	256544039	15295111	105919738	2507337	26010651	5837286	13935252	82586107
2	Vneshtorgbank	9	27880178	6051022	7512448	8128274	204948	7934234	1962333	1754440
3	Inkombank	-	22232134	1989918	11228759	2406843	3141094	4580170	744224	2079300
4	ONEXIM Bank	0	20559354	2888576	11001564	2745128	5444812	5210433	266726	169453
5*	MOSBUSINESSBANK	-	17717616	1038238	556014	1309682	1495809	1552564	481439	13782267
6	Russian Credit	47	16262670	1156165	3744658	3924636	1484055	1013230	351422	1139980
7	Tokobank	16	14464418	1131315	1084580	1874055	298390	3001239	282709	394220
8	Stolichniy Bank Sverezheniy	14	13860459	1299284	3316666	4534299	981569	1458213	175425	4016402
9	Menatep	19	12229470	972424	3216375	1658982	4465525	3287845	210575	622536
10	National Reserve Bank	0	11225462	163869	2154018	3733060	1862525	283352	645948	2447065
11	Most Bank	8	11013431	605308	1093991	2623968	486944	1750507	129213	135553
12*	Promstroybank	70	10142435	829569	3956137	863161	1932444	504010	301488	508837
13	MFK	-	10138941	1984696	2466714	4629611	1787972	3294976	512766	264117
14	Moscow Industry Bank	34	10075322	908944	2052653	62513	1310639	111688	365371	373187
15	Alpha Bank	17	9891903	400053	1106801	1304343	2104838	1150058	75347	251701
16*	BANK "SAINT PETERSBURG"	22	9346177	232123	744503	33794	275189	106247	56424	68072
17	Imperial Bank	8	8558776	1589110	4073838	766886	2204605	3064039	429943	206541
18	Vozrozhdeniy	62	8412828	651204	3040451	794038	1354222	553603	583388	277892
19	Mezhdonarodni Moscow Bank	-	8259551	1200089	4899429	955937	0	1620223	290712	675984
20	Promishlenno-Stroit. Bank	43	8160232	799411	2642633	383487	1331410	453046	306230	544942

#	BANK	NUMBER OF BRANCHES	TOTAL ASSETS	AMOUNT OF REGISTERED CAPITAL	TOTAL DEPOSITS	AMOUNT of RESOURCES	AMOUNT OF RUBLE LOANS	FOREIGN CURRENCY LOANS	TOTAL PROFIT	STATE SECURITIES
21	Unekombank	71	8022207	749472	1889154	852538	786839	282612	6418	109950
22	Avtobank	12	7671469	1513021	2234406	3135538	1438222	642011	913948	1583780
23	Guta Bank	2	6921019	427282	3134764	2035220	377680	415837	66093	662367
24	Gazprombank	20	5370763	662129	2741012	497887	1127072	570058	265402	164464
25	Mezhdunarodniy Prom. Bank	4	5130999	1180948	2716097	705706	1370981	1649108	18283	230523
26	Mezhkombank	9	4581861	579417	2078814	924948	127232	786352	167271	682164
27	Moskovskiy National. Bank	-	3728163	315717	-	-	-	-	265052	-
28	Torybank	2	3516600	203996	876560	1095890	88974	69613	137193	373493
29	Mosstroiekonom-bank	36	3468778	372045	1159223	229	1216464	78044	221485	9959
30	Omskpromstroi-bank (Omsk)	21	3100529	262055	393997	18012	257343	27003	62172	64770
31	Neftekombank	6	2829701	577343	599123	434249	267578	635682	41775	104225
32	Bashkreditbank (Ufa)	4	2756321	1096673	512388	32528	387186	222239	418147	388011
33	Konversbank	12	2566419	302024	1527390	237144	540556	279236	167353	210538
34	Enicei (Krasnoyarsk)	36	2322724	179895	576022	21499	363498	73594	102737	52032
35	Kuzbassprombank (Kemerova)	27	2309971	325409	1039390	43712	1007679	97057	36021	134121
36	Mastear-Bank	-	2286945	35653	71819	1000	55293	5327	8659	24971
37	MDM	2	2073279	613617	346406	377612	458675	931178	340865	385185
38*	PETROVSKIY COMMERCIAL BANK (ST. PETERSBURG)	21	1990665	184927	244799	70318	293785	210149	4885	93807
39	Uraltransbank (Ekaterinburg)	9	1822751	180039	185073	20473	352024	15366	143143	250
40	Chelindbank (Chelyabinsk)	33	1747192	346434	456444	0	352982	48306	98583	75825

#	BANK	NUMBER OF BRANCHES	TOTAL ASSETS	AMOUNT OF REGISTERED CAPITAL	TOTAL DEPOSITS	AMOUNT of RESOURCES	AMOUNT OF RUBLE LOANS	FOREIGN CURRENCY LOANS	TOTAL PROFIT	STATE SECURITIES
41	Zapsibkombank (Tumen)	34	1715568	252607	774882	9180	428909	48238	129009	101496
42	KOPF	-	1690790	311024	239856	978330	322621	197864	222128	657756
43	Baltiiskiy Bank (St. P)	9	1604188	210137	388577	66744	239683	220807	36923	637
44	Bashprombank (Ufa)	34	1597457	211897	725095	152243	358370	136628	42458	6375
45	Postpromstroi-bank (Rostov-na-Doni)	23	1576527	85812	253569	78869	402324	26223	23736	1634
46	InterTEKbank	2	1565542	478770	499508	251869	423307	471075	57380	8531
47	Zenit	0	1538627	118929	769818	375094	125467	254340	77663	278442
48	Probiznes-bank	0	1525955	183075	196469	81516	299202	98453	88275	291174
49	Rosestbank (Tolyatti)	1	1506242	381851	565241	54799	384604	56225	243691	171514
50	Promradtexbank	6	1499220	105062	655090	274172	331297	158558	27557	120999

*See Unit 4 for more information. All banks are based in Moscow unless otherwise noted. Contact each bank directly for additional information.

EPILOGUE

No discussion of banking, which is the processing of money, which is the tool of economics, which is the study of man's exercise of his creative ability, would be complete without mention of the source of this ability to create, The Creator.

God's laws are forever unchanging and can be known to his creations through our communication with him. It takes a lot of faith to be an atheist but for those with such faith the chaos around us simply is. For those who prefer a more optimistic alternative by which to be guided, God offers consulting services.

It is quite clear that the responsibility for poor government is the responsibility of the people who elect it. If incompetent officials were not tolerated they would be replaced. There is an old saying. "People get the kind of government they deserve." The person placed in the post of an official can be changed every week, but nothing will change until people find their beliefs and place people in office who share their morality, spiritual philosophy, and logic, and who will implement policies friendly to the population and conducive to their economic productivity. Term limits, not career politicians.

We have not learned or remembered that power cannot be taken. It must be given. We have lost our identity and forgotten whom we really are. Two thousand years ago we were reminded who we are. Since then, with all the mental work we have engaged into make this a better world, the results can be likened to pouring water in to a swollen river. The solution lies in giving up our mortal sense of existence and acknowledging that, "I of myself can do nothing." The secret to success lies in rediscovering our God. The absence of that word in any economic plan is a real clue to the reason for its poor results.

Taken in the context of whom we are, the answers are within us. The solution could start tomorrow. We have the free will to procrastinate or to remember who is with us: He who is with us is perfectly aware of what is to be done, and by keeping our minds focused on that Presence, the Spirit will work through our awareness to accomplish everything easily, effortlessly and creatively. We have no cause to worry.

The U.S. dollar has inscribed upon it, "In God We Trust." What better time to reaffirm that we indeed do... Have Faith.

BIBLIOGRAPHY

1. Astakhov, V.P, "Securities Markets;" Moscow, 1995.
2. Banking Affairs/Pod reg. V.I. Kolesnikova and L.P. Krolivestkoui. M.: Finance and Statistics, 1995
3. Banking Encyclopedia for Russia; ETA. Moscow, 1995.
4. Bank "St. Petersburg" PLC, Annual Report; 1993, 1994, 1995, 1996
5. Beloglazava, G.H., "Commercial Banks Conditions in the Financial Markets." L.:Izd.LFZE, 1991
6. Bukato, Viktor I., Banks and Banking Operations in Russia; Moscow, Russia. Finance and Statistics, 1996.
7. Business and Banking, Newspaper
8. Business in the Russian Free Market; Bukato, Corbin, Lapidus, Lvov. Mir House. 1995
9. Laws of the Russian Federation about banking, securities markets, and settlements. 1994, 1995, 1996
10. Lvov, Yuri I., Banking and the Financial Markets; St. Petersburg, 1995
11. Economics and Zhizhin (Life), Newspaper
12. Financial Izvestia, Newspaper
13. Izvestia, Newspaper
14. Mikhailova, Elena B., "Corporate Securities." Business International; 1996 "Financial Markets in the Russian Federation" 1992
15. Mirkin, Y.M.,"Valuable Papers and Securities Markets." Moscow, "Perspectiva," 1995.
16. MosbusinessBank, Annual Report; 1993, 1994, 1995, 1996
17. Petrovskiy Commercial Bank, Annual Report; 1994, 1995, 1996
18. Promstroybank (Industry & Construction Bank), Annual Report; 1993, 1994, 1995, 1996.
19. St. Petersburg Commercial Banks Association, "Bulletin of St. Petersburg Commercial Banks Association - Financial Markets." (V.A. Antonov, Dr. S.A. Gurjanov, A.R. Davlitsarov, Dr.V.A. Dolbiozhkin, Dr.V.V. Platonov, Dr.V.V. Titov, E.N. Chetvergov, A.I. Yazev, E.V. Shilina, Editor: Dr.Vladimir V. Platonov, and Translator: Tatiana V. Baibakova). 1996.
20. Torkanovskiy, Professor V.S., "Financial Markets and its Financial Institutions." St. Petersburg, AO "Komplekt" 1994

AUTHORS
Alumni of Saint Petersburg State
University of Economics and Finance

Professor Mikhail K. Lapidus
Russian Doctor of Economics
Born in 1924 and a veteran of World War II. He worked in the State
Bank from a common clerk, to the President of the Leningrad Branch for twenty-
five years. He then became a professor and taught at the St. Petersburg State
University of Economics and Finance for twenty-five years. He helped establish
the first three commercial banks in Russia, and has since consulted in all spheres
of the economy. He has lived in the United States for five years and studies
English. He has published over eighty-five works, including eighteen textbooks,
reference books, and monographs.

Professor Leonid S. Taraseivich
Director of Saint Petersburg State
University of Economics and Finance
Born in 1937. Currently, he is the Director of Saint Petersburg State
University of Economics and Finance. He has worked and taught at all levels in
the University, which is the biggest and one of the oldest University's in
Russia. He has helped to establish close relations with many Western academic
institutions and organizations, including those in the U.S., Germany, France,
Eastern Europe, and the C.I.S. countries. He is a political scientist and
economic, financial, and banking specialist. He has published in Russia many
books, booklets, textbooks, reference books, and articles about economic
conditions and banking activities.

296

Viktor I. Bukato, Ph.D.
President of Mosbusinessbank
15 Kuznetsky Most
Moscow, 103780, Russia

Born in 1939. Graduate of the Saint Petersburg State University of Economics and Finance. He is currently the President of Mosbusinessbank, one of the ten largest banks in Russia today. He is a member of the Banking Council advising the Russian government on banking issues. He has published in Russia many books, booklets, textbooks, reference books, and articles about economic conditions and banking activities.

Yuri I. Lvov, Ph.D.
President of Bank "St. Petersburg" PLC
8 Admiralteiskaya Embankment
Saint Petersburg, 190000, Russia

Born in 1946. Graduate of the Saint Petersburg State University of Economics and Finance. After receiving a Bachelor of Economics degree, he began his work in the State banking system. In 1990, he became the President of Bank "Saint Petersburg," one of the top banks in the city and in the top twenty banks of Russia. He participated in the early development of private commercial banks in Russia. He lectures at the Saint Petersburg State University of Economic and Finance. He has published in Russia many books, booklets, textbooks, reference books, and articles about economic conditions and banking activities.

David I. Traktovenko, Ph.D.
Chairman of the Management Board of Industry & Construction Bank
Promstroibank
38 Nevsky Prospect
Saint Petersburg, 191011, Russia
Graduate from Saint Petersburg State University of Economics and Finance. Began working in a branch of the State bank in Kolpino. He participated in the early development of private commercial banks in Russia. In 1996, he became the Chairman of the Management Board of Industry & Construction Bank, the top bank in the North-Western region of Russia.

Yuri Golovin, Ph.D.
President, Petrovskiy Commercial Bank
8 Ruzovskaya Street
Saint Petersburg, 198013, Russia
Born in 1962. Graduate of the St. Petersburg State University of Economics and Finance. Began work in the military as a financial officer of a regiment, then he worked in the State bank, Promzhlenno-Stroitelnovo Bank of Russia. He worked as the Chief book-keeper in a construction company and then the Chief book-keeper of a branch of a commercial bank. Since 1990, he has been the President of Petrovskiy Commercial Bank, in the top forty banks of Russia.

Dr. Pyotr Joannevich van de Waal-palms
President, Palms & Company, Inc.,
Investment Bankers (1934-1997)
United States of America
Email: russia@aa.net
WWW home page: http://www.aa.net/~russia
Russian Ministry of Education:
Palms Free Electronic Russian Public
Library of 1000 Great Books Home page:
http://www.informika.ru/windows/books/gutenb/list.html

Dr. van de Waal-Palms, a delegate to the Yeltsin-Clinton Summit and participant in the New York Stock Exchange board-room meetings with CEO's of America's leading industries and Russia's Prime Minister, began teaching market economics at the Moscow Business School and Leningrad Management School in 1989, later teaching at the Russian Academy of Science. He is President of the international investment banking firm Palms & Company, Inc. (1934-1997) which was the first American corporation licensed by the USSR government to operate in the USSR. Please visit the following internet URL's for more information and business opportunities.

Buying Agent
http://www.aa.net/~russia/trade/palagent.html
Financing of 180 days or longer if certain Russian banks will guarantee.
http://www.aa.net/~russia/trade/forfaiting.html
Export
Customers in 40 countries for whatever you produce.
http://www.aa.net/~russia/trade/palexport.html
Currency Exchange
We can provide dollars in any country outside Russia directly to your bank accounts, or create bank accounts for you with the top ten banks in the world. All that is needed is to deposit rubles to our accounts in Russia. No messing with Moscow Interbank Currency Exchange, no having to buy and import something with the dollars you buy. No cross border transfer of either currency. You could call it, two interest free loans of dollars and rubles.

Exchange Rate

If the MICEX rate is 5806 then the rate would be 6967 - which is approximately the difference in Moscow between the interest rate on ruble denominated loans, and dollar denominated loans reflecting the devaluation of the ruble as it occurs daily.

http://www.aa.net/~russia/currency/palcurrency.html
http://www.aa.net/~russia/currency/palcurrency2.html

Capital Investment

For Russian companies interested in renovating their production:

http://www.aa.net/~russia/capital/palcapital.html
http://www.aa.net/~russia/capital/palcapital2.html
http://www.aa.net/~russia/capital/palcapital3.html

Off-shore Incorporation and Banking

Incorporate any Russian company in one of 13 tax free countries, and open bank accounts for them with major World Banks.

http://www.aa.net/~russia/banking/palbanking 2.html

Money Management

For pension funds and investment funds in Russia, guaranteed 30% with no risk or more if losses for them are not covered. Safe from Russian inflation, devaluation, fixed exchange rates, currency exchange risks.

http://www.aa.net/~russia/pensions.palpension.html
http://www.aa.net/~russia/pensions.palpension2.html
http://www.aa.net/~russia/pensions.palpension3.html

Palms & Company is a major buyer of hundreds of millions of dollars of commercial debt of Russian companies, where it is accompanied by a Sovereign Accreditation of the Russian Federation.

To revitalize the 6 aero space vehicle manufacturers and get them customers for vehicles and launches at Plesetsk and Baykonur:

http://www.aa.net/~russia/satellitelaunch.html

Much of this is in both Russian (KOI cyrillic fonts) and English as well.
Books for Russian ethics and business principles:

http://www.eskimo.com/~palbank

"A Course in Miracles"

http://www.aa.net/~russiapaleth2.html

For more information, please email:
mirhouse@sky.net

Russian Related Links on the WWW

http://www.mirhouse.com/ruslinks.html